D1010780

SUPREMELY POLITICAL

SUNY Series in the Presidency: Contemporary Issues
John Kenneth White, Editor

SUPREMELY POLITICAL

The Role of Ideology and
Presidential Management
in Unsuccessful Supreme
Court Nominations

John Massaro

STATE UNIVERSITY OF NEW YORK PRESS

Published by
State University of New York Press, Albany

©1990 State University of New York

For information, address State University of New York
Press, State University Plaza, Albany, N.Y., 12246

Library of Congress Cataloging-in-Publication Data

Massaro, John, 1941-
    Supremely political: the role of idology and presidential management in
unsuccessful Supreme Court nominations/John Massaro.
        p.   cm.—(SUNY series in the presidency)
    Includes bibliographical references.
    ISBN 0-7914-0301-7.—ISBN 0-7914-0302-5 (pbk.)
    1. Judges—United States—Selection and appointment.   2. United
    States. Supreme Court—Officials and employees—Selection and
    appointment.   3. Executive power—United States.   4. United States.
    Congress. Senate—Powers and duties.   I. Title   II. Series.
    KF8776.M335   1990
    347.73'14—dc20
    [347.30714]   89-21622
                                                                                CIP

10 9 8 7 6 5 4 3 2 1

CONTENTS

ACKNOWLEDGMENTS

THE DELICIOUS PLEASURE in completing this book is enhanced by the opportunity to acknowledge those who provided kindness and assistance over the long course of its preparation. The staffs at the following institutions were most considerate and efficient in providing support for my research and writing: National Endowment for the Humanities, Lyndon Baines Johnson Library, Nixon Presidential Materials Project, Margaret Chase Smith Library Center, Richard B. Russell Memorial Library, Gerald R. Ford Foundation, the NYS/UUP Professional Development and Quality of Working Life Committee, and the Clerical Center of Potsdam College of the State University of New York. I would also like to acknowledge the efficient work of those at the State University of New York Press, especially the efforts of Production Editor Elizabeth Moore.

Members of the academic communities at Southern Illinois University at Carbondale, Nasson College, University of Southern Maine, and Potsdam College of the State University of New York have consistently expressed genuine interest in my study of unsuccessful Supreme Court nominations and for that I am most appreciative. In particular, I would like to thank Randall Nelson for always being an excellent model of a demanding and caring teacher; Stephen L. Wasby not only for editing portions of the manuscript but for always insisting on my best effort; John White for believing in the worth of this project; and Sandy Schram for his friendship and gentle persistence in encouraging my return to the academic world. I would also like to acknowledge the many friends who helped in completing the project by directly assessing my research efforts, offering a kind word of encouragement, or simply providing a warm and inviting distraction. Included among this group are Calvin Senning, Peter Poor, Richard Del Guidice, Joan Schram, Judy Durham, Richard D'Abate, Fred and Barbara Aiello, Madelaine and Larry Ries,

Joan and Bob Wuerthner, Cindi and Steve Kostis, David and Kay Brown, and with happy memories, Garrett C. Clough and Wescott Merrow.

Es and Art Hessman, my beloved parents-in-law, generously provided me the opportunity to become a professional political scientist as well as a quiet place to begin the early writing of this manuscript, a role later assumed no less caringly by Karen and John Blank. My mother and father, Irene and Palmo, made the sacrifices for their children that deserve so much more in return than I can offer. I only hope my acknowledgment of their devotion and support serves as some small repayment for all they have given me. The gentleness and strength of my sister, Jeanne, brother, Frank, and sister-in-law, Valerie, helped my resolve in the dark winter of 1986. During my parenting of this book, my sometimes neglected, always loved children, John-Paul, Summer, and Aries, provided all any father could ask: they have remained kind and good people. Finally, I must recognize the one individual without whom this book would have been far less joyfully completed, if completed at all. She will remain forever in my mind as the daughter Es and Art loved and the daughter-in-law Palmo would have treasured. In their memory, I dedicate this book to my cherished spouse and best friend, M. Kimberlin Hessman Massaro.

INTRODUCTION

THE UNSUCCESSFUL Supreme Court nominations of Robert K. Bork and Douglas Ginsburg in 1987 raise anew the question of why the United States Senate periodically rediscovers its power of advice and consent and refuses to confirm a nominee to the high court.[1] As of October, 1988, the Senate has refused to confirm no fewer than twenty-six of the Supreme Court nominations it has considered, (see appendix 1).[2] While it is widely recognized that in the aggregate approximately one of five Supreme Court nominations will be refused confirmation, the likelihood of a specific nomination's being turned down has been less predictable, in part because the Senate's use of its power of advice and consent has simply not been consistent. For example, from 1789 to 1900, the Senate refused to confirm twenty of eighty-five Supreme Court nominations, generating a denial rate approaching one in four. However, high court nominees in this century have fared far more favorably, with the Senate turning down only six of fifty-seven nominations, a rate just over one in ten. Indeed, writing in 1965 and noting the Senate had refused to confirm only one Supreme Court nominee since 1894, one scholar boldly predicted that future rejections would be unlikely.[3] A short time later, the Senate, beginning in 1968, defied this optimistic forecast by refusing to confirm three nominations to the Court within the span of eighteen hectic months.

This chain of events began when Associate Justice Abe Fortas's nomination to succeed Earl Warren as chief justice of the United States was withdrawn by President Lyndon Baines Johnson on October 4, 1968, shortly after senators favoring confirmation failed to terminate a filibuster designed to block consideration of the nomination. At that time, Johnson also withdrew the nomination of United States Court of Appeals Judge Homer Thornberry, of Texas, whom he had selected to succeed to the vacated associate justice seat upon the anticipated approval of Fortas as chief justice. Johnson stepped down from the presidency in January,

1969, without having named a replacement for Chief Justice Warren, who continued to serve through the term of the Court which ended in June, 1969. By that time, in addition to the vacancy created by Chief Justice Warren's retirement, the Court was left with another opening due to Associate Justice Fortas's resignation on May 14, 1969, amid charges of judicial impropriety and the threat of impeachment occasioned by his association with financier Louis E. Wolfson.

President Richard M. Nixon quickly won Senate approval of Warren Earl Burger, Chief Judge of the United States Court of Appeals for the District of Columbia, to be Warren's replacement as chief justice. But the Republican president ran into considerable difficulty in attempting to gain the Senate's consent to a replacement for Associate Justice Fortas. Nixon's nomination of United States Court of Appeals Judge Clement F. Haynsworth, Jr., of South Carolina, to succeed Fortas was rejected by a 55-45 vote on November 21, 1969. A short time later, a second attempt by the president to fill the Fortas vacancy failed when the Senate voted 51-45, on April 8, 1970, to reject the nomination of United States Court of Appeals Judge G. Harrold Carswell, of Florida.

The Senate's rediscovery of its power of advice and consent in the 1968-1970 period raises several key questions providing the central focus of this study. Why did the Senate, after so long a period of submission, suddenly refuse to confirm three nominations to the Supreme Court within the span of eighteen months? What particular factors respectively led to the Senate's disapproval of the Fortas, Haynsworth, and Carswell nominations? Are the cases of Fortas, Haynsworth, and Carswell separate, idiosyncratic events or do they reflect a discernible pattern of factors associated with unsuccessful nominations? Can the identification of a discernible pattern point to the development of a common framework for improving our understanding of the Senate's refusal to confirm Supreme Court nominees? If so, what might this common framework reveal regarding the Senate's role in refusing to confirm Supreme Court nominations in the past, including the Bork and Ginsburg cases of the very recent past? And finally, what implications do the answers to these questions hold for the Presidency, the Senate, and the Supreme Court regarding future nominations?

This study provides answers to these questions by focusing upon the factors associated with the Fortas, Haynsworth, and Carswell refusals and developing an explanation of the Senate's action on these nominations. This explanation will in turn be employed to assess not only the recent refusals to confirm Bork and Ginsburg but all unsuccessful Supreme Court nominations. As the following chapters will indicate, the explanation of the Senate's action will emphasize the rich interplay among the three leading factors associated with unsuccessful Supreme Court nominations. These factors include two which have been widely recognized by scholars, the Senate's perception of the nominee's ideology and the timing of the nomination, and a less appreciated one, presidential management of the confirmation process.

Several significant aspects of this study improve upon others that have dealt with unsuccessful Supreme Court nominations.[4] Narrowing the array of significant factors to three provides a clearer and more understandable explanation of the Senate's role in unsuccessful nominations. Additionally, the development of a common framework of analysis distinguishes this study from several excellent but specific treatments of the Fortas, Haynsworth, and Carswell cases.[5] While helpful, these specific treatments have in part accounted for the criticism that "most attempts to analyze the modern [Supreme Court selection] process have produced few reliable generalizations."[6] The development of a common framework of analysis responds to that criticism. Finally, and most importantly, this study highlights presidential management of the confirmation process and in so doing elevates to its rightful significant status a factor which has been unappreciated in earlier studies. As will be demonstrated, the factor of presidential management provides the key to understanding not only the Senate's reassertion of its power of advice and consent in the 1968-1970 period but the recent unsuccessful nominations of Bork and Ginsburg as well.

THE IMPORTANCE OF THE SELECTION PROCESS

Before beginning the analysis of the key factors associated with unsuccessful Supreme Court nominations, some introductory comments regarding the judicial selection process are in order. That process, especially in regard to Supreme Court justices, can be one of the most important endeavors in which any president or senator engages. Several considerations support this view.

Fundamentally, the selection process determines who will become a member of the Supreme Court and share in the significant power exercised by that high tribunal. Excluding the president, a justice of the Supreme Court has been considered to hold "more actual power than any other individual in American public life."[7] This power springs in large part from the generally accepted view that the interpretation of both constitutional and statutory law bears the indelible stamp of the people who serve on the Supreme Court. Accordingly, a searching awareness of the process through which individuals become or fail to become justices is of crucial importance in understanding the Supreme Court as a dynamic institution within the United States political system.[8]

The selection process is also important because it can influence what is perceived as the proper role of a judge in the United States political system. The enduring controversy whether a judge should be a finder or maker of law is often at the heart of the debate over Supreme Court nominees. Indeed, were the Senate to disregard such qualifications as competence and ethics and focus exclusively on a nominee's party affiliation, one might anticipate the reputation as well as the expected role of justices as fair-minded, non-partisan proponents of law would be undermined and altered. Furthermore, it is not inconceivable that should the Senate's and/or the public's role expectation of Supreme Court justices undergo drastic change, the justices' own perception of their role would soon reflect this change. Accordingly, an examination of the Senate's refusal to confirm Supreme Court nominees can provide a useful perspective on the conflict surrounding the proper role of a judge in the United States political system.

Although the Constitution has established that the appointment of Supreme Court justices be subject to the advice and consent of the Senate, it is silent about what criteria the Senate should use in carrying out this important function. Understanding the potential power held by Supreme Court justices and their freedom from direct election by the people, the importance of the criteria employed in staffing the Court becomes readily apparent. For example, most citizens would likely agree that a major criterion should be the legal capability of the nominee. However, one comprehensive study of the selection process has concluded that opposition to Supreme Court nominees generally has not been based on the qualifications or lack thereof of the individuals appointed.[9] Closely related to the question of what criteria have been employed in the selection process is the question of what criteria should be employed. A thorough understanding of the selection process can make a significant contribution by providing data on what criteria have been employed in the past, a necessary step toward assessing what criteria should be employed in the future.

Finally, the selection process is important because its repercussions can affect the relationship between the president and the Senate. The strife and bitterness sometimes caused by the Senate's consideration of

Supreme Court nominees can be the origin of friction between the Senate and the president, jeopardizing an otherwise smooth working relationship between these branches. At least one president, Woodrow Wilson, voiced the opinion that it was in dealing with nominations that the most friction arises between the president and the Senate.[10]

Focusing upon the Fortas, Haynsworth, and Carswell cases, this study seeks to contribute to what is known about the selection process by providing an explanation of unsuccessful nominations built upon the key factors of ideology, timing, and presidential management. Chapter 1 presents an analysis of the key role each nominee's ideology (as perceived by members of the Senate) played in bringing down the Fortas, Haynsworth, and Carswell nominations, as well as an examination of the role of timing in the Fortas case. Chapters 2, 3, and 4 respectively highlight the role of presidential management in the Fortas, Haynsworth, and Carswell nominations. An explanation of why, in the 1968-1970 period, the Senate struck down these three nominations after a long spell of acquiescence in the president's choices is provided in chapter 5. This chapter also draws upon the interplay among the factors of ideology, timing, and presidential management in presenting an overarching explanation of unsuccessful nominations and in discussing the contribution this explanation can make toward better understanding not only the role of the president and the Senate in the selection of justices but also that of the Supreme Court in the United States political system. Finally, chapter 6 examines the unsuccessful nominations of Bork and Ginsburg.

1. IDEOLOGY AND TIMING IN THE FORTAS, HAYNSWORTH, AND CARSWELL NOMINATIONS

> It is simply a matter of judicial philosophy.
> —Senator Ernest F. Hollings

THE DOMINANT ROLE OF IDEOLOGY

The major factor leading the Senate to turn down the nominations of Abe Fortas,[1] Clement F. Haynsworth, Jr.,[2] and G. Harrold Carswell[3] was the perceived ideology of the nominees. In all three instances, senators consistently favored or opposed the nominations on the basis of whether or not they were in accord with the basic philosophy they believed the nominees would rely upon in deciding cases once they assumed their positions on the Court.[4] Most senators apparently accepted the view that a justice's basic philosophy will have a profound effect on the decisions he/she renders as a member of the Supreme Court.

The dominant role of ideology is not instantly recognizable in the Fortas, Haynsworth, and Carswell cases because of the presence of other factors which conceivably could have led senators to oppose confirmation. As the following discussion will indicate, sufficient information was available for senators to oppose confirmation on several grounds. The three leading factors which could have conceivably moved senators to oppose confirmation can be classified as follows: (1) the nominee's ideology, (2) the nominee's party affiliation, and (3) non-ideological considerations. A discussion of the information available to senators which was pertinent to each of these factors follows.

1

The Ideology Factor

Senator Sam J. Ervin, Jr. (D, N.C.) has maintained that the best way to ascertain a Supreme Court nominee's ideology is to analyze his previous opinions when and if he has had prior judicial experience.[5] Fortas, Haynsworth, and Carswell all had previous judicial experience. Consequently, they had participated in many judicial decisions which gave some indication of their ideologies.

It is not surprising, therefore, that each nominee's judicial record became a major concern in the Senate's deliberations. Even less astounding, assessment of Fortas's, Haynsworth's, and Carswell's ideology on the basis of their previous judicial records led to charges by their supporters that their past decisions were being misinterpreted. Opponents of the nominations were criticized for basing their assessments on a few selected decisions rather than on the nominee's complete judicial record. Supporters, especially in the Haynsworth and Carswell deliberations, maintained it was unfair to draw conclusions about a lower court judge's ideology from those cases in which higher court precedent clearly demanded the decision at hand.[6] These decisions only demonstrated that the nominee was obedient to precedent set by a higher court and, according to supporters of the nomination, indicated little about his basic ideology.

The following brief discussion of the various judicial decisions senators considered in assessing each nominee's ideology does not present the complete debate occasioned by these matters. The emphasis has been placed upon selected decisions which conceivably led some senators to oppose the nominations on ideological grounds.[7]

In appraising Fortas's ideology, conservative senators appeared to have been particularly upset over the nominee's siding with the 5-4 majority in *Miranda* v. *Arizona*.[8] In this controversial case, the Supreme Court held that confessions obtained without informing a criminal suspect of his rights could not be used as evidence in any subsequent prosecution. Also alienating some Senate conservatives was Fortas's joining the 6-2 majority in *United States* v. *Robel*[9] in which the Court declared unconstitutional a provision of the Subversive Activities Control Act of 1950. The nullified provision had made it illegal for a member of a Communist action group under final orders to register with the Subversive Activities Control Board to work in defense plants regardless of the quality and degree of membership. Finally, conservative senators were concerned with Fortas's participation in what they perceived to be the Warren Court's unwise and dangerous loosening of state and federal obscenity standards.[10]

The Senate's perception of Haynsworth's ideology tended to be based upon several cases in which he participated while serving on the United States Court of Appeals for the Fourth Circuit. Liberal senators were particularly concerned with the nominee's record in cases involving civil rights and/or labor-management relations. Among the former cases, senators pointed to *Simkins* v. *Moses H. Cone Memorial Hospital*[11] and noted Haynsworth's dissent from a ruling that a hospital receiving federal funds could no longer discriminate on the basis of race. Also cited was *Green* v. *The School Board of New Kent County, Virginia.*[12] In *Green*, Haynsworth joined the majority upholding Virginia's "freedom of choice" statutes. Liberal senators were particularly upset with the nominee's position in *Green* on two counts. In their view, Haynsworth had failed to anticipate the Supreme Court's repudiation of the "freedom of choice" statutes as had other members of the panel. In addition, they argued the nominee continued to favor the "freedom of choice" approach even after it had been unanimously repudiated by the Supreme Court.[13]

In regard to Haynsworth's record in the area of labor-management relations, pro-labor senators pointed to the case of *NLRB* v. *S. S. Logan Packing Co.*[14] In *Logan*, Haynsworth wrote the majority opinion categorically rejecting the use of authorization cards as a means of determining whether a union had the support of a majority of a company's employees. While authorization cards had generally been accepted as binding by the NLRB whenever the employer had previously committed unfair labor practices designed to hinder a fair election, Haynsworth's opinion allegedly rejected the use of the cards in all cases.[15] Opponents also cited *Darlington Manufacturing Co.* v. *NLRB.*[16] In addition to the soon-to-be-discussed ethics issue raised by Haynsworth's participation in this case, pro-labor senators noted the nominee joined the majority ruling that an employer had an absolute right to shut down part of his business even if it had been done to "chill unionism." Organized labor argued this decision would make it impossible to organize textile workers in the South.[17]

In the deliberations over Carswell's nomination, liberal senators were particularly concerned about what they perceived to be the nominee's less than satisfactory position on racial matters. These senators charged that the history of litigation leading to the case of *Steele* v. *Board of Public Instruction of Leon County, Florida,*[18] indicated Judge Carswell had deliberately delayed the revision of a grade-a-year desegregation plan until 1967 despite a higher court ruling in February, 1965, rejecting such a plan.[19] An additional case cited was *Singleton* v. *Board of Commissioners of State Institutions.*[20] In *Singleton*, Carswell dismissed for mootness a suit calling for the desegregation of a Florida reform school. Carswell had concluded that because a youngster was no longer detained at the reform school, he lacked standing to sue for desegregation of the institution. The court of appeals reversed this decision noting that because the average stay of a child at the reform school was shorter than the time required for litigation, Carswell's ruling would have virtually made it impossible ever to challenge the obvious unconstitutional segregation at the reform school. Opponents concluded Carswell had clearly misused the doctrine of mootness in this case in order to delay desegregating reform schools in northern Florida.[21]

It should also be noted that in addition to Carswell's decisions as a federal district judge, liberal senators cited several incidents in the nominee's public and private life which, in their view, were indicative of his less than satisfactory ideology on racial matters. While a more complete discussion of these incidents is presented below, particularly upsetting to these senators were Carswell's delivery of a 1948 white supremacy speech while he was seeking elective office; his 1956 involvement in avoiding the desegregation of a country club, while serving as a United States attorney; and his reported hostile demeanor to civil rights attorneys appearing before him in court.

The Party Factor

All senators involved in the consideration of the nominations obviously knew the party affiliations of the respective nominees. Fortas was widely recognized as a long-standing member of the Democratic party and Haynsworth and Carswell were easily identified as Republican party members. This information alone may have been sufficient to generate the opposition of senators inclined to oppose a nomination for purely partisan considerations without any additional reflection on the nominee's ideology or on any other factors. Accordingly, the ensuing analysis must and will assess the role of party in leading senators to oppose the nominations.

The Non-Ideological Factors

In addition to considerations of ideology and party, senators could have been moved to oppose these nominations on various non-ideological grounds including the nominees' ethics, judicial competence, and judicial temperament. These considerations are described as non-ideological because senators of diverse ideologies will generally agree that a nominee who obviously fails to meet basic standards of competence, ethics, and temperament should not be confirmed. In all three cases, at least some non-ideological considerations, discussed immediately below, entered into the Senate's deliberations and conceivably could have led to the opposition of some senators.

The non-ideological grounds for opposing the Fortas nomination related to the nominee's ethics. Fortas became vulnerable to the charge of ethical insensitivity by continuing to advise President Johnson while serving on the Court on several matters of national importance, such as the Vietnam War and the ordering of federal troops into Detroit to quell the 1966 riots. By remaining an advisor to the president, Fortas placed himself in a possible conflict of interest situation in that decisions the chief executive made pursuant to his advice may later have come before the Court for review. Opponents of the Fortas nomination were quick to point out Canon 24 of the Canons of Judicial Ethics required a judge "should not accept inconsistent duties, nor incur obligations, pecuniary or otherwise, which will in any way interfere or appear to interfere with his devotion to the expeditious and proper administraton of his official functions."[22]

Fortas also confronted opposition on ethical grounds when it became known he had accepted the surprisingly high fee of $15,000 for conducting a nine-week seminar at the American University Law School during the summer of 1968. While the amount of the fee would have supplied support for those senators looking for a reason to attack Fortas's sense of propriety, the manner in which the seminar was funded provided additional grounds for opposition. Funds to support the seminar were raised by Paul A. Porter, Fortas's close friend and former law partner, who solicited the money from five prominent businessmen likely to be affected by future Supreme Court decisions related to their ventures. This arrangement spurred Senator Strom Thurmond (R, S.C.) to allege that the seminar provided a convenient conduit through which Fortas's former law firm could supplement his judicial compensation.[23] To Senator Richard B. Russell (D, Ga.), the arrangement appeared to have put Fortas in violation of Canon 25, which required a judge not to enter into any business relation which might bring his personal interests into conflict with the impartial performance of his official duties.[24]

Haynsworth, like Fortas, was attacked for lacking the sense of propriety expected of a Supreme Court justice. Among the issues allegedly reflecting adversely on the nominee's ethical sensitivity was his participation as a federal court of appeals judge in cases involving litigants who had a business relationship with Carolina Vend-A-Matic Company

(CVAM), a firm in which Haynsworth held a substantial interest and in which he had reportedly served as a director until late 1963.[25] To opponents of the nomination, Haynsworth's participation in these cases clearly put him in violation of Canon 13, which required that a judge "should not suffer his conduct to justify the impression that any person can improperly influence him or unduly enjoy his favor." Opponents suggested Haynsworth might be inclined to favor the litigant with whom his firm did business.

Haynsworth's sense of propriety was also attacked on the ground that he had been less than candid in testimony before the Senate by claiming he had divested himself of all directorships of corporations upon being named to the federal bench in 1957. Contrary to this testimony, records indicated he was listed as both a vice-president and a director of CVAM until 1963.[26]

Opponents of the nomination also criticized Haynsworth for failing to excuse himself in cases in which he had a direct financial interest in one of the litigants.[27] Senator Birch Bayh (D, Ind.) cited this action as clearly violating Canon 29, which, according to the Ethics Committee of the American Bar Association, required a judge to refrain from exercising any judicial discretion in cases where he owns stock in one of the litigants.[28]

Carswell's promotion to the Supreme Court was opposed on the dual grounds that he lacked the judicial temperament required of a Supreme Court justice and that he possessed, at best, mediocre legal ability. This latter charge is typified by the testimony of Louis H. Pollak, Dean of the Yale Law School, before the Senate Judiciary Committee that Carswell "presents more slender credentials than any nominee put forth in this century."[29] Further reflecting adversely on Carswell's competence, at least in the view of many opponents of the nomination, were the results of a study conducted by the Ripon Society and the Law Students Concerned for the Courts. This study concluded Carswell's inadequate legal ability was purportedly indicated, among other considerations, by his reversal rate of forty percent, which was a full ten percentage points above the average for all federal district judges in the fifth circuit.[30]

Carswell's lack of the proper judicial temperament was allegedly indicated by several incidents brought out in testimony before the Senate Judiciary Committee. In 1948, while running for the Georgia state legislature, Carswell had made a speech in which he stridently endorsed white supremacy. Carswell's speech stated in part: "I yield to no man . . . in the firm vigorous belief in the principle of white supremacy."[31] Although he later repudiated the idea of white supremacy before the

Judiciary Committee considering his nomination, opponents remained unconvinced he could ever approach cases involving racial matters in the evenhanded manner demanded of a Supreme Court justice.

Opponents also pointed to Carswell's 1956 involvement, while serving as United States Attorney for the Northern District of Florida, in setting up a private corporation to take over a Tallahassee municipal country club. The nominee's participation in this incorporation, purportedly undertaken to avoid an order to desegregate the all white public club, coupled with repeated reports that as a federal district judge he had been rude and hostile to civil rights attorneys, were cited by opponents as additional evidence that Carswell lacked the judicial temperament expected of a potential Supreme Court justice. Also reflecting adversely on the nominee's judicial temperament, according to some of his opponents, were reports he had sold property in 1966 with a restrictive racial covenant written into the deed and had signed an affidavit in 1953, when he was United States Attorney, chartering an all white booster club for the Florida State University football team.

Ramifications from the country club incorporation also called into question Carswell's candor before the Senate Judiciary Committee considering his nomination. On January 26, 1970, the night before Carswell first appeared before the Judiciary Committee, two representatives of the American Bar Association's Committee on the Federal Judiciary visited the nominee in his Washington hotel room. The ABA representatives extensively discussed the country club incorporation with Carswell and reportedly showed him the official papers designating him as an "incorporator." The ABA representatives left the meeting convinced the nominee had played such a minor role in the incorporation that it should not disqualify him for a seat on the Supreme Court. However, in testifying before the Judiciary Committee the next day, Carswell claimed his recollection of details of the incorporation transaction was vague, denied he had been an incorporator of the club, and, despite the previous night's meeting, implied he had not recently seen the documents of incorporation. Some opponents cited this testimony before the Judiciary Committee as indicating the nominee's evasiveness and lack of candor, which in turn reflected his lack of the proper judicial temperament to serve on the Court.

The preceding discussion of the non-ideological charges raised against the Fortas, Haynsworth, and Carswell nominations does not present a complete review of the substantive Senate debate on these issues. All three nominees had both their opponents and supporters who either emphasized these charges or reiterated the proffered rebuttals.[32] What is important at this point is that these charges were raised and debated in the Senate and senators had the opportunity to consider them in deciding whether to support or oppose the nominations.

Ideology or Non-Ideology?

The dominant role of ideology would not be recognized if one were only to examine the Senate debate on the nominations and the public statements of most senators. For while there is unanimous agreement among senators that a Supreme Court nominee's ethical sensitivity and legal expertise should be scrutinized before the vote on confirmation, there is less accord on whether a prospective Supreme Court justice's ideology should also be closely examined. The prevailing view in the Senate, at least as publicly expressed at the time of the Fortas, Haynsworth, and Carswell nominations, was that the president is entitled to nominate a Supreme Court justice on the basis of the nominee's ideology and party, and the Senate is to consent to the nomination barring the development of legitimate non-ideological grounds upon which to base opposition to confirmation.[33]

An important development follows from this situation. When senators are given the opportunity to base their opposition to a Supreme Court nomination on non-ideological considerations, they will be inclined to cite those considerations in any public statements on the nomination. Being less universally accepted and therefore more controversial, senators will tend to avoid stating that their opposition is based upon party and ideological considerations when other grounds are present.

This inclination of senators to base their publicly expressed opposition to a Supreme Court nomination on non-ideological considerations complicates analysis of the Fortas, Haynsworth, and Carswell cases. As outlined above, in all three instances at least some non-ideological considerations involving the nominees' sense of ethics, level of judicial competence, or degree of judicial temperament entered into the Senate's deliberations. The presence of charges calling into question Fortas's and Haynsworth's ethical sensitivity and Carswell's competence and judicial temperament raises an important question. Did senators who were reluctant to oppose these nominations publicly on party and/or ideological grounds, employ the non-ideological and non-partisan issues of ethics, competence, and/or judicial temperament to conceal the real basis of their opposition?

The Non-Ideological Smokescreen. Senators belonging to different political parties and/or dissimilar ideological groups will nevertheless agree that a Supreme Court nominee obviously tainted by serious ethical infractions or lacking the requisite degree of legal expertise or judicial temperament should not be approved by the Senate. This is so because despite party and ideological differences, most senators, if not all, use approximately the same general standards in evaluating the sense of propriety, level of competence, and degree of judicial temperament of a prospective Supreme Court justice.

Accordingly, it can reasonably be expected that when charges are raised which call into question a nominee's ethics, competence, or judicial temperament, the percentage of senators within the different parties or ideological groups opposing the nomination on these grounds will be roughly the same. Any wide divergence between Democrats or Republicans, liberals or conservatives, in opposing the nomination will suggest that the proffered charges, rather than having been appraised with objectivity, were evaluated with a party and/or ideological bias.

Table 1 indicates that on the Fortas cloture roll call sixty-five percent (thirty-five of fifty-four) of the Democrats in the Senate voted in favor of terminating debate, while only twenty-nine percent (ten of thirty-four) of the Senate Republicans were so inclined. The wide divergence between Democrats and Republicans indicates that the standards of ethical sensitivity were not consistently applied by members of both parties.

Table 1

Party Affiliation and the Cloture Vote on the Fortas Nomination

	Votes For Cloture	Votes Against Cloture	Total	Percent in Favor
Democrats	35	19	54	65%
Republicans	10	24	34	29%
Total	45	43	88	51%

Source: U.S., *Congressional Record,* 90th Cong., 2d Sess., 1968, p. 28933.

It can be argued that a cloture roll call does not truly reflect each senator's position on the merits of the Fortas nomination, for several reasons. In voting on cloture, there are some senators who always oppose terminating debate irrespective of the merits of the issue involved. On the other hand, there are senators who maintain the president is entitled to a direct vote on all nominations forwarded to the Senate. Therefore, these latter senators may very well vote to terminate a filibuster on a nomination even when they intend to oppose the nomination on its merits. While analysis of a cloture vote does present some of these problems, it should be noted that the roll call on cloture was the only one which either directly or indirectly pertained to the Fortas nomination. Furthermore, it is believed that the cloture roll call reflects how more than enough of the senators would have voted on a direct vote to justify the conclusions reached in this analysis.

The data presented in tables 2 and 3 indicate when the Senate was considering the nominations of Republicans Haynsworth and Carswell, it was the GOP senators who were more inclined than their Democratic colleagues to support the nominations. Table 2 shows sixty percent (twenty-six of forty-three) of Senate Republicans voted to confirm the Haynsworth nomination while only thirty-three percent (nineteen of fifty-seven) of Senate Democrats did the same. Similarly, the data on the Carswell nomination presented in table 3 indicate sixty-eight percent (twenty-eight of forty-one) of the Republicans favored confirmation as opposed to only thirty-one percent (seventeen of fifty-five) of their Democratic counterparts. In both cases, wide divergences between Democrats and Republicans appear again.

Table 2

Party Affiliation and the Vote on the Haynsworth Nomination

	Votes For Confirmation	Votes Against Confirmation	Total	Percent in Favor
Democrats	19	38	57	33%
Republicans	26	17	43	60%
Total	45	55	100	45%

Source: U.S., Congressional Record, 91st Cong., 1st Sess., 1969, p. 35396.

These wide divergences between Democrats and Republicans in voting on the Fortas, Haynsworth, and Carswell nominations warrant the conclusion that the charges leveled against each nominee were not appraised objectively by senators. In the Fortas and Haynsworth cases, both Democrats and Republicans apparently applied a less severe standard when assessing the propriety of a nominee who shared their party affiliation than when appraising the fitness of one belonging to the opposition party. In evaluating Carswell's competence and judicial temperament, Republicans clearly appeared to have applied less severe standards than their Democratic colleagues.

Table 3

Party Affiliation and the Vote on the Carswell Nomination

	Votes For Confirmation	Votes Against Confirmation	Total	Percent in Favor
Democrats	17	38	55	31%
Republicans	28	13	41	68%
Total	45	51	96	47%

Source: U.S., Congressional Record, 91st Cong., 2d Sess., 1970, p. 10769.

There is additional evidence of the Senate's less than objective application of ethical standards in the Fortas and Haynsworth deliberations. Some close observers of the Supreme Court have contended Fortas and Haynsworth both transgressed the bounds of judicial propriety.[34] Their contention lends support to the conclusion that in both instances a reasonable doubt as to each nominee's judicial propriety had been raised. It also suggests that under an objective application of ethical standards, neither Fortas nor Haynsworth deserved confirmation by the Senate.

Were senators to have applied their ethical standards objectively in regard to both Fortas and Haynsworth, one would expect a high degree of consistency on both roll calls. Senators who opposed Fortas's elevation to the chief justiceship because of his alleged lack of ethical sensitivity would also oppose Haynsworth's nomination as associate justice for the same reason. Conversely, senators who supported Fortas and believed the ethical charges were not serious enough to merit Senate disapproval would likewise overlook these charges in considering Haynsworth's qualifications to serve on the Court.

Contrary to the expected pattern of consistency, analysis of the Fortas and Haynsworth roll calls reveals of the seventy-eight senators who took part in both roll calls, only eight followed the consistent pattern. (Appendix 2 presents each senator's position on the roll calls.) No less than seventy senators apparently favored a strict ethical standard in one case and a less rigid standard in the other, indicating considerations other than the nominees' perceived ethics entered into the Senate's deliberations.

Party Affiliation or Ideology? The preceding analysis hinted that party affiliation appeared to be an important consideration in determining the severity of the standards senators applied in assessing each nominee's ethics, competence, and judicial temperament. It would be premature, however, to conclude that party affiliation was the major factor in the Senate's disapproval of the nominations. Another factor more significant than party affiliation played the dominant role, and that factor was the Senate's perception of each nominee's ideology.

Demonstrating the dominant role of ideology in the Senate's refusal to confirm Fortas, Haynsworth, and Carswell necessitates a comparison of the factors of ideology and party affiliation to determine which one better explains Senate voting on the nominations and can justifiably be deemed dominant. To aid in making this comparison, an "ideology index" has been constructed which indicates the extent to which senators were inclined to support the interests of lower or less privileged economic and social groups in the United States. The index or score, which represents the percentage of time each senator voted in accordance with the interests of lower or less privileged economic and social groups on selected key roll calls in 1968 and 1969, was designed specifically to tap two distinct political ideologies extant at the time of the Senate deliberations that have been labeled "reform liberalism" and "conservatism."[35] Reform liberals strongly support political equality, place a greater emphasis than conservatives on social and economic equality, and seek a somewhat reduced role for property rights, materialism and individual self-interest in the United States political system. Conservatives, on the other hand, are grudging about the use of government for social purposes and are prone to value property over equality. (Appendix 2 presents more detailed information on the ideology index, including the scores for all senators and their votes on the Fortas, Haynsworth, and Carswell roll calls.)

Obviously, no single index can ever adequately represent something as complex as an individual's ideology. Nevertheless, indexes similar to the one employed here to reflect an individual's ideology have been utilized in previous voting studies.[36] Accordingly, the ideology index used in the following analysis can justifiably be interpreted to mean, the higher the index, the more "liberal" the senator.

It is now possible to compare ideology to party affiliation and determine which factor better explains Senate voting on the Fortas, Haynsworth, and Carswell nominations. Tables 4, 5, and 6 respectively present the relationship between ideology and Senate voting on the Fortas cloture motion and on the Haynsworth and Carswell nominations. In these tables, the Senate is divided along ideological rather than party lines. In all three tables, senators with indexes higher than at least half of their Senate colleagues who participated in the specific roll call in question are classified as "Liberals." Conversely, those roll call participants in the Senate with scores placing them among the lower half of senators likewise participating in the specific roll call are designated as "Conservatives." (It should be noted that in the tables and in subsequent pages the terms "Liberal" and "Conservative" are used to refer to the categories established by the ideology index. The terms "liberal" and "conservative," lower case, are employed to refer to the more generic and usual ideological descriptions suggested by these terms.)

Table 4

Ideology and the Cloture Vote on the Fortas Nomination

	Votes For Cloture	Votes Against Cloture	Total	Percent in Favor
Liberals	40	4	44	91%
Conservatives	5	39	44	11%
Total	45	43	88	51%

Note: Senator Charles E. Goodell (R, N.Y.) succeeded to the Senate seat of the assassinated Robert F. Kennedy on September 10, 1968, and did not participate in enough roll calls in that year to permit a fairly representative ideology index for him. Having, however, a 1969 index of eighty-three, which placed him in the upper third of liberal senators, Goodell has been classified as a "Liberal" for this table.

Table 5

Ideology and the Vote on the Haynsworth Nomination

	Votes For Confirmation	Votes Against Confirmation	Total	Percent in Favor
Liberals	6	44	50	12%
Conservatives	39	11	50	78%
Total	45	55	100	45%

Note: Senators George D. Aiken (R, Vt.), Marlow W. Cook (R, Ky.), and Mike Mansfield (D, Mont.) all had indexes of fifty-eight, which put them in a tie for the fiftieth "Conservative" position. Senator Cook was assigned to this position on the basis of his 1969 rating by the liberal interest group Americans for Democratic Action (ADA). Cook's ADA rating of fifty indicated that in the ADA's view he was more conservative than either Aiken or Mansfield, who were rated fifty-six and seventy-two respectively. For the ADA ratings for 1969, see *Congressional Quarterly Weekly Report*, February 20, 1970, pp. 567-576.

Table 6

Ideology and the Vote on the Carswell Nomination

	Votes For Confirmation	Votes Against Confirmation	Total	Percent in Favor
Liberals	2	46	48	4%
Conservatives	43	5	48	90%
Total	45	51	96	47%

Note: Senators Cook, Aiken, and Mansfield tied here for the final "Liberal" position (see note to table 5). Mansfield was assigned to it, again on the basis of 1969 ADA ratings.

One method of comparing the relationship between ideology and Senate voting on the nominations with the relationship between party affiliation and Senate voting is to count the "deviants." In analyzing the relationship between party affiliation and Senate voting, deviants are those senators who voted inconsistently with their party affiliation if one assumes senators always favor the nomination of their own party member and oppose that of an opposition party member. In analyzing the relationships between ideology and Senate voting on the nominations, deviants are those senators who voted inconsistently with their ideology if one assumes senators will always support the nomination of an individual perceived to be in agreement with their ideology and oppose the nomination of anyone deemed to be in disagreement. Of the two factors, party affiliation or ideology, the one generating the fewer deviants can be said to provide the better explanation of Senate voting on the nominations.

Table 4 indicates that dividing the Senate in half along ideological lines when analyzing voting on the Fortas cloture motion generates only nine deviants. This compares favorably with the twenty-nine deviants produced when the Senate was divided along party lines in table 1, and the voting on the cloture motion analyzed. The more consistent relationships between ideology and Senate voting on the nominations is further evidenced by examining the data for the Haynsworth and Carswell cases. Table 5 reveals that seventeen deviants are generated by employing ideology to explain Senate voting on the Haynsworth nomination, whereas thirty-six deviants are exhibited when party affiliation was used in table 2. Likewise, table 6 shows only seven deviants when ideology is employed to to explain Senate voting on the Carswell nomination, as opposed to the thirty deviants produced when party affiliation is used in table 3. In all three nominations, ideology is indicated to be a more convincing factor than party affiliation in explaining Senate voting on the Fortas cloture roll call and on the Haynsworth and Carswell nominations.

An additional method for comparing ideology with party affiliation in determining which factor better explains Senate voting on the Fortas, Haynsworth, and Carswell nominations is provided by an index of likeness. This index measures the difference between two groups in their voting on a specific roll call.[37] Simply defined, the index of likeness is the complement of the difference between the respective percentages voting "yea" in two groups. The index is obtained by calculating the percentage of members of each group that voted in favor of the measure, subtracting the smaller percentage from the larger, and subtracting that remainder from one hundred. The index varies from zero to one hundred, with the former representing complete dissimilarity and the latter complete similarity in the groups' voting response. For example, if one hundred percent of each group votes in support of a nomination, the response of each group is identical. This is also the case when each group splits eighty percent to twenty percent or sixty percent to forty percent. In each case, the percentage of group members voting in the affirmative would be exactly the same. Accordingly, this similarity would be reflected by an index of likeness of 100. This can be illustrated by calculating the index of likeness for two groups which have each split eighty percent to twenty percent on a specific nomination. The fact that each group supported the nomination at an eighty percent rate produces an index of likeness of one hundred $(100 - [80 - 80] = 100)$. Conversely, when (and only when) one hundred percent of the members of one group favor the nomination and zero percent of the other group support it there is complete dissimilarity between the groups, and a resultant index of likeness of zero $(100 - [100 - 0] = 0)$.

Whether ideology or party affiliation better explains Senate voting can be determined by comparing the indexes of likeness for the Senate groups divided along ideological lines, "Liberals" and "Conservatives," with the indexes of likeness for the groups divided along party lines, Democrats and Republicans. A working hypothesis is that the indexes of likeness for "Liberals" and "Conservatives" on the Fortas, Haynsworth, and Carswell votes will all be lower than the indexes for Democrats and Republicans on these same three roll calls. The basic rationale underlying this hypothesis is that whichever factor, ideology or party, produces greater dissimilarity in group voting (i.e., a lower index of likeness) provides the better explanation of the Senate's refusals to confirm.

Table 7 sets out the indexes of likeness for the Senate groups divided on the basis of ideology and party affiliation for the roll calls on the Fortas, Haynsworth, and Carswell nominations. In the Fortas case, the index of likeness for Democrats and Republicans, based upon the data of table 1, is sixty-four. This index indicates some dissimilarity in voting on cloture when the Senate is divided along party lines. However, the index of likeness for "Liberals" and "Conservatives" on the same roll call, based upon the data of table 4, is much lower, at twenty. Clearly, greater dissimilarity in Senate voting on the Fortas cloture motion is produced by dividing the Senate along ideological rather than party lines. Similarly, the index of likeness of thirty-four for "Liberals" and "Conservatives" voting on the Haynsworth nomination, based upon data presented in table 5, is much lower than the index of seventy-three for Democrats and Republicans reflected by table 2. Finally, in the Carswell case, the index of fourteen for "Liberals" and "Conservatives" based upon table 6 is substantially lower than the Democrat and Republican index of sixty-three based upon the data presented in table 3. The hypothesis presented above is convincingly supported. In all three cases, the indexes of likeness for "Liberals" and "Conservatives" are considerably lower than the comparative indexes for Democrats and Republicans, indicating substantially greater dissimilarity in Senate voting on the nominations when ideology rather than party affiliation is the basis for dividing the Senate into two distinct groups for the purpose of analysis.[38]

Table 7
Indexes of Likeness

	Party Affiliation	Ideology
Fortas cloture vote	64	20
Haynsworth vote	73	34
Carswell vote	63	14

Ideology: A Closer Look. What now appears evident is that in the key roll calls on the Fortas, Haynsworth, and Carswell nominations, ideology rather than party affiliation or non-ideological considerations offers the best explanation of Senate voting. A supportable conclusion is that despite the pronounced accusations of ethical insensitivity launched against Fortas and Haynsworth, the dual charges of incompetency and unjudicial temperament leveled at Carswell, and the surface party line voting evident in all three cases, the major factor leading to the Senate's refusals to confirm the three nominations was each nominee's ideology as perceived by the members of the Senate. Senators generally voted for or against the nominations on the basis of whether or not they approved or disapproved of the basic philosophy upon which they believed the nominee would rely in deciding cases once he assumed his position on the Court.

Additional evidence of the dominant role of ideology can be gleaned from the public and heretofore private comments of senators who participated in the deliberations. These senators can, of course, only speak directly for themselves. However, their reported comments provide an indication of the ideological motivations likely underlying the actions of other, more circumspect, senators, who were reluctant to attribute their opposition to ideological considerations when less controversial considerations were available. If some senators demonstrably made the link between a nominee's past judicial record and his ideology and openly proclaimed their opposition on this ground, it is likely their colleagues also made the connection even if the members of this latter group remained silent about the true basis for their disapproval.

In the Fortas case, there were several senators who publicly or privately expressed the ideological considerations underlying their opposition to the nomination. Even before the nomination was announced, at least two senators privately informed the president that they would oppose Fortas's confirmation because his record on the Court reflected an unsatisfactory ideology. Senator Robert C. Byrd (D, W.Va.) apprised a White House official the day before the Fortas nomination was announced that he would do "everything in my [Byrd's] power" to block confirmation by the Senate. It was Byrd's view that Fortas's record on the Supreme Court revealed the nominee to be a "leftist" undeserving of becoming chief justice of the United States.[39] Senator Russell B. Long (D, La.) also told a Johnson aide prior to the announcement of the nomination that he could not support confirmation. According to the Louisiana Democrat, Fortas was "one of the dirty five" Supreme Court justices who consistently "sides with the criminal against the victims of the crime."[40]

After the Fortas nomination had been announced, these senators and others continued to proclaim publicly and privately that it was the nominee's ideology which gave rise to their opposition to confirmation. Byrd subsequently told his West Virginia constituents his objection to Fortas's confirmation rested solely upon the nominee's "judicial philosophy and actions while serving on the Court."[41] In addition, Byrd confided that he opposed Fortas because the associate justice was in favor of "forced integration and leniency toward Communists, atheists, and other immoral people."[42] Long made known to the public he disapproved of the nomination because of Fortas's Supreme Court decisions supporting the rights of criminal suspects.[43]

In addition, Senator John Stennis (D, Miss.) publicly announced that his opposition to the Fortas nomination stemmed from the nominee's judicial record, which clearly indicated he was "aligned in personal and judicial philosophy with the 'liberal wing' of the Court."[44] Stennis's Mississippi colleague, James O. Eastland, powerful chairman of the Senate Judiciary Committee, openly concluded that Fortas's "opinions and decisions as an associate justice clearly demonstrate that his judicial philosophy disqualifies him for this high office [the chief justiceship]."[45]

According to Senator John L. McClellan (D, Ark.), Fortas's "legal and general philosophy" and the "specific ideologies reflected in several major decisions in which he has participated" demanded a negative vote on confirmation.[46] The hostility of McClellan's opposition to Fortas is indicated by the Arkansas Democrat's private comment to a White House aide, made before the nomination had been forwarded to the Senate. McClellan confided he was looking forward to having "that SOB formally submitted to the Senate" so that he could fight the nomination.[47]

Senator Ernest F. Hollings (D, S.C.) publicly avowed that his opposition to Fortas's confirmation as chief justice was "simply a matter of judicial philosophy."[48] Likewise, Senator Richard Russell (D, Ga.) noted his "principle objection" to Fortas was that "as Chief Justice he would extend 'Warrenism' for another fifteen or twenty years."[49]

Fortas's "undoubted proficiency as a lawyer," according to Senator Spessard L. Holland (D, Fla.), could not make up for his greatest deficiency—a "most liberal personal, legal, and judicial philosophy."[50] A White House aide seeking the Florida Democrat's support for the nomination, reported Holland was "absolutely opposed to Fortas for Chief Justice." The aide noted Holland opposed Fortas because if confirmed he would become a most effective leader of the "Warren Court and its philosophy" which the Florida Democrat had always opposed.[51] Holland also confided to a constituent that he opposed the nomination because of Fortas's "ultra-liberal, left-wing philosophy."[52]

Some senators expressing ideological opposition to the nomination were convinced that in the event Fortas became chief justice, the Supreme

Court would continue to make policy decisions they believed had already caused great unrest in the country. Senator Ervin, of North Carolina, publicly claimed that by joining the Court majority in the *Miranda* case, Fortas participated in creating new rules of evidence which were responsible for permitting "multitudes of murderers, rapists, burglars, robbers, and thieves to go unwhipped of justice."[53] According to a report of a White House staffer, the North Carolina Democrat believed the *Miranda* decision was a dangerous and unneeded re-writing of the basic legal document of the United States. Leaving little doubt as to where this led, Ervin concluded he "was opposed to anyone whose philosophy would permit a re-writing of the Constitution by the Court."[54]

Senator Norris Cotton (R, N.H.) openly informed his constituents he opposed the Fortas nomination because as chief justice the nominee "will perpetuate the policies of the Warren Court for many years to come, and that . . . would be a catastrophe." According to the New Hampshire Republican:

> The Warren Court has . . . protected criminals to the detriment of law and order. It has interfered with state legislatures and local elections. It has ignored the fundamental doctrine of separation of powers of Congress to legislate and the President to execute. It has banished prayer or recognition of God from our public schools. It has nullified laws passed by Congress to safeguard the Nation against subversion by Communism.[55]

Fortas's joining the majority in Warren Court decisions in the obscenity area appeared to have aroused significant Senate opposition. According to Senate Minority Leader Everett Dirksen (R, Ill.), this opposition was heightened by the fact that "a good many" senators took advantage of the private screening of sexually-explicit films arranged by the Judiciary Committee.[56]

While the link between the films and Fortas's ideology may have been an oblique one, several senators remained convinced that any nominee who failed to conclude that these films were obscene possessed an ideology too far to the left to deserve confirmation as chief justice. Senator Thurmond concluded:

> Justice Fortas has voted to reverse obscenity convictions in 35 of 38 cases since he became an associate justice. Testimony before the Judiciary Committee made clear that these decisions have opened the floodgates for pornographic material of all kinds, and created chaos in the efforts to enforce laws against such materials.[57]

In addition, Senator McClellan, having viewed one of the films, was reportedly "convinced that any senator who saw it would vote against the nomination."[58] Senator Milton R. Young (R, N.D.) who informed a White House aide on September 10, 1968, that he would vote for Fortas's confirmation, contacted another aide a few days later and withdrew his pledge of support. According to the second aide's report, Young confided he could not vote for Fortas "because of the movies."[59] Senator B. Everett Jordan (D, N.C.) privately informed the White House he could no longer support the nomination because of constituency pressure stemming in large part from "Fortas's position on pornography."[60] Senator Frank J. Lausche (D. Ohio) reportedly told a colleague he had assessed some of the motion pictures recently judged to be non-obscene by Justice Fortas and concluded he "would never vote to confirm a man who would approve the films."[61] Finally, both Senate Majority Leader Mike Mansfield (D, Mont.) and Minority Leader Dirksen confirmed that the "'dirty movies' issue had taken its toll on Fortas."[62]

The Haynsworth confirmation battle generated its share of senators who publicly and/or privately opposed the nomination on ideological grounds after having made the link between the nominee's judicial record and his ideology. Senator Fred R. Harris (D, Okla.) publicly traced his opposition to confirmation to Judge Haynsworth's legal opinions. According to the Oklahoma Democrat, these opinions revealed the nominee's "judicial philosophy" to be incompatible with "modern and progressive legal thought."[63] The conclusion that Haynsworth's prior judicial record reflected "some of the most regressive judicial thinking" in matters of race and labor avowedly led Senator Harrison A. Williams, Jr. (D, N.J.) to oppose confirmation.[64]

In addition, Senator Charles H. Percy (R, Ill.) openly based his opposition to confirmation on the nominee's ideology, citing Haynsworth's record in school desegregation and labor-relation matters. In Senator Percy's view, this record showed Haynsworth's failure to be "sufficiently sensitive to the needs of the men with whose fate he would deal."[65] Senator Clifford P. Case (R, N.J.) publicly concluded that the nominee's judicial record reflected a "degree of insensitivity to human rights unfitting the tribunal to which the American people look as the ultimate protector of constitutional guarantees."[66] Senator Mark Hatfield (R, Ore.) privately conveyed to President Nixon that he would vote against confirmation because "his greatest concern for the nomination related to the civil rights convictions of Judge Haynsworth."[67]

Senator Edward W. Brooke (R, Mass.) eventually voted against confirmation after he had unsuccessfully urged President Nixon, in a private communication, to withdraw the nomination. The private letter from the only black member of the Senate to the president conveyed his conviction that Haynsworth's "treatment of civil rights issues is not in keeping with the historic movement toward equal justice for every American citizen."[68]

There is an oblique reference suggesting that even conservative Senator Len B. Jordan's (R, Idaho) decision to vote against confirmation may have stemmed in part from the nominee's perceived lack of commitment to the equal treatment of the races. Jordan confided to a friend shortly before the crucial Senate roll call that he had "some difficulty" with the nomination because he was convinced Haynsworth was the "stalking horse for the Supreme Court" of the very conservative, prosegregationist Senator Strom Thurmond of South Carolina.[69] While Thurmond had in fact recommended someone other than Haynsworth for the position, there is little doubt the South Carolina Republican was very pleased with the nomination of Haynsworth.[70]

As in the Fortas case, implicit in this ideological opposition was an awareness that once Haynsworth joined the Court he would play a major role in shaping public policy. Senator Edmund S. Muskie (D, Maine) opposed the nomination because Haynsworth's promotion to the Supreme Court would "further encourage those resisting meaningful desegregation."[71] Senator Walter F. Mondale (D, Minn.) publicly opposed confirmation because of the nominee's record in civil rights cases, noting that Haynsworth's elevation to the Supreme Court would "affect the course of civil rights enforcement for a generation."[72]

Senator Jacob K. Javits (R, N.Y.) also publicly testified to the related policy and ideological considerations underlying his opposition to confirmation. As the New York Republican told his Senate colleagues:

> I have found, on reviewing the written opinions of Judge Haynsworth, particularly in racial segregation cases, that . . . his views on the application of the Constitution to this most critical constitutional question of our time are so consistently out of date, so consistently insensitive to the centuries-old injustice which we as a nation have caused our black citizens to bear, that I could not support the introduction of Judge Haynsworth's judicial philosophy into the Nation's highest court.[73]

Finally, Assistant to the President Peter M. Flanigan, in a post-roll analysis, implicitly confided to a friend that because pressure groups opposed to Haynsworth's social philosophy were able to convince enough senators to make the link between the nominee's ideological record and his future behavior on the Court, many of these senators went on to vote against confirmation. According to Flanigan, "the combined forces of civil rights and labor groups coupled with the smoke surrounding the ethical issue proved to be too much to overcome.[74] Flanigan's view is shared by no less an authority than John D. Ehrlichman, Assistant to the President for Domestic Affairs, who concluded Haynsworth "was not confirmed because of a highly expert, expensive and intensive campaign by organized labor and the civil rights groups."[75]

In the Carswell case, it is difficult to determine from the public and private statements of senators whether their opposition rested upon considerations of ideology or judicial temperament. The remarks of some senators were limited solely to what they perceived to be the nominee's unsatisfactory ideology in regard to obtaining fundamental rights for all citizens. The criticism of other senators, however, seemed to go well beyond this concern. For example, Senator Stephen M. Young (D, Ohio) clearly was objecting to more than Carswell's purported conservative ideology in noting confirmation should be denied because the nominee was a "bigot."[76] Young's criticism struck at the very essence of a judge — the will to decide cases without allowing personal prejudices to interfere. On the other hand, Senator Brooke, of Massachusetts, publicly based his opposition to confirmation on the nominee's lack of "true dedication to the principle of equal rights under law."[77] In contrast to Young, however, the Massachusetts Republican was careful to point out he did not believe Carswell was a "racist."[78]

The distinction between senators' opposing Carswell because of his alleged conservatism or because of his purported racism is important. As has been indicated, senators will disagree on whether a Supreme Court nominee should ever be opposed on ideological grounds. However, there appears to be little discord, if any, in the Senate regarding considerations of racial bigotry. All senators would no doubt agree an undisputed racist should not serve on the Supreme Court. And while this distinction is important, a determination of whether opposition to confirmation was based upon grounds of ideology or temperament is not necessary in demonstrating that some senators made the link between Carswell's previous record and his policy preferences. In this context, the difference between conservatism and racism is one of interpretation; either would nonetheless provide senators with some evidence of a nominee's policy preferences. Those senators opposing Carswell because he was a conservative as well as those senators disapproving because he was perceived as a racist understood that either interpretation of Carswell's previous record indicated he would side with the conservatives on civil rights issues.

Most senators making the link between Carswell's record and his ideology emphasized the nominee's previous decisions on racial matters. Senator Javits was among those senators who voiced their concerns publicly, noting these decisions revealed Carswell's "desire to slow the movement toward equal opportunity for all Americans insofar as it can be established by law."[79] Senator Daniel K. Inouye (D, Hawaii) also noted publicly that he was compelled to oppose confirmation because of the nominee's "philosophy on one of the most critical issues facing our Nation today—civil rights."[80] Senator Charles E. Goodell (R, N. Y.) likewise openly grounded his opposition to confirmation on what he perceived to be Carswell's "basic insensitivity to fundamental civil rights issues, which are essential to our survival as one, indivisible nation."[81] Senator Richard Schweiker (R, Pa.), who had originally come out in support of Carswell when assured the nominee was a "racial moderate," reportedly quietly withdrew his support when he was convinced this was not the case.[82] The Pennsylvania Republican eventually voted against confirmation.

Finally, Assistant Attorney General William H. Rehnquist, destined to be an associate justice of the Court and Chief Justice of the United States, noted the impact that Carswell's as well as Haynsworth's ideology, perceived in their lack of strong support for civil rights, had on the Senate's refusals to confirm.

> It is evident from our experience in the Haynsworth and Carswell confirmation fights that a demonstrable "red neck" hostility to civil rights on the part of a nominee, or a personal animus against any minority, could well prove fatal to chances for confirmation.[83]

The selected comments of senators and other participants in the confirmation process presented in the preceding pages indicate that in the Senate deliberations on the Fortas, Haynsworth, and Carswell nominations, senators clearly could and did make the link between each nominee's previous judicial record and his ideology. Furthermore, the roll call analysis convincingly demonstrated that the voting of most senators on the nominations was primarily influenced by their perception of each nominee's ideology. These two facts in combination clearly indicate that most senators, despite their many public statements to the contrary, appraised the nominations by reviewing each nominee's previous record and deciding whether or not they were sympathetic to the ideology reflected therein.

This leads to the inescapable conclusion Fortas, Haynsworth, and Carswell were denied confirmation because a sufficient number of senators, whether they publicly expressed it or not, opposed the nominations on ideological grounds. As will be developed in the next section as well as in the following chapters, other factors played key supporting roles in the Senate's negative action. Nevertheless, the dominant factor leading the Senate to refuse to confirm all three nominations was the perceived ideology of the nominees.

TIMING AND THE FORTAS NOMINATION

As subsequent chapters will indicate, opposition stemming solely from the perceived ideology of the nominees would not have been sufficient to bring about the Senate's refusal to confirm the nominations of Fortas, Haynsworth, and Carswell. While ideology played the leading role, the drama of the Senate's disapproval of these nominations would not have occurred without the presence of several additional supporting factors not the least of which in the Fortas case was the point in time at which the vacancy occurred on the Court.

The unfavorable timing of the Fortas nomination was linked to President Johnson's surprising March 31, 1968, announcement that he would not be a candidate for re-election. Consequently, when the Fortas nomination was announced on June 26, 1968, it was not only forwarded to the Senate in the heightened partisan atmosphere extant shortly before a presidential election, it also bore the signature of a so-called "lame-duck" president.[84] Senators were no less aware than the general public that there would soon be a new occupant in the White House with the same power to nominate Supreme Court justices as that momentarily held by Johnson.

The timing of the Fortas nomination made the effort to win Senate confirmation more difficult in several ways. It was the lame-duck nature of the nomination which provided the common ground underlying early Republican opposition to confirmation. Senate Republicans had the opportunity to oppose confirmation for any one of several reasons ranging from sincere concern about Fortas's sense of propriety to more ideological and/or partisan considerations. However diverse the motivations behind their opposition, the lame-duck nature of the nomination enabled most of these GOP senators to base their opposition on the commonly shared principle that this influential and important position should only be filled by an individual appointed by the soon-to-be-elected president.

The significant influence of the lame-duck nature of the nomination in unifying early Republican opposition was evident from the time Fortas was nominated. On the same day Fortas's name was sent to the Senate, no less than nineteen Republican senators issued a joint statement expressing their opposition to confirmation. The statement was significantly devoid of any mention of the diverse grounds for opposition and concentrated instead on the nineteen's common ground for seeking to block confirmation. It read in part:

> The next Chief Justice of the United States and any nominees for vacancies on the Supreme Court should be selected by the newly-elected President of the United States, after the people have expressed themselves in November's election. We will, therefore, because of the above principle and with absolutely no reflection on any individuals involved, vote against confirming any Supreme Court nominations of the incumbent President.[85]

The firmness of this early Republican opposition is indicated by the fact that not one of the nineteen senators who initially signed the statement later voted in favor of cutting off debate in order to allow the Senate to consider the Fortas nomination directly. For the most part, the original signers of the statement unswervingly upheld the principle expressed in their initial proclamation on the nomination. Typical of this group was Senator Howard H. Baker, Jr. (R, Tenn.) who after having signed the statement in June, 1968, continued to tell constituents well into August, if not later, that his opposition stemmed essentially from considerations of timing. Baker noted he opposed confirmation because

> the election of a President and of one-third of the Senate is imminent; and . . . the new President, whoever he is, and the 91st Senate will be closely attuned to the American people and will have a sounder grasp of that which is best for the country.[86]

Evidence also suggests that this initial bloc of GOP opposition to the nomination in turn encouraged several conservative Democrats to oppose confirmation. Senator Russell, of Georgia, who eventually played a key role in blocking the nomination in the Senate, reportedly was initially inclined to favor confirmation. Although the Georgia Democrat never warmly endorsed Fortas, he intended to support confirmation because he was purportedly convinced sufficient opposition to defeat the nomination could not be mustered and maintained in the Senate. It was Russell's initial view that the early GOP opposition to Fortas reflected by the joint policy statement would crumble under pressure from the

White House and the Republican leadership.[87] But after being convinced by Senator Robert Griffin (R, Mich.) that the nineteen Republicans who signed the statement would not waver under this pressure, the Georgia Democrat decided to put his not inconsiderable weight behind the move to block the nomination.[88]

Another important consequence of the Fortas nomination's being forwarded to the Senate late in Johnson's last year in office was that it provided the anti-Fortas forces with a political setting they could use to their advantage. Senators opposed to a nomination are always free to resort to a filibuster or other delaying maneuvers to block a direct vote on confirmation. But these tactics become especially effective, and hence more attractive to senators opposed to confirmation when the nomination is made late in a president's term and the chief executive is prohibited from or elects not to seek an additional term.[89] This is so for several reasons. A lame-duck president is obviously deprived of the opportunity of resubmitting the nomination at the next session of Congress. In addition, a departing president soon finds his powers of pressure, patronage, and persuasion muted more and more with each tick of the clock. Furthermore, the political arithmetic clearly favors those intent on blocking the nomination through the use of filibuster. Ordinarily, a majority vote of participating senators is needed to defeat a nomination outright. However, by employing a filibuster, a mere third of the Senate can usually prevent the termination of debate and thereby effectively and permanently block consideration of the nomination. (A cloture motion to terminate debate on an issue requires today the favorable votes of three-fifths of the Senate. Senate rules in effect at the time of the Fortas deliberations in 1968 required the positive votes of at least two-thirds of the senators present and voting.)

The strategy of the anti-Fortas forces was to prevent a direct vote on confirmation. When Majority Leader Mansfield requested the Senate, on September 4, 1968, to begin consideration of the Fortas nomination, senators opposed to confirmation launched a debate on the procedural issue of whether to take up the nomination. Their intent was to avoid a direct vote on the nomination and thereby defeat confirmation. The majority leader soon filed a cloture petition designed to terminate discussion and enable the Senate to consider the nomination directly. However, on October 1, 1968, Mansfield's effort to invoke cloture failed to win the requisite support of at least two-thirds of the senators present and voting. Consequently, debate on the procedural issue could have gone on indefinitely had not Johnson conceded defeat by withdrawing the nomination on October 4, 1968.

The use of delaying tactics was particularly significant because of the presence of an impressive amount of evidence indicating that, had the Senate voted directly on the nomination, Fortas would have been confirmed as chief justice. Assuming senators who either voted for or were otherwise recorded in favor of cloture would also have voted for confirmation, and vice-versa, the following pattern emerges. There were forty-five senators who voted for cloture and presumably would have supported confirmation and forty-three who cast ballots against cloture and would likely have opposed confirmation on a direct vote. In addition, two senators who did not vote on the cloture motion, Frank Church (D, Idaho) and Wayne Morse (D, Ore.), were paired in favor of terminating debate and can be counted as being in favor of the nomination. Conversely, five other senators who did not vote on the cloture roll call, George D. Aiken (R, Vt.), Margaret Chase Smith (R, Maine), Alan Bible (D, Nev.) , Allen J. Ellender (D, La.) and Ernest Gruening (D, Alaska), were either paired or announced against terminating debate and can be considered to have been against the nomination. This suggests that forty-seven senators supported confirmation and forty-eight opposed.

There were, however, five additional senators who neither voted nor expressed a position on the cloture roll call. These five were Thruston B. Morton (R, Ky.) , E. L. Bartlett (D, Alaska) , Edward Long (D, Mo.), George S. McGovern (D, S.D.), and George A. Smathers (D, Fla.). Evidence presented below indicates that all five of these senators were inclined to favor cloture and, presumably, would have supported confirmation on a direct vote.

Although Senator Morton was among the group of Republicans who initially issued the joint policy statement opposing the nomination, evidence exists suggesting he would have supported confirmation. Early in July, 1968, after the statement had been released, Morton reportedly expressed the opinion it was "unfortunate" his name appeared on the GOP declaration of opposition. Contrary to the view expressed in the statement, he purportedly intended to vote for cloture and for confirmation.[90] In addition, a White House memorandum circulated shortly before the cloture vote notes Morton as being "right" on cloture and confirmation.[91] Finally, a distinguished home state newspaper reported on the day of the cloture vote that Morton was in favor of confirming the Fortas nomination.[92]

Additionally, two of the four Democratic senators unrecorded on cloture, Bartlett and Long, had respective ideology indexes of eighty and fifty-three, placing them among the Senate "Liberals" who had consistently favored confirmation. Bearing in mind the generally consistent relationship demonstrated above between ideology and Senate voting on the nomination, as well as the pull of party loyalty, one could reasonably speculate that Bartlett and Long would have supported both cloture and confirmation. Additionally, there is evidence that less than one week before the cloture vote, Bartlett told a presidential aide he would vote in favor of cloture in the event his support were really needed.[93] While there is no evidence indicating Long's attitude toward the nomination at the time of the cloture vote, the Missouri Democrat reportedly had been "particularly enthusiastic" about the prospect of Fortas becoming chief justice.[94] While this report reflects Long's thinking early in the Senate's deliberations, immediately after the nomination had been announced, it should be noted there is no evidence indicating the senator ever lost his enthusiasm for Fortas's promotion to the chief justiceship. The only other report on Long's position suggests that as late as August 13, 1968, he was still considered by the White House to be solidly in favor of confirmation.[95]

The two other Democrats unrecorded on cloture, McGovern and Smathers, had respective ideology indexes of forty and seven, which indicate they were not among the Senate "Liberals" who consistently favored confirmation. Nevertheless, there is evidence supporting the conclusion that these two senators would also have supported cloture and confirmation. Shortly before the cloture vote, McGovern was recorded by the White House as being in favor of Fortas's confirmation.[96] In a post-nomination correspondence, McGovern has confirmed that at the time of the cloture vote he was leaning in favor of confirmation.[97] In regard to Smathers, a White House communication on September 16, 1968, less than three weeks before the vote to terminate debate, noted that the Florida Democrat "will vote for cloture if his vote is needed."[98]

The evidence presented above suggests the likelihood that all five of the unrecorded senators would have favored confirmation on a direct vote. Their anticipated pro-confirmation votes make the speculative tally on the nomination fifty-two for confirmation and forty-eight opposed.

There is additional evidence supporting the conclusion that Fortas would have been confirmed as chief justice had there been a direct vote on the nomination. At least five senators who voted or announced against cloture and were counted above as likely to oppose confirmation may have subsequently favored cloture. These five were Aiken, Cotton, Smith of Maine, Winston L. Prouty (R, Vt.), and Howard W. Cannon (D, Nev.). Evidence presented below suggests these senators clearly conveyed the impression to the White House that they would eventually switch their positions and cast ballots in favor of terminating debate.

A White House memorandum circulated shortly before the cloture roll call notes that Aiken, Cannon, Cotton, and Smith would all eventually support the motion to terminate debate. For example, Aiken is noted as committed to voting for cloture "after a reasonable debate." In addition, Smith is described as being for cloture "if she could be on the floor."[99] Additionally, a White House communication written shortly before the cloture roll call characterizes Prouty as being "right on cloture if the vote doesn't come too soon."[100] In the event there had been a second roll call on cloture, the evidence presented above indicates that these five senators would have voted in favor of cutting off debate. Continuing to assume a vote to terminate debate suggests support for confirmation, the anticipated switch of these five senators indicates the Senate would have favored the Fortas nomination by a fifty-seven to forty-three margin.

There exists still more evidence indicating the Fortas nomination would have been confirmed if voted upon directly. At least five other senators who publicly opposed cloture or who were unrecorded on the motion were reportedly inclined to favor confirmation on a direct vote. These five senators were J. Caleb Boggs (R, Del.), J. W. Fulbright (D, Ark.), Wallace F. Bennett (R, Utah), Roman L. Hruska (R, Neb.), and James B. Pearson (R, Kan.)

A White House memorandum dated September 24, 1968, less than two weeks before the cloture vote, "confirmed" Boggs as being "right on the Fortas and Thornberry nominations."[101] Fulbright, according to a White House staffer's August 22, 1968, report, "strongly indicated that he would vote for confirmation of Fortas."[102] Another White House report concluded that while Bennett would make "a very partisan speech attacking the nominations," he "will probably vote for Fortas."[103] On August 1, 1968, Fortas's former law partner, Paul A. Porter, who played a key role in trying to round up support for the nomination, intimated that Hruska and Pearson as well as Smith, of Maine, would likely support confirmation.[104] Porter noted that Hruska "has privately expressed great admiration for Fortas and unless sheer political expediency changes him, he is believed to be a favorable."[105] Pearson, according to Porter, had "represented to mutual friends his intention to support the nominations."[106] Assuming these five senators would have eventually followed their privately expressed inclination to favor the nomination, the anticipated tally on a direct vote was sixty-two in support of Fortas's confirmation and thirty-eight opposed.

Support from others for the admittedly speculative conclusion reached here, that substantially more senators than the needed majority were prepared to support Fortas's confirmation, is readily available. Most senators opposed to confirmation agreed that without the filibuster, Fortas would have been confirmed as chief justice.[107] A White House aide charged with keeping a tally on the nomination has remained convinced Fortas would have easily won a majority on a direct vote.[108] Another White House staffer maintains there were "at least seventy votes" in favor of Fortas's confirmation.[109] After counting "close to sixty-five votes in favor of confirmation," Porter concluded, "the problem, of course, is [the] filibuster and cloture."[110] Finally, as interested an observer as fellow nominee Homer Thornberry later remarked:

> I have the feeling and have always had the feeling, that if Mr. Justice Fortas's name had come up at that time, if it had not been for the filibuster and they [the senators] had been allowed to reach that name, that he would have been confirmed.[111]

The evidence presented above regarding the analysis of the cloture vote, the expressed intentions of various senators, and the particular effectiveness of delaying tactics in a presidential election year, justifies the conclusion that despite the presence of significant ideological opposition, Fortas would have most certainly been confirmed to be chief justice had the nomination been made at any time other than in the last months of Johnson's final term. Therein lies the tale of the significance of timing in the Fortas defeat.

Support for the conclusion reached here that timing was a significant factor contributing to Fortas's defeat is not difficult to find. Both Johnson and Fortas have intimated that some of the negative votes on the cloture motion, so lethal to the hope for confirmation, stemmed from the perceived lame-duck status of the nomination. Fortas and Johnson reportedly agreed that once the president had announced on March 31, 1968, that he would not be a candidate for re-election, he "let some of the senators feel they could . . . oppose him with impunity."[112] In addition, a White House aide actively involved in dealing with the Senate in the doomed struggle for confirmation also has testified to the deadly impact Johnson's announced decision not to seek re-election had on the nomination. In response to a question on whether Johnson's decision not to seek re-election weakened his power in Congress, the aide answered: "I think there's no doubt about that. I think that if we had been allowed to vote on the Fortas nomination, we could have carried that very easily."[113] Additionally, shortly before the crucial cloture roll call, Senator Percy, a supporter of the Fortas nomination, testified to the hostile atmosphere in the Senate, occasioned by election year politics and Johnson's decision not to run. The Illinois Republican reportedly told a White House aide "people close to the President just are not going to be well received in the Senate between now and the election."[114] Porter attributed the opposition's success in blocking Fortas's confirmation to the unfortunate timing of the nomination, which had occasioned "a classic case of erosion of presidential power."[115]

Finally, no less an authority than Senator Griffin, of Michigan, who had waged the early and lonely fight against the nomination, and who steadfastly held together GOP opposition to confirmation despite intense White House pressure, has testified to the influence of timing on Fortas's demise. Queried on whether Johnson's announced retirement had hindered the effort to get the Fortas nomination through the Senate, the Michigan Republican answered:

> When the nomination was first submitted, there was every reason to believe—and I'm sure they did believe down at the White House— that there were lots of votes in the Senate to confirm it. The fact that President Johnson had announced he wasn't going to run had little impact at first. It would be more difficult, however, to evaluate the impact farther down the road, in the crunch.[116]

There can be little doubt the perceived lame-duck status of the nomination made timing a significant factor contributing to the Senate's refusal to confirm Abe Fortas as Chief Justice of the United States.

2. PRESIDENTIAL MANAGEMENT: THE FORTAS NOMINATION

A Fortas-Thornberry package would
be in real trouble.
> —Senator Russell B. Long

I did not anticipate there would be
any opposition.
—President Lyndon Baines Johnson

THE KEY ROLE played by ideology in the Senate's refusals to confirm Fortas, Haynsworth, and Carswell, and the contributing role of timing in the case of Fortas, raise the question of whether these two factors have been influential in previous unsuccessful nominations. Had ideology and timing been consistently significant in past unsuccessful nominations, their presence in the three more recent refusals to confirm might denote the continuation of a revealing pattern and point toward a common framework for analyzing previous unsuccessful nominations and the Senate's seeming rediscovery of its power of advice and consent in the post-1968 period.

Of the 139 nominations made to the Supreme Court through 1986, only twenty-four, approximately seventeen percent, failed to gain confirmation by the Senate. (See appendix 1.)[1] The rate at which the Senate has refused confirmation increases sharply, however, when the nominations have been made amid two conditions which would appear to enhance opposition stemming from considerations of ideology and timing. These two key conditions are (1) that a majority of the senators considering the nomination did not share the same party affiliation as the president, and (2) the nomination was forwarded to the Senate in the last full year of a president's term or in what is commonly referred to as the interregnum period after a new president had been elected.[2] While there have been only fourteen nominations made amid *both* of these adverse conditions, no less than ten, a substantial seventy-one percent, have failed to gain Senate approval.[3] This suggests the significant roles of ideology in the Fortas, Haynsworth, and Carswell cases and timing in the Fortas deliberations were not unprecedented.

The Senate's action thus far assessed in the Fortas, Haynsworth, and Carswell cases sheds some light, if only by implication, on the reasons why nominations made under these two adverse conditions have been turned down at such an unusually high rate. Analysis of the key roll calls on the Fortas, Haynsworth, and Carswell nominations indicated what had initially appeared to be party-oriented voting was actually ideology-oriented voting. Given the consistent although sometimes imperfect relationship which has long existed between party affiliation and ideology, it is not difficult to understand why the Supreme Court nominees of presidents whose party was in the minority in the Senate have failed to gain confirmation at a relatively high rate.[4] More than likely, those nominees ran into ideological opposition similar to that experienced by Fortas, Haynsworth, and Carswell.

It is also not difficult to comprehend why nominations made late in a president's term or in the interregnum period have been turned down by the Senate at a comparatively high rate. The Fortas case, where the nomination was so vulnerable to tactics of delay that a minority of senators could block confirmation, clearly indicates the key role of timing. Most certainly, those previous nominees who had the unenviable distinction of being nominated to the Supreme Court in a president's last full year in office or in the interregnum period faced similar opposition stemming from the unpropitious timing of their nominations.

It is crucial to note, however, that the Fortas, Haynsworth, and Carswell cases do not neatly fit into the pattern created by the ten of fourteen unsuccessful nominations forwarded at unfavorable times to Senates in which the president's party was in the minority. All three nominations were forwarded to the Senate when only *one* of the two key conditions was present. Fortas's nomination was indeed sent to the Senate late in Johnson's last year in office but the president's Democratic party held a substantial majority in the Senate. Conversely, while the GOP was the minority party in the Senate during the deliberations on Republican President Nixon's nominations of Haynsworth and Carswell, these nominations were made early in the president's term. Consequently, it is not possible to attribute the Senate's refusals to confirm Fortas, Haynsworth, or Carswell to the presence of both of the adverse conditions making opposition stemming from considerations of ideology and timing more pronounced.

It is also unlikely that the presence of only one of the adverse conditions would be sufficient to bring down the Fortas, Haynsworth, and Carswell nominations. Through 1986, Supreme Court nominations forwarded to Senates in which the president's party was in the minority but at a favorable time (i.e., at time other than in the last full year of a president's term or in the interregnum period) were turned down at a twenty-one percent rate (four of nineteen), while nominations made at unfavorable times but considered by Senates in which the president's party was in the majority were refused confirmation seven percent of the time (one of fourteen). This yields a refusal rate of approximately fifteen percent (five of thirty-three) for nominations made amid only one of the adverse conditions, a rate not markedly different from the overall Supreme Court nomination refusal rate at the end of 1986 of approximately seventeen percent (twenty-four of 139) and significantly different from the seventy-one percent rate (ten of fourteen) when both conditions were present.

These data suggest a more thorough explanation of the Senate's refusals to confirm Fortas, Haynsworth, and Carswell requires at least one additional supporting factor. A simple but revealing fact provides a clue to that factor's identity. From 1789 to 1968, only two of the twenty-five Supreme Court nominations submitted under only one of the two adverse conditions strongly associated with unsuccessful nominations were refused confirmation.[5] Presidents Johnson's and Nixon's failure to gain Senate approval of their Supreme Court nominees under circumstances where many previous presidents had succeeded raises an interesting question. Can any of the crucial opposition leading to the Senate's refusals to confirm Fortas, Haynsworth, and Carswell be attributed to a factor best described as "presidential management" of the confirmation process?

THE FACTOR OF PRESIDENTIAL MANAGEMENT

Whenever a vacancy occurs on the Supreme Court, there are certain considerations clearly beyond the control of anyone, including the president. Party composition in the Senate and the timing of the vacancy are two obvious examples. Although presidents can endeavor to control the timing of a vacancy by attempting to persuade a justice to step down from the Court at an opportune time, these two factors are generally "givens" which set the framework in which the chief executive is forced to operate. But, there are other factors over which the president can have substantial control and through which he can significantly influence the Senate's deliberations on the nomination; it is here that presidential management—the degree of prudence, astuteness, and skill demonstrated in overseeing the confirmation process—can become a most important consideration.

A basic assumption underlying the concept of presidential management is that ultimate accountability for gaining Senate confirmation of a Supreme Court nomination rests with the president because the Constitution grants that office sole authority to nominate a particular individual to serve on the court. The president is generally responsible for managing the confirmation process so as to guard against the nominee's encountering avoidable damaging Senate opposition. He may elect to delegate key tasks and even extensive responsibility to subordinates in various stages of the confirmation process, but any failure to gain confirmation of a Supreme Court nomination traceable to opposition generated by the chief executive or his associates is ultimately a presidential failure.

Presidential management includes two key stages, a pre-nomination stage and a post-nomination stage. Within each, the chief executive is called upon to plan, oversee, and administer key tasks associated with the confirmation process. In the pre-nomination stage, the president's two principal responsibilities are (1) directing the screening process to assure the availability of complete, reliable information on potential nominees and (2) overseeing, if not directly undertaking, both the devising of an overall strategy of confirmation and the selecting of a nominee capable of gaining Senate approval. In the post-nomination stage, the president is responsible for (1) overseeing and controlling the adoption and execution of tactics appropriate to carrying out the overall strategy successfully, and (2) taking care that positive relationships are generally maintained with senators to provide the most favorable atmosphere possible for the nomination during the Senate's deliberations.

The key to understanding the Senate's refusals to confirm the Fortas, Haynsworth, and Carswell nominations lies in an appreciation of the roles Presidents Johnson and Nixon played in these defeats. Both presidents failed to exercise the astute management called for in attempting to gain Senate approval of the nominations. President Johnson's management of the Fortas nomination is the subject of the remainder of this chapter. The following two chapters address, respectively, President Nixon's management of the Haynsworth and Carswell nominations.

PRESIDENT JOHNSON AND THE FORTAS NOMINATION

On June 26, 1968, Chief Justice Earl Warren's desire to retire was officially announced and President Johnson nominated Associate Justice Abe Fortas as Warren's potential successor.[6] Homer Thornberry was nominated to Fortas's seat on the Court contingent upon Senate approval of Fortas as chief justice. The Senate Judiciary Committee hearings, held from July 11 through July 23, focused on Fortas's judicial philosophy and his extrajudicial activities, especially his continued involvement in advising President Johnson while serving on the Supreme Court. Fortas testified before the Committee for four consecutive days beginning July 16.

The Senate recessed on August 2, 1968, for the national nominating conventions, with the Judiciary Committee not having reported the Fortas nomination. When the Senate reconvened in September, Fortas was asked to retestify before the Judiciary Committee but refused to accept the Committee's invitation to appear. Nevertheless, the Judiciary Committee held two additional days of hearings on September 13 and 16, focusing primarily upon the Warren Court's obscenity decisions and Fortas's being paid a $15,000 fee for conducting a nine-week seminar at American University in the summer of 1968. Despite Fortas's refusal to reappear for additional questioning, the Judiciary Committee, on September 17, voted 11-6 to report the nomination favorably to the Senate.

When Majority Leader Mike Mansfield (D, Mont.) requested, on September 24, 1968, that the Senate proceed to consider the Fortas nomination, anti-Fortas senators prepared to stage a filibuster in order to block a direct vote on the nomination. Seeking to curtail the filibuster, Mansfield filed a cloture motion that required a two-thirds majority of all participating senators to terminate debate. When the pro-Fortas forces could only muster a slim 45-43 majority in favor of cloture on October 1, it was clear the filibuster could not be ended and the nomination was doomed. Shortly after the unsuccessful cloture vote, Fortas requested that the president withdraw the nomination, and on October 4, 1968, Johnson obliged.

Selecting a Vulnerable Nominee

President Johnson contributed to the Senate's disapproval of the Fortas nomination by selecting a nominee vulnerable on grounds of judicial impropriety. Some senators employed this issue to conceal the ideological and/or partisan basis of their opposition at the same time others were led to disapprove of the nomination out of genuine concern about the nominee's alleged lack of sufficient ethical sensitivity. Whether the opposition emanated from a disingenuous or bona fide concern about the nominee's sense of judicial propriety, the opportunity to oppose confirmation on this ground would not have occurred had Johnson not selected a vulnerable nominee.

Ethics as a Cover Issue. The analysis of the cloture roll call in chapter 1 clearly indicated that despite the Senate's publicly expressed concern with Fortas's sense of propriety, most senators' estimation of the seriousness of this charge was closely related to their ideological viewpoints. This suggests that much of the hubbub surrounding Fortas's sense of ethics was employed to conceal the ideological considerations underlying many senators' opposition. Use of ethics as a pretext or cover issue is logically consistent with the previously mentioned reluctance of senators to base their opposition to a Supreme Court nomination on ideological and/or partisan grounds when there exist politically safer reasons upon which to rest their disapproval.

More thorough and effective presidential oversight of the pre-nomination screening process would have provided more options for President Johnson. Neither Fortas nor Thornberry was subjected to an FBI investigation at the time of their nominations in 1968. In attempting to justify the administration's reluctance to check out the nominees, Attorney General Ramsey Clark explained, "You don't run a new FBI investigation on a sitting judge."[7] As a result of this approach, the attorney general as well as other White House advisors did not know all they could have known about the nominees in order best to advise the president. For example, Attorney General Clark has testified that the $15,000 seminar fee arrangement between Fortas and American University which so concerned many senators had come as "a complete surprise to all of us, and I'm sure to the President."[8]

Had a more thorough, effective pre-nomination screening of Fortas been undertaken, the president might have had a greater appreciation of Fortas's liabilities and settled upon another nominee with a similar ideology but free from non-ideological and non-partisan criticism. By way of illustration, if White House advisors, already aware of Fortas's extensive involvement in counseling the president while serving as associate justice, had uncovered the details of the fee arrangement with American University earlier and thereby had the opportunity to assess fully the potentially damaging impact of these events, Johnson might have been persuaded to forward a less controversial chief justice nominee for consideration by the Senate.

Ethics as a Legitimate Issue. While many senators utilized the issue of ethical insensitivity to shield their ideological objections to the Fortas nomination, others appeared to have been genuinely influenced by that consideration in arriving at their decision to oppose confirmation. For example, Senator Thomas J. Dodd (D, Conn.) appears to have been primarily influenced by ethical considerations in deciding to cast his vote against cloture, a vote that cannot be explained on party grounds. As Dodd's ideology index of sixty clearly placed him among the "Liberals" who had consistently favored cloture, ideological considerations do not provide a satisfactory explanation of his vote. Indeed, that Dodd was the only "Liberal" among the Democrats to oppose cloture strongly implies that ethical considerations played a primary and genuine role in his vote on the roll call.

This conclusion is supported by Dodd's particular sensitivity at this time to charges of impropriety due to his June 23, 1967, censure by the Senate for his own ethical infractions. Dodd would no doubt have found it extremely uncomfortable to support the nomination of a fellow party member under attack for ethical infractions so soon after his own censure on similar grounds. Shortly before the cloture roll call, Dodd privately told a White House aide he was inclined to oppose Fortas's confirmation because of American University's $15,000 payment to the nominee.[9] Although some senators employed this issue to conceal ideological or partisan opposition to the nomination, given Dodd's relatively liberal ideology and Democratic affiliation, there is little reason to doubt his private message to the White House conveyed the genuine motive behind his disapproval of the nomination and his negative vote on cloture.

Republican John Sherman Cooper (R, Ky.), whose ideology index of seventy-three clearly placed him among Senate "Liberals," provides another example of a senator who appeared genuinely moved by the ethics issue. On July 3, 1968, months before Fortas's receipt of the American University seminar fee had been uncovered, the administration was very confident Cooper would support both cloture and confirmation. According to a White House report, Cooper told fellow Kentuckian and GOP colleague Senator Thruston Morton that he supported the Fortas nomination.[10] Once the seminar fee incident became a matter of public knowledge, however, Cooper's support for the nomination began to waver. On September 20, 1968, he told a White House aide that, while he still supported the nomination, the seminar fee problem troubled him and others supporting confirmation "more than any previous charge against Justice Fortas."[11] By October 1, 1968, the ethics issues had apparently succeeded in bringing about his opposition to confirmation. As Cooper told the Senate shortly before the cloture vote, "the relations of Justice Fortas with former law clients in connection with the lecture series has caused me to have grave doubts about the propriety of this nomination."[12] The senator went on to conclude that he would vote for cloture on principle but would not vote in favor of confirmation on a direct vote.

It will never be known precisely to what extent the ethical charges raised against Fortas entered into the decisions of senators to oppose cloture. While the Dodd and Cooper cases suggest some senators were sincerely moved by these allegations to oppose the Fortas nomination, the roll call analysis of chapter 1 indicates many senators utilized the charges as a smokescreen to conceal the ideological basis of their opposition. Nevertheless, it remains clear that Johnson's failure to select a nominee free from serious accusations of ethical insensitivity enabled senators to employ these charges in either a genuine or feigned matter and thereby played a pivotal role in the Senate's refusal to confirm.

Overseeing Confirmation Strategy

President Johnson can also be held responsible for the adoption of a strategy for confirmation which, rather than increasing support for the nomination, generated additional opposition against Fortas. A closer look at Johnson's misguided efforts in his futile attempt to win the chief justiceship for his old friend, Abe Fortas, will support this conclusion.

In a March 31, 1968, speech to the nation, Johnson made what he considered the most "unselfish" decision in his life and withdrew as a presidential candidate.[13] In expounding upon his reasons for not seeking re-election, the president appeared to be taking the high road, promising that the spirit of non-partisanship would be the beacon guiding his actions in his remaining days in office.[14]

If a few months later the president had approached the selection of Warren's replacement in the spirit of unselfishness and non-partisanship promised in his March 31 address, he may not have encountered stiff opposition to his attempt to appoint Warren's successor. Rather than following this high road course, however, Johnson soon conveyed that his approach to seeking a replacement for Warren would be free from neither the reality nor the appearance of personal and partisan concerns. The forfeiture of the high road strategy is evident in at least three areas: the nature of Chief Justice Warren's retirement announcement, the coupling of the Fortas nomination with that of Homer Thornberry, and the unseemly and calculated use by the White House of the issue of anti-Semitism.

Warren's "Retirement". On June 26, 1968, in announcing the chief justice's intention to retire at an unspecified future date, President Johnson stipulated Warren's resignation would not become effective until "such time as a successor is qualified."[15] That stipulation soon became a cause celebre.

The contingent nature of Warren's retirement upset many senators. Whether or not it was Johnson's intention, he appeared to offer the Senate a choice—a dubious choice to some senators—to confirm Fortas or have Warren withdraw his intention to retire and continue to serve indefinitely as chief justice. Senator Paul J. Fannin (R, Ariz.) denounced the contingent retirement plan as a cheap trick of "political maneuvering."[16] Senator Gordon Allott (R, Colo.) was reportedly livid at what he perceived to be a "deep plot" designed to dictate to the Senate the choice of the next chief justice.[17] Senator Sam Ervin (D, N.C.) testily concluded: "It comes down to this, that the Senate must confirm Mr. Fortas as Chief Justice or return Mr. Warren as Chief Justice."[18] Senator Robert Griffin (R, Mich.), whose leadership of the GOP forces opposed to Fortas was crucial to the outcome, testified after the defeat of the nomination that it was the nature of Warren's retirement that had propelled him to work so actively against confirmation. "My initial concern and opposition to the nomination," noted the Michigan Republican, "sprang from the fact that it had all the earmarks of a political maneuver."[19]

Warren has since insisted his only intention in agreeing to make his departure contingent upon confirmation of a replacement was to assure that the Court would not be left without a chief justice. Both the former chief justice and the White House noted that during Warren's long tenure on the Court two incidents had occurred which called for a special session during the summer recess. With at least the possibility that a similar incident could happen in the summer of 1968, and in the interest of maintaining continuity in the office of the chief justice, Warren reportedly agreed to leave the effective date of his retirement to the president.[20] The chief justice also noted he had "no further discussion or understanding" beyond this with the president.[21]

Despite this disclaimer, a White House memorandum describing a meeting between the chief justice and the president on June 13, 1968, the day Warren informed Johnson of his intention to retire, indicates there was further discussion between these two men on the matter of a chief justice designee. According to the memorandum, the departing chief justice urged President Johnson to replace him with someone whose views were similar to his [Warren's] own.[22]

Even though Warren's June 13, 1968 letter to the president contained the key phrase "effective at your [Johnson's] pleasure," there is some evidence the chief justice originally had fully intended to retire immediately and not make his stepping down contingent upon Senate confirmation of his successor.[23] Warren's colleagues on the Court, who most likely would have been aware of the chief justice's intention, apparently were convinced he was leaving the Court forthwith. According to one report, the other justices "believed that he [Warren] had resigned effective immediately, and were looking around for somebody to sign writs in Warren's absence."[24]

In accepting Warren's June 13 letter, the president could have made the chief justice's retirement effective immediately or at a definite date in the future. However, the president's June 26, 1968, letter to Warren acknowledging the chief's intention to leave the Court carefully specified the retirement would not become effective until "such time as a successor is qualified."[25] In agreeing to the exchange of letters and despite his reported initial intention to retire immediately as well as the desire to keep his retirement from becoming a political issue,[26] Warren acquiesced in the contingent retirement plan.

Fortas also appears to have been actively involved in the contingent retirement plan. A June 24, 1968, preliminary draft of President Johnson's June 26, 1968, letter to Warren bears the initials "AF" which signify Abe Fortas.[27] This preliminary draft contains the following opening paragraph:

> I acknowledge receipt of your retirement letter. I accept this with the greatest regret, to become effective (when your successor takes office?)[28]

Fortas's likely involvement in designing the nature of Warren's retirement is consistent with the associate justice's private but extensive participation in most phases of the struggle for confirmation. For example, Fortas appears to have played key roles in setting up his friend and former law partner, Paul A. Porter, as the "central clearing house on information and assignments" regarding the confirmation effort as well as in lining up support for the nomination from senators and influential private citizens.[29] Even though Fortas prepared the original draft of the June 26 letter, the reference in the draft to a contingent retirement for Warren is in the form of a question, indicating final approval clearly rested with the president.

According to one account, when President Johnson met with Warren on June 13, 1968, and was informed of the chief justice's intention to retire, both men wanted to make sure it was Johnson who appointed Warren's successor. Later that day, Warren forwarded his letter to the president making his retirement effective at Johnson's pleasure. After securing Fortas's assent to becoming chief justice, Johnson set about ensuring that in the event he was deprived of naming Warren's successor, Warren could continue to serve beyond 1968. Relying on the language suggested by Fortas, Johnson's acceptance of Warren's intention to retire was made contingent upon the qualification of a successor. Johnson deliberately included this language to enable Warren to withdraw his retirement in the event something went wrong with his plan to handpick the chief's successor.[30]

Additional evidence that the contingent retirement scheme was hatched by President Johnson is supplied by then Deputy Attorney General Warren Christopher. Christopher included the following statement relative to the contingent retirement in a chronological summary of the Fortas and Thornberry cases prepared for the White House shortly after the nominations had been withdrawn by the president.

> On June 25 . . . the President indicated to the Attorney General that he wanted great care taken on the reply to the letter of retirement from the Chief Justice, the President indicating that he would like to accept the retirement in a manner to make it effective upon the qualification of Warren's successor, and to enable the retirement to be withdrawn if the successor does not qualify.[31]

While the evidence indicates that the president conceived the contingent retirement scheme, the possibility exists the plan may not have originated with him. While unlikely, it remains possible that the plan was first suggested by Warren, Fortas, or others who met with Johnson before the announcement of the nominations, and who shared the president's goal to have him name Warren's successor. However, the important point is not whether the retirement plan originated with the president or with someone else. What is most meaningful is that the contingent retirement concept could not have been implemented without the president's approval. That fact alone justifies the conclusion Johnson bears prime responsibility for any opposition to the Fortas nomination which can be attributed to the contingent retirement plan.

The charges of partisan maneuvering on the part of the president stemming from the contingent nature of Warren's retirement became more credible and continued to draw more adherents in the Senate in part because of the president's reluctance to do anything to alter the situation. At least two pro-Fortas senators advised the president to squelch the charge once and for all by requesting a definite date of retirement from Warren. On July 11, 1968, Senator Albert Gore (D, Tenn.) suggested to the president that he have another exchange of letters with the chief justice in order to lessen the growing partisan opposition to Fortas occasioned by the contingent retirement scheme. The Tennessee Democrat saw this as the only way of finally "removing all doubts" as to Warren's intention to retire.[32] The same course of action was also reportedly recommended to the president by Senator George Smathers (D, Fla.).[33] Johnson, however, declined to follow this suggestion and as a result lost the opportunity to lessen some of the opposition raised against Fortas's confirmation.

The controversy surrounding the contingent nature of Warren's retirement helped erase any advantage Johnson could have hoped to gain by proclaiming his adherance to a non-partisan stance. Republican senators and others whom the Johnson administration accused of playing partisan politics with the Supreme Court by using the threat of a filibuster to block a direct vote on the nomination could easily parry the attack by citing the contingent retirement scheme. Fortas's opponents could credibly raise the countercharge it was the White House that initially involved the choice of the next chief justice in partisan politics by resorting to the retirement scheme. For example, Senator Roman L. Hruska (R, Neb.) responded to charges that Senator Griffin and his supporters were unwisely involving the Supreme Court in politics in opposing Fortas by noting "if the opposition to . . . confirmation is political, it is because the timing and the fact of the resignation are also political."[34]

In addition, senators opposed to the nomination were also able to point to the conclusion drawn by important members of the president's own party on the partisan considerations underlying the unique nature of Chief Justice Warren's "retirement." By way of illustration, it was Democratic Senator John L. McClellan of Arkansas who concluded Warren

> does not intend to retire until and unless the Senate confirms Mr. Justice Fortas as his replacement. Any attempt by the present incumbent or any presumption that he has any right, legal or otherwise, to, in effect, name his replacement clearly goes beyond the purview of any official duty or responsibility and transgresses the historic and vital separation of powers upon which this government rests.[35]

The charge of partisan maneuvering leveled against the president by opponents of the nomination, purportedly incensed by the contingent nature of Warren's retirement, may or may not have been justified. Indeed some anti-Fortas senators who cited this issue in expressing opposition to confirmation may have employed it as others did the ethics issue, i.e., as a shield to conceal the real motivations behind their disapproval. Nevertheless, the possibility that this issue could be employed at all, in either a sincere or an insincere manner, stemmed from Johnson's decision to go ahead with the contingent retirement plan as well as from his refusal to take any action to lessen opposition occasioned by the plan. This realization underscores Robert Shogan's conclusion that the "indefinite timing of Warren's retirement, with the implication of forcing the Senate to choose between Warren and Fortas, served only to antagonize the opposition and to tarnish the nominations."[36]

A Lack of Balance. President Johnson also unwisely passed up an opportunity to gain broader support in the Senate for his chief justice designee when he coupled the Fortas nomination with that of Homer Thornberry. Thornberry, a Texas Democrat, was a close friend of the president's. When Johnson moved up to the Senate, Thornberry had taken his old congressional seat and had been with the president through his heart attack in 1955, his unsuccessful campaign for the presidency in 1960, and his succession to the White House on the day of John F. Kennedy's assassination.[37] Johnson had also named Thornberry to the United States Court of Appeals for the Fifth Circuit.

In nominating Fortas, Johnson was asking the Senate to accept a Democrat, a liberal, and his close personal friend as the next chief justice of the United States. In the spirit of non-partisanship expressed in his March 31 address, or simply in a pragmatic attempt to win Senate confirmation of the nominations, Johnson could have selected as Fortas's replacement a distinguished moderate-to-conservative independent or Republican or, that being an overly cautious and extreme move, at least a Democrat with whom he was not closely associated. This approach would have at least given those senators who reacted negatively to Fortas's perceived ideology and/or party affiliation some reason to support the confirmation of both nominations. The president elected not to follow this approach.

The nominations of Fortas and Thornberry meant that Republicans in the Senate were being asked not only to approve two perceived Democratic "cronies" of the president's but also to deprive the next president, whom they hoped would be a Republican, of the opportunity of filling these vacancies. Given this situation, there is little doubt GOP Senators would have been more inclined to support the Fortas nomination had it been balanced by the designation of a nominee perceived more favorably by them.[38]

Additionally, several key Southern Democrats believed the coupling of Thornberry's nomination with Fortas's represented the unattractive pairing of two staunch liberals. Senator Richard Russell came to the conclusion that despite Thornberry's Texas background, he "had ruled on civil-rights matters like a Yankee liberal judge."[39] Senator Robert C. Byrd (D, W.Va.) was another who believed Thornberry should be opposed because he was "sympathetic to the liberal majority on the Court."[40] Senator Russell Long (D, La.) directly indicated to the president that he would not likely support Thornberry because in the Louisiana Democrat's view, the nominee was a "liberal."[41]

These senators and other conservatives no doubt felt Johnson was asking them to approve two liberal nominees to serve on a Supreme Court many of them believed had already moved too far to the left. When the president coupled the Fortas and Thornberry nominations, they were given little incentive to support confirmation. In the view of these senators, the presence of a bona fide conservative nominee for Fortas's associate justice seat would have represented a more ideologically balanced approach to staffing the Court and may have encouraged them to withhold their opposition.

In addition, that both Thornberry and Fortas were the president's close personal friends caused some senators to conclude the nominations smacked of "cronyism," reducing the chances for confirmation. They might have been willing to approve one intimate friend of the president but not two. As expressed by Senator Griffin, other chief executives had nominated personal friends to prestigious positions but never before had any president been so bold as to make two such nominations at the same time.[42] Evidence that Griffin's views were widely shared even by supporters of the nominations is indicated by a report circulated at the White House that "one well-known administration senator, talking with colleagues in the cloakroom, remarked caustically, 'This appointment is the crassest kind of cronyism.' "[43]

Finally, both opponents as well as supporters of the nominations seriously questioned whether Thornberry possessed the requisite legal ability expected of a Supreme Court justice. Among those senators opposed to the nomination and expressing concern about Thornberry's ability were Byrd of West Virginia, Wallace F. Bennett (R, Utah), and Norris Cotton (R, N.H.). Bennett, who eventually opposed both nominees, had initially been inclined to support Fortas but had disapproved of Thornberry from the start as a "hack."[44] Byrd was reportedly "particularly concerned about Thornberry's qualifications."[45] Cotton concluded that Thornberry is "a fine gentleman, but he is not Supreme Court material."[46]

While criticism of Thornberry's legal ability by opponents of the nominations was to be expected, even those favoring the nominations shared the view that the Texas judge was not of Supreme Court caliber. For example, Senator Harrison A. Williams, Jr. (D, N.J.) strongly supported Fortas but reportedly complained privately about the Thornberry nomination.[47] Senator Jacob K. Javits (R, N.Y.) publicly announced support for Fortas but was described in a White House report as having "reservations as to Thornberry."[48] A Justice Department official reported pro-Fortas Senator Clifford P. Case (R, N.J.) to be "privately outraged by the appointment of Thornberry, thinking it a bad appointment."[49] Finally, a White House staffer, queried on whether the Thornberry nomination undermined support for Fortas, responded:

> I think that hurt a little bit. I recall talking to one senator, who said that . . . "I can go along on Abe Fortas. But I served with Thornberry over in the House, and he just isn't qualified to be a member of the Supreme Court." He said "Of course, I'm going to swallow hard and vote for him, but that's a mistake." This was a good friend of the President's.[50]

The failure of the president to couple the nomination of a chief justice with that of a more attractive associate justice is even more surprising given that several White House advisors and respected Johnson intimates urged the president to do just that. Secretary of Defense Clark M. Clifford encouraged the president to name as Fortas's successor an outstanding constitutional and trial lawyer of unimpeachable and impeccable standing with the American Bar Association. In addition, it was Clifford's judgement that the nominee for Fortas's seat should also be a Republican.[51] Harry C. McPherson, Jr., Special Counsel to the President, had suggested coupling the Fortas nomination with that of either Washington, D.C., attorney Hugh Cox "for sheer intellectual brilliance and character" or Senator Thomas H. Kuchel (R, Calif.) on grounds "it would be hard for Republicans to oppose him."[52] Deputy Special Counsel to the President Larry Temple only succeeded in inviting Johnson's wrath when he suggested the selection of Thornberry would hinder the Fortas nomination because opposition senators could more credibly accuse the president of appointing individuals to the Supreme Court on the basis of "personal favoritism and personal friendships."[53] The president could not even be deterred from naming Thornberry by the concurrence in Temple's comments of no less a Johnson intimate and friend of the Texas judge than Lady Bird Johnson.[54] Finally, Louisiana Democrat Russell B. Long reportedly cautioned the president shortly before the nominations were announced that if forwarded to the Senate, "a Fortas-Thornberry package would be in real trouble."[55]

The conclusion reached here regarding President Johnson's lack of astute presidential management in coupling the Fortas and Thornberry nominations is endorsed by at least two other observers. Shogan notes that "while the President could do nothing to conceal his long friendship with Fortas, he could certainly have selected as the other nominee someone further removed from him personally and politically than Homer Thornberry."[56] Mike Manatos, a special assistant to the president, concluded, "it . . . would probably have been better if he'd [President Johnson] sent Fortas up and then dangled out another spot on the Supreme Court for a more conservative type. The southerners and some Republicans might have bought that."[57]

The Anti-Semitism Issue. President Johnson also contributed to the Senate's negative action by his approach to the anti-Semitism issue. His involvement with this matter once again helped to erase any advantage he hoped to gain by appearing to be the statesmanlike, non-partisan chief executive he proclaimed he would be in his March 31, 1968, address.

Some groups and perhaps even one senator opposed Fortas because he was Jewish. The National Socialist White People's Party, predictably upset with the prospect of a Jewish chief justice, set up a telephone recording urging callers to oppose Fortas and describing the nominee as a "despicable Jew with a 'red' record that smells to high heaven."[58] A White House staffer not only claimed "there was a lot of anti-semitism in the whole struggle" but reported one unidentified southern senator's saying to a Dixie colleague, "you're not going to vote for that Jew to be Chief Justice, are you?"[59] Porter attributed his friend's defeat to "the evil forces of bigotry."[60] Indeed, Fortas himself noted some of the opposition to his confirmation stemmed from anti-Semitism.[61]

Despite these reports, there is little evidence senators decided to oppose the nomination on religious or ethnic grounds. On the contrary, there exists significant evidence indicating anti-Semitism was never a factor leading senators to oppose Fortas. Minority Leader Everett Dirksen retrospectively concluded the charge some senators opposed Fortas for anti-Semitic reasons was "without any real warrant or justification."[62] Senator Javits, a Jew, liberal, and strong supporter of Fortas, willingly came to the aid of those senators who opposed the nomination and were subsequently criticized for being anti-Semitic. The New York Republican both privately and publicly expressed the view there was no hard evidence that anti-Semitism was an issue in the controversy.[63] Finally, a

White House aide noted that while some irresponsible fringe groups mounted an anti-Semitic campaign against Fortas, "none of the members of the Senate . . . even those that were opposing the nomination thought well of this."[64]

Most, if not all, senators soundly condemned the bigoted charges of the anti-Semitic groups opposing the nomination. Accordingly, one would expect the anti-Semitism issue would never have surfaced in the Fortas deliberations or, if it did arise, would soon have died out. The intriguing question is why this issue was so consistently and so prolongingly raised in these deliberations. The answer to that question points to the president's unstatesmanlike, partisan approach to this delicate issue.

Substantial evidence exists indicating Johnson was instrumental in both raising and keeping alive the issue of anti-Semitism. At the beginning of the Senate's deliberations on the Fortas nomination, the president reportedly sought to pressure reluctant senators by warning them, at least implicitly, that opposition to Fortas would open them to the charge of being biased against Jews, an indictment sure to alienate their Jewish constituents and contributors. One report notes that the president began making veiled threats of his intended use of the anti-Semitism issue before the nominations were even announced. Shogan describes a June 27, 1968, meeting between the president and Senator Dirksen:

> Then Johnson brought up something that was to become the ugliest aspect of the controversy that lay ahead. It would be well for senators, Republican as well as Democrat, to bear in mind that Fortas stood to become the first Jewish Chief Justice in the nation's history. His none too subtle point was that it would be foolhardy for politicians of either party to risk antagonizing Jewish votes, not to mention Jewish financial contributors, in an election year.[65]

Evidence also exists indicating that Johnson not only threatened to use the anti-Semitism issue to pressure senators into supporting Fortas but did so use the issue. One White House report boasts that seventy-five Jewish leaders were contacted to work on Fortas's behalf and concludes, "we have gotten the Jews wound up."[66] While it is unclear what issues were used by the White House to get Fortas's Jewish supporters so motivated, more than likely the anti-Semitism issue was among them.

The assertion that Johnson calculatedly exploited the anti-Semitism issue gains credibility from additional reports he privately employed the bigotry charge to rally support for the nomination. Shogan notes:

Word spread on Capitol Hill that senators opposing the nominations would risk retaliation from Jewish voters. Lyndon Johnson had made that very point to Everett Dirksen and some [senators] strongly suspected LBJ of inspiring the talk. In fact, soon after he announced the nominations, the President, in private chats with newsmen, had made clear his belief that there was more than a bit of prejudice behind the opposition to Fortas. These assertions could not be attributed to him, and the press treated them gingerly. Nevertheless, the anxiety among dissident senators was fed by reports from home. Some Jewish constituents were expressing concern about opposition to Fortas, and Jewish leaders were pointedly rallying to Fortas's support.[67]

In addition, a White House document sent to the president reflects one aide's effort to follow the administration's apparent strategy of pushing the anti-Semitism issue without appearing to promote it. After noting that he had spoken to an editor "about a Fortas editorial along the lines we discussed," the aide reported that the newspaper official "wondered whether the issue of anti-semitism should be openly raised, and by inference attributed to some of the opposition." The aide apparently did not reject the suggestion out of hand. On the contrary, his report appears to signal White House acceptance of the tactic by concluding:

> I said that if I were writing the editorial, I would warn the opponents that there are reactionary voices being raised over the nomination, and that those who have more acceptable purposes in opposing Fortas might find themselves in bed with anti-semites.[68]

There is also evidence that the White House used the anti-Semitism issue in a vain attempt to secure Republican presidential candidate Richard Nixon's support for the Fortas nomination. The administration tried to convince Nixon that his failure to speak out strongly on Fortas's behalf would be interpreted as an act in tacit support of the filibuster blocking Senate consideration and thereby cost him significant Jewish support in the November election. A letter written by Porter to a Nixon supporter, Republican Senator Thruston B. Morton of Kentucky, is indicative of this effort by the White House. Porter's letter noted:

> A lot of people who feel about Abe [Fortas] as I do are convinced a word from Dick Nixon would do the job. The Court obviously will be an issue in this [presidential] campaign in any event but I do not believe it would become such a massive controversy if these nominations were out of the way. There is the ugly prospect of undertones of anti-semitism and bigotry that could be involved.[69]

President Johnson's approach to the anti-Semitism issue worked against Fortas's chances for confirmation in at least two significant ways. Because the president not only initially raised the specter of anti-Semitism but also calculatedly kept the subject alive, any leverage the White House sought to gain from use of the issue was soon negated. Opponents of the nomination could convincingly and often righteously counter the anti-Semitism charge raised against them by pointing to the White House's callous exploitation of this issue and by criticizing the pro-Fortas forces for recklessly raising the groundless but still inflammatory charge of anti-Semitism.[70] In addition, any support Johnson sought to gain for the nominations by sticking to the high road of nonpartisanship was undermined by what appeared to be a crass and partisan use of the anti-Semitism issue.[71]

Fuel for the Filibuster. President Johnson's tactics in the battle for confirmation undermined the Fortas nomination in other ways. It was evident early in the confirmation battle that the tactics of the anti-Fortas forces "were geared toward delay."[72] These opposition senators, aware their major ally was time, realized that the longer they could delay action on the nomination, the better the chances for defeating it. In this situation, it became essential that the president and the pro-Fortas forces do everything they could to avoid giving the opposition any excuse for prolonging Senate consideration of the nomination.

At the outset of the battle for Fortas's confirmation, Johnson appeared to appreciate the fatal impact any prolonged slowdown might have on the nomination. His reported remarks to a group of White House aides charged with planning a successful strategy for confirmation included the following prophetic comment:

> We're going to be in trouble on this. We've got to get this thing through, and we've got to get it through early because if it drags out we're going to get beat . . . I know that Senate. If they get this thing drug out very long, we're going to get beat.[73]

Despite the president's apparent awareness of the necessity of avoiding any extended delay, his approval of the contingent retirement plan and the coupling of the Fortas and Thornberry nominations played into the hands of the anti-Fortas forces by providing opposition senators with debating material they could use to slow down Senate consideration of the nominations.[74] The conditional nature of Warren's retirement led to an extensive debate in the Judiciary Committee on whether any vacancy really existed on the Court. Because Chief Justice Warren had not definitely retired, Senator James O. Eastland, chairman of the Senate Judiciary Committee, and Senator Sam Ervin (D, N.C.) contended that there was no need to consider either the Fortas or Thornberry nomination. In their view, there would be no vacancy on the Court until a definite date had been set for Warren's retirement.[75] The coupling of the Fortas and Thornberry nominations also gave opposing senators the opportunity to consume precious time discussing the merits of a president naming personal friends to prestigious positions.[76]

In retrospect, the opportunity for delay was needlessly given to the opposition forces by the president. The prolonged debate generated by these events could have been avoided by the president's early rejection of the contingent retirement plan and by the selection of a nominee more attractive to opposition senators than Thornberry. In turn, the avoidance of or the immediate blunting of the issues generated by the retirement scheme and the Fortas-Thornberry package would also have given the president leverage in his effort to move the Senate to consider the Fortas nomination directly. A more convincing case could have been made to the public that much of the extended debate in the Senate was designed solely to avoid a direct vote on whether to confirm Fortas. However, and as a result of the president not taking these steps, opponents were successful in stretching out the Senate's consideration of the Fortas nomination until after the Democratic and Republican national conventions were completed in August, 1968.

The extended delay in Senate consideration of the Fortas nomination proved even more important after Congress reconvened in September. By that time, events at the conventions had begun to cast dark shadows over Fortas's prospects for confirmation. Nixon's designation as the Republican presidential candidate amid the balmy atmosphere of Miami, and Hubert H. Humphrey's selection as the Democratic nominee in the turmoil of Chicago signaled that a Nixon victory in November was a strong possibility and that a Republican and more conservative chief justice was in the offing if the Fortas nomination could be permanently derailed.

Delaying Senate consideration of the Fortas nomination until after the nominating conventions had been concluded also contributed significantly to hardening the opposition of conservative Democrats to confirmation. It can be assumed conservative Democrats in the Senate would have been inclined to support Fortas out of party loyalty, if for no other reason, had the Republicans nominated a more liberal presidential candidate than Nixon. For example, had Governor Nelson A.

Rockefeller of New York won the presidential nomination, these conservative Democrats would have had reason to expect Rockefeller's nominee for chief justice would be as liberal, if not more liberal than Fortas, and a Republican as well. These conservative Democrats may very well have preferred a liberal Democrat to a liberal Republican as the next chief justice, although not being particularly pleased with either one.

With the prospects for a Nixon victory in the 1968 election looking bright, the Fortas and Thornberry nominations faced severe jeopardy. One report notes, "the climate on Capitol Hill when Congress returned in early September was less favorable than ever toward Lyndon Johnson's nominations."[77] There appears to have been more than coincidence in the fact that conservative Senate Democrats Eastland of Mississippi and Harry F. Byrd, Jr., of Virginia did not announce their opposition to the Fortas nomination until shortly after Nixon had been designated the Republican presidential nominee.[78] Very likely the prospects of a Nixon victory in November and of a more conservative chief justice solidified the opposition of these two senators to Fortas's confirmation. Johnson was convinced these considerations cemented Eastland's opposition to Fortas. "Eastland had received assurances", Johnson later wrote in his memoirs, "that if he blocked the Fortas nomination and the Republicans captured the White House, a chief justice more to his liking would be appointed."[79]

Eastland's opposition to the Fortas nomination played a crucial role in contributing to its defeat. According to White House insiders, the Judiciary Committee chairman seriously undermined the nomination when he "strung the hearings along for months."[80] Another report adds that Eastland's announced opposition prompted Majority Leader Mansfield and Minority Leader Dirksen to warn the president that the prospects for Fortas's confirmation had become bleak.[81] Additionally, President Johnson has directly testified to the decisive impact Eastland's opposition had on Fortas's chances for confirmation. After being informed of the Mississippi Democrat's unequivocal opposition, the president glumly concluded the White House "probably could not muster the votes to put the Fortas nomination through."[82]

The delay in considering the nomination, augmented by Johnson's tactics, also afforded opposition senators sufficient time to uncover and publicize the key issue of the $15,000 seminar fee the nominee had received from American University. It will be recalled that Fortas had accepted the fee for conducting a nine-week seminar at American University Law School during the summer of 1968. And while the amount of the fee raised some eyebrows in the Senate, the manner in which the seminar was funded generated additional criticism. Funds to support the project were raised by Fortas's close friend and former law partner Porter, who had solicited the money from five prominent businessmen likely to be involved in litigation before the Supreme Court.

Knowledge of the American University fee arrangement, which reportedly came as a "complete surprise" to the White House and "disappointed" and "troubled" Johnson, did not surface in the Senate until early September, 1968, some two months after the Fortas nomination had been announced.[83] Had Johnson taken steps to avoid or shorten the delay in Senate consideration of the nomination, the cloture roll call and perhaps even the direct vote on Fortas might have taken place before the beginning of September. It is the conclusion of at least one observer that had the president employed different tactics, "Fortas's nomination might well have been confirmed before the disclosure of the $15,000 American University fee."[84]

Delay in considering the nominations was significant because the resultant disclosure of the $15,000 seminar fee reportedly played a pivotal role in the Senate's refusal to confirm Fortas. In the opinion of many observers, the opposition generated by the disclosure of the fee doomed the Fortas nomination. One White House advisor concluded:

> The key thing that really broke our back was the revelation that Justice Fortas had received some fifteen thousand dollars from Amderican [sic] University for delivering some lectures while he was a member of the Supreme Court. Even our most ardent supporters found this to be sort of an objectionable thing with them. They were upset about it.[85]

White House Special Assistant Joseph Califano reportedly noted that the American University incident was "the straw that broke the camel's back."[86] Another White House aide concluded that the $15,000 fee arrangement was instrumental because it "put the nails in the coffin."[87] In addition, the seminar fee has been described as the "one final unexpected blow" that "demolished" any hope of Fortas's confirmation.[88]

The significant impact the $15,000 fee arrangement had in the Senate can be gauged by the extent to which this incident caused concern even among senators who were supporting the administration on the cloture roll call.[89] As noted above, Senator Cooper reportedly confided to a White House aide his deep concern about the seminar fee arrangement. Majority Leader Mansfield as well as Minority Leader Dirksen informed the White House that "the $15,000 fee, while a secondary issue, has been hurtful, particularly since Paul Porter raised the money."[90]

Mansfield also told his senate colleagues that while he would support the Fortas nomination, the episode of the $15,000 fee was "unfortunate because it breaches the extraordinary insulation which must exist between the Supreme Court and other branches of the government and private interests."[91] Finally, Senator Hugh Scott (R, Pa.) reportedly confided to the White House his view that the surfacing of the fee arrangement "had struck a damaging blow to the Fortas case."[92]

The controversy surrounding the American University fee also apparently had a notable impact on senators who eventually disapproved of the Fortas nomination and/or voted against terminating debate.[93] And while it is difficult to ascertain whether these senators used the $15,000 fee issue in a sincere or disingenuous way, its effect can nonetheless be seen in the number of senators who switched from supporting the nomination and/or cloture after news of the payment was disclosed. Senator Griffin claimed at least three defectors from the pro-Fortas camp because of the $15,000 arrangement: Senators J. Caleb Boggs (R, Del.), Roman L. Hruska (R, Neb.), and James B. Pearson (R, Kan.).[94] Boggs and Hruska had apparently favored Fortas's confirmation before disclosure of the $15,000 payment to Fortas. During July, 1968, Hruska described Fortas as a "fine man and the best lawyer on the Court" and confided to the White House he would vote for Fortas.[95] Boggs had been consistently listed by the administration among those senators who were in favor of cloture and confirmation. However, after disclosure of the fee arrangement, his switch to opposing Fortas was described by White House aides as "bad news."[96] Confirming the accuracy of Griffin's claim, Hruska, Boggs, and Pearson all voted against terminating debate on the Fortas nomination.

On August 13, 1968, the White House included Senators Allen J. Ellender (D, La.), B. Everett Jordan (D, N.C.), J. W. Fulbright (D, Ark.), and John J. Sparkman (D, Ala.) among "those southerners who will support Fortas."[97] A few weeks later, after the $15,000 payment was made public, none of these four senators sided with the administration in its effort to terminate debate on the Fortas nomination.

It is both ironic and significant that when Ellender reportedly pledged his support of Fortas shortly after the nomination was announced, he reserved the right to retreat from this position if "something develops that shows him [Fortas] to be a real scoundrel." The Louisiana Democrat confided he would support both Fortas and Thornberry "unless something is developed in the hearing, such as fraud, etc., which would make one or both undesirable." "With this exception, which I do not expect", concluded Ellender, "the president can count on my support."[98] No doubt the $15,000 seminar fee arrangement became the unanticipated exception leading Ellender to withdraw his support.

The American University payment to Fortas also appeared to have played a significant role in influencing Senators Thomas J. Dodd (D, Conn.) and Richard Russell (D, Ga.) to oppose the nomination. As noted above, shortly after the disclosure of the $15,000 fee, Dodd told a White House aide he might have to vote against confirmation. Senator Russell attributed his opposition to the nomination at least in part to the seminar fee. In a September 26, 1968 private letter to Johnson, the Georgia Democrat stated that the fee arrangement made it "impossible for me to support Justice Fortas."[99]

President Johnson and the Senate

President Johnson's most serious misjudgments in attempting to win confirmation of the Fortas nomination occurred in his dealings with the Senate. This conclusion is most surprising in view of Johnson's reputation for understanding the Senate better than any previous occupant of the White House. Notwithstanding this reputation, evidence suggests the president made at least two fundamental errors in his effort to appoint Warren's successor. He relied almost exclusively on the judgment of a few select senators, notably his old buddies, Russell and Dirksen. In addition, and perhaps as a direct result of this limited reliance on a few senators, he failed to assess correctly the mood of the Senate and consequently adopted a confirmation strategy destined for failure.

Before the Fortas and Thornberry nominations were announced, Johnson reportedly consulted with Senators Russell, Dirksen, and Eastland. This consultation left the president with the understanding that Russell and Dirksen clearly were committed to supporting the nominations. In addition, Eastland, while not definitely committed, reportedly responded favorably enough to the Fortas-Thornberry package to leave the president with the impression that he could count on his support.[100]

As Johnson sized up the Senate, the support of Russell and Dirksen was essential if the door leading to confirmation were to be unlocked. Russell's backing was counted upon to lessen, if not eliminate, the anticipated opposition of some southern senators to Fortas. Dirksen's support was expected to offset any prospective opposition on the part of Senate Republicans.[101]

The president's approach toward gaining Senate approval of his nominations soon backfired for several related reasons. The limited reliance on Russell's and Dirksen's assessments of the mood of the Senate toward the nominations resulted in Johnson's severely narrowing the range of potential nominees considered by the White House and adopting an unsound strategy for confirmation. In addition, this limited reliance led the president to ignore the advice and warnings of other senators, especially in regard to the negative response in the Senate to the Fortas-Thornberry package. The evidence also suggests that the president either misjudged the firmness of Russell's and Dirksen's commitment to support Fortas and/or acted in such a way as to alienate these two senators and lose their support.

Limited Senate Consultation. Beyond consulting with Russell, Dirksen, and Eastland, there is little evidence Johnson contacted any other senators before announcing the Fortas and Thornberry nominations. A White House aide actively involved in the effort to win confirmation of the Fortas nomination has testified to the president's almost exclusive reliance on a few senators, especially Russell and Dirksen:

> I don't think he confided in anybody else. I'm inclined to think that almost from the outset he thought of Fortas for the chief justiceship and thought of Thornberry for the other position, and then went through the process of eliminating all of the other possibilities.[102]

The president's decision not to consult more broadly in the Senate hurt Fortas's chances for confirmation. Senator McClellan, particularly incensed about not learning of the president's decision to nominate Fortas and Thornberry until the public announcement of the nominations, noted:

> I'm only the second ranking man on the [Judiciary] Committee, yet no one bothered to consult me. They talked to everybody else. . . . I wonder if we ought not have real long hearings. Find out about the "deal" which was made, and then talk to me.[103]

It is doubtful whether the decidedly conservative McClellan would have ever come around to supporting Fortas. His ideology index of zero indicated a strong inclination to oppose Fortas's elevation to the chief justiceship on ideological grounds. Nevertheless, had the president consulted even briefly with the senator prior to the public announcements of the nominations, McClellan's opposition may have been softened. At the least, a meeting between the president and McClellan might have cleared up the latter's suspicions of a "deal" and encouraged him to withdraw his threat to string out the hearings. As it was, the Arkansas Democrat was soon to be described as being "vehemently opposed" to the Fortas nomination.[104] His opposition was pivotal because at the very time the White House was seeking speedy action on the nominations, the Arkansas Democrat delivered on his threat to delay Senate consideration. According to a White House report, McClellan was extremely influential in critically prolonging the Judiciary Committee's deliberations.[105]

Two other southern senators who opposed the Fortas nomination noted their concern about the president's failure to consult with them before announcing the nominations. Senator John G. Tower (R, Tex.), who was under the impression the president was going to nominate Arthur Goldberg for the chief justiceship instead of Fortas, was reportedly "a little upset that he did not get contacted before the announcement."[106] Senator Russell Long (D, La.) was described in one White House report as being "disinterested" in the nominations because "no one at the White House has called him."[107]

Johnson's reluctance to heed the advice of anyone other than Russell and Dirksen committed the White House to pursuing a confirmation strategy founded on unreliable and misleading information. This is especially so in regard to the president's response to the advice reportedly offered by Judiciary Committee Chairman Eastland. The day before Fortas and Thornberry nominations were announced, when the opportunity to select another nominee for the chief justiceship and/or adopt a different confirmation strategy still existed, Eastland warned Johnson that the Senate would never confirm the Fortas and Thornberry nominations. According to the Mississippi Democrat, there would definitely be a filibuster against the Fortas nomination that could only end in defeat for the president.[108]

Eastland also expressed to the president his misgivings about the White House strategy of relying upon Russell and Dirksen to hold in check the respective opposition of Southern Democrats and Republicans. The Judiciary Committee Chairman prophetically noted that despite their purported commitment to the president to support the nominations, both would eventually desert the administration and oppose Fortas's confirmation.[109] A retrospective and lengthy memorandum by a Justice Department official prepared months after the defeat of the nominations confirms the report of Eastland's advice.

> On June 25 at 1:05 p.m., Senator Eastland told the Attorney General that a filibuster was already being organized against Fortas (though his nomi-

nation had not yet been sent up) and that if it started against Fortas, it would include Thornberry. Eastland reported that he had talked to eight or ten Senators who were very bitter and outspoken against Fortas, and he commented that he had never seen so much feeling against a man as against Fortas. Eastland went on to say, however, that the nomination would probably be approved if both Dirksen and Hruska supported to carry it [sic]. Later in the afternoon, Senator Eastland commented that Dirksen was acting strangely, though it appeared that the President had won him over. At this point, Eastland predicted that a filibuster against Fortas would be a success.[110]

This same memorandum notes that on June 27, the day after the nominations were announced, Eastland informed the White House that Russell would not fulfill the critical role assigned to him in the strategy designed to gain confirmation for Fortas and Thornberry. It was Eastland's view that despite assurances given to the president, Russell "was not going to vote for Fortas and that all the Southerners would oppose Fortas and would not vote for cloture if there was a filibuster."[111]

Several post-mortem explanations of the demise of Fortas's hopes for confirmation point to the contributing role played by the president's failure to comprehend the hostile mood of the Senate toward the nominations. One report attributed Fortas's remarkable fall from grace to "a major miscalculation on the part of President Lyndon B. Johnson."[112] Another noted the president had "badly misjudged the political atmosphere that quickly enveloped the nomination."[113] Fortas's trusted friend Porter traced the defeat to "several innocent miscalculations—the most important being a failure to recognize the depth and fanaticism of the opposition."[114]

Finally, Johnson implicitly admitted his error in not consulting more widely on the nominations and in not heeding the more pessimistic and, in retrospect, more realistic warnings of other senators such as Eastland. After the nominations were withdrawn, the president told the national press he simply "did not anticipate that there would be any opposition."[115] Had the president been willing to listen to a more diverse collection of senators and been more receptive to reports he apparently did not want to hear, the opposition could have been anticipated and, perhaps, controlled.

The President and Senator Dirksen. Throughout his years in the presidential office, Johnson had worked closely with Dirksen in securing the passage of legislation.[116] Indeed, the minority leader was described by the president as the key figure in enlisting the support of moderate Republicans to choke off a filibuster when the Senate, for the first time in history, voted cloture on a civil rights bill, paving the way for Congressional approval of the landmark Civil Rights Act of 1964.[117] No doubt Johnson remembered Dirksen's pivotal role in the 1964 struggle and anticipated that the Illinois Republican would play a similar part in the battle for Fortas's confirmation. However, by 1968, the mood of the Senate as well as Dirksen's ability to control his party colleagues had undergone some changes.

Dirksen's role in the Johnson-devised strategy for confirmation was so crucial one would have expected the president to have been certain the Illinois Republican's support of Fortas was solid and enduring before submitting the nominations to the Senate. Surprisingly, evidence suggests the president committed the White House to this strategy even though he was obviously aware Dirksen's support for confirmation was shaky. In this regard, there is Eastland's aforementioned warning, conveyed to the White House before the nominations were announced, that Dirksen would renege on his commitment to the president to support the nominations. There is also Dirksen's reputation for an "infinite capacity for changing his mind."[118] More important, there is Johnson's direct personal testimony to the effect that he was aware of the unsteady nature of Dirksen's pledge to support Fortas. At the very beginning of the battle for confirmation, the president reportedly made the following prophetic statement about the nomination to a group of his aides:

> Dirksen will leave us. Just take my word for it. I know him. I know that Senate. If they get this thing drug out very long, we're going to get beat. Ev Dirksen will leave us if we get this thing strung out very long.[119]

At first, the president's reliance on Dirksen's backing appeared to be a wise strategy. The Illinois Republican's support of the Fortas nomination did indeed lessen some early opposition to confirmation. The minority leader reportedly convinced Senator Hruska not to endorse the policy statement, launched by Senator Griffin and signed by nineteen Republicans, opposing all Supreme Court nominations made by the departing president in his closing months in office.[120] In addition, Dirksen denounced the sentiments expressed in the policy statement and reportedly persuaded four of its signers, Wallace F. Bennett (Utah), Milton R. Young (N.D.), Hiram L. Fong (Hawaii), and Thruston B. Morton (Ky.) to support the nomination.[121] The Illinois Republican was also given credit for derailing Griffin's effort to get the Credentials Committee of the Republican National Convention to adopt a strong "anti-crony" resolution aimed at the nominations and for foiling the Michigan senator's bid to have the Republican Platform Committee take a formal position in opposition to Fortas.[122]

Despite these early efforts, Dirksen eventually backed off from actively supporting Fortas's confirmation. By August, 1968, Dirksen was being described as approaching the prolonged delay in the Senate's consideration of the Fortas nomination without any "enthusiasm, confidence, or sense of outrage."[123] On September 27, 1968, the Illinois Republican announced he would not support the cloture motion, and he voted against terminating debate a few days later.[124]

Dirksen's decision to vote against cloture was reportedly as pivotal a factor in the Senate's refusal to confirm Fortas as his expressed and active support of the nomination was to have been in the president's confirmation strategy. The *Chicago Tribune* noted Dirksen's "complete reversal" to a position in opposition to terminating debate had the effect of swinging "four or five Republicans to the anti-cloture side."[125] Another report concluded that the Illinois Republican's "flip at the last minute means almost sure defeat for the cloture movement."[126] In the view of the *Christian Science Monitor*, once Dirksen announced his opposition to cloture, "few Fortas supporters in the Senate retained any hope at all that the associate justice could be confirmed."[127]

Confirming the devastating impact of Dirksen's defection are the reports of several individuals closely involved in the Senate's deliberations. Griffin, cautiously aware of the minority leader's potential clout with GOP colleagues, told reporters that Dirksen's switch had greatly bolstered the hopes of senators opposing the Fortas nomination.[128] Majority Leader Mansfield asserted that Dirksen's defection would "sure as hell" hinder the chances of terminating the filibuster dooming the nominations.[129] One White House aide described the Dirksen reversal as a "serious blow" to Fortas's hopes for confirmation.[130] Another hastened to advise the president that "in anticipation of the unhappy result of Senator Dirksen's new posture, may I respectfully urge that you send up a new nomination for Chief Justice as soon as . . . feasible."[131] Finally, no less an intimate in the associate justice's battle for confirmation than Carolyn C. Agger Fortas, an astute lawyer and spouse of the chief justice nominee, has testified to the crucial impact of Dirksen's reversal. The nominee's wife confided to her friend, Lady Bird Johnson, that Dirksen's turnabout on cloture had sounded the death knell for the nomination.[132]

Why did Dirksen defect from the pro-Fortas camp and vote against cloture? There is little doubt the charges of impropriety raised against Fortas made it increasingly more difficult for the Illinois Republican to support the nomination. The senator personally attributed his opposition to these charges, insisting he would not have initially supported the nomination had he known of the $15,000 fee Fortas received from American University."[133] According to Dirksen, his original promise to the president to support Fortas was based upon his current knowledge of the nominee's record and was subject to change if "something highly derogatory" were to be uncovered.[134]

Dirksen also publicly based his opposition on Fortas's siding with the 6-3 majority in *Witherspoon* v. *Illinois*, holding unconstitutional any death sentence imposed or recommended by a jury from which potential jurors voicing general objections to or expressing conscientious or religious scruples against the death penalty had been excluded.[135] Dirksen expressed the concern that as a result of this decision, twenty-four convicted murderers in Illinois, including Richard Speck, the 1966 slayer of eight Chicago nurses, would have their convictions reviewed and possibly set aside.[136]

Despite his public comments, Dirksen's disenchantment with the Fortas nomination appears to have been generated by considerations other than the *Witherspoon* decision or the nominee's sense of propriety. Reviewing his actions regarding the Fortas nomination in an interview conducted less than six months after the cloture vote, Dirksen did not even mention the *Witherspoon* case. In addition, he pointed to the seminar fee arrangement as a highly visible factor in the decision of others opposing Fortas but not necessarily in his own. As Dirksen put it:

> Well, there was the $30,000. That's all that was needed. Well, *they* read a lot of significance into the fact that Justice Fortas's law partner interested himself in getting this money and then later, of course, it was testified that the fee for the lecture to the Justice was $15,000, half of that sum. Well, *there are those* who thought that that was a rather untoward thing and it shouldn't have happened and pretty soon it began to scream from the front pages.[137]

In the same interview, Dirksen describes the events reflecting on Fortas's sense of propriety as "all these little things . . . that had an impact on the country."[138] Finally, Dirksen's office continued to express strong support of the Fortas nomination in response to constituent inquiries at least as late as September 20, 1968, a week *after* the $15,000 seminar fee had surfaced and been aired in the Senate Judiciary Committee.[139]

What then was the motivating factor behind Dirksen's critical defection? It appears the Illinois Republican did not feel strongly about either

opposing or supporting the Fortas nomination. What was most important to the minority leader and what he felt most strongly about was his
being perceived as playing a decisive role in events as momentous as
those determining the next chief justice. Whether Fortas was confirmed
or not, Dirksen believed it essential to his own reputation as a power to
be reckoned with that he appear to control the margin between victory
and defeat.

Consequently, at the early stages of the confirmation battle, when
Senate approval of the nomination seemed a certainty, Dirksen lined up
with the pro-Fortas forces. He actively lobbied in support of the nomination in order to leave the impression Fortas's confirmation would be
due to his efforts on the nominee's behalf. Support of this analysis can
be drawn from the remarks of Senator Cooper who observed to a White
House aide during the thick of the confirmation battle that Dirksen is
"throwing a lot of sand in everybody's eyes and no doubt would like to
come out as the savior of the nomination after a while."[140] In addition,
early in the confirmation fight, Dirksen repeatedly assured White House
aides of victory, confidently proclaiming "*we* will win this one."[141]

In retrospect, Dirksen's approach to the Fortas nomination was simple and direct. Being neither pleased nor displeased with the prospect of
seeing Fortas as chief justice but confident the nomination would win
Senate approval, the minority leader decided to get what he could out of
the situation by working with the White House. Early in the confirmation process, he believed he had nothing to lose by supporting a nomination inevitably expected to gain the Senate's consent.

Dirksen had much to lose, however, after the nomination's long
delay in the Senate and the growing opposition of a coalition of southern Democrats and Republicans made confirmation uncertain if not
unlikely. With this turn of events, Dirksen found his reputation and
power in the Senate seriously threatened by an intraparty revolt against
his leadership. To continue to support the cloture motion in the face of
its likely defeat would run the risk of providing Senator Griffin, the
aggressive and ambitious leader of the anti-Fortas forces, with a spring-
board from which he could launch a serious challenge to Dirksen's position as minority leader.

The Illinois Republican was painfully aware a party leader does
not enhance his reputation for leadership by ending up on the losing
side on an issue as important as the selection of the next chief justice of
the United States. Also nagging at Dirksen was the realization that in
addition to his ending up on the losing side, many of his GOP colleagues who had spurned his leadership on the nomination were des-

tined to find themselves on the winning side. An Illinois newspaper familiar with the pragmatic maneuvers of the minority leader described the events leading up to the cloture vote as "a natural situation for a Dirksen flip."[142]

The very real threat Dirksen's handling of the Fortas nomination held for his leadership position is illustrated by an editorial appearing in the press even after the Illinois Republican had switched and joined the anti-Fortas forces of Senator Griffin. The editorial avowed Griffin's success in the face of Dirksen's opposition shows the minority leader "doesn't always command the support of his troops" and "raises questions about Republican Senate leadership." The specific question advanced in the editorial was: "Will Senator Everett M. Dirksen be back as the Senate Republican leader in 1969?"[143]

Faced with the likelihood of an embarrassing and dangerous defeat, Dirksen's public statements to the effect he opposed cloture because of the nominee's sense of propriety and the *Witherspoon* decision appear to have been self-serving if not misleading. According to the Illinois Republican's biographer, these statements were simply "flimsy attempts to rationalize his change."[144] The more likely motivation behind the pivotal switch was Dirksen's desire to detach himself from a losing cause and thereby avoid what he viewed as a costly personal defeat. In the sometimes paradoxical tradition of a pragmatic leader, Dirksen led where the Republican majority wanted to go.[145]

In summary, President Johnson's strategy of relying on Dirksen to play a crucial role in the battle for Fortas's confirmation was faulty on at least two counts. In limiting his pre-nomination consultations with senators to Dirksen and a few others, the president had unwisely set up a situation in which he would be provided with only a narrow and potentially inaccurate assessment of the mood of the Senate. As a result, Dirksen's erroneous assessment that the early modest GOP opposition to the Fortas nomination would crumble in the face of pressure from the White House and from the minority leader's office became the president's assessment as well, leading him to be caught off guard when the opposition held firm.[146] Compounding the problem raised by limited Senate consultation, Johnson then linked his ill-conceived strategy for confirmation to the continued support of the fickle Senator Dirksen. The president should have anticipated and been prepared to make adjustments in the likely event Dirksen reneged on his pledge of support. There is simply no reason for the president to have overlooked or to have failed to anticipate what many observers already knew about the Illinois Republican, to wit:

Senator Dirksen's support cannot be compared, say, to the support of a dependable garter. It is rather like the wind, which comes and goes according to natural laws we cannot hope to comprehend—and sometimes it hasn't even been there at all.[147]

The President and Senator Russell. As previously noted, the president counted upon Senator Russell's support of the Fortas and Thornberry nominations to lessen some of the opposition which might arise on the part of the southern Democrats. Senator Russell never fulfilled this role. Instead, bitter feelings emanating from the Senate's consideration of the Fortas-Thornberry package not only culminated in the Georgia Democrat's actively opposing Fortas's confirmation but also severely threatened the warm and longtime friendship which had existed between Johnson and Russell. The story behind the Georgia Democrat's pivotal opposition to the Fortas nomination and the chilling of the relationship between the president and the senator is a complex one, involving the rough and tumble world of bureaucratic intrigue, judicial politics, and presidential decision-making.

On February 13, 1968, Russell recommended that President Johnson nominate Alexander A. Lawrence to fill a vacancy on the federal court for Georgia's southern district. Russell described Lawrence as an "able, ethical, and dedicated lawyer" who will make "an outstanding judge." He also urged the president to "take some action in this matter without undue delay" because the dockets of the southern district were so congested.[148] In response to Russell's request, the president immediately asked Attorney General Ramsey Clark to do some preliminary checking on Lawrence.

In a May 13, 1968, memorandum, Clark recommended the president not make the Lawrence nomination.[149] The attorney general noted while Lawrence was an able lawyer, there was considerable evidence his appointment would "continue segregationist views on the bench." Clark cited disturbing reports that, in 1958, Lawrence made an anti-integration speech highly critical of the Supreme Court and its handling of the *Brown* decision, which called for the end of segregated schools in the South. Clark reported Lawrence as standing by the anti-integration sentiments expressed in his 1958 speech as recently as March 27, 1968. Clark also noted that an individual who had known Lawrence for thirty years attributed to the southern attorney a statement to the effect that the only way to solve the race problem was to get rid of the Negroes. The attorney general also pointed to reports that rumors of Lawrence's consideration for a federal judgeship had aroused the opposition of the

NAACP and other organizations representing minority groups throughout the South. To these groups, Clark noted, the nomination of Lawrence
"would mean that segregationist judges are still being appointed in 1968."

The attorney general's memorandum then turned to the impact the
president's refusal to make the Lawrence nomination would have on
Russell. Clark noted he had recently met with Russell and informed
him he could not recommend the Lawrence appointment. Clark went
on to alert the president the Georgia Democrat had expressed the view
that in the event the Lawrence nomination was not made, he, Russell,
would be "deeply hurt" and would never feel the same way about the
president. If the president should decide not to nominate Lawrence, Clark
suggested Russell be told that the president could not do so in light of
the attorney general's negative recommendation.[150] In this way, the attorney general rather than the president would "take the heat" from the
disappointed Georgia Democrat.

In response to the attorney general's report, Johnson elected to delay
making a final decision. The attorney general was instructed to advise
Russell further investigation was still required before a final decision
could be made. Johnson also told Clark that while he did not want to
make an appointment which would in any way undermine the federal
judiciary's efforts to desegregate the South, he valued Russell's judgment and friendship and did not want to do anything to offend him.
The president's obvious desire not to offend Russell is evident in his
reported instructions to Clark:

> If we come to the final conclusion that we can't appoint him [Lawrence],
> then we'll come to that conclusion. We'll cross that bridge. But if there's
> any way at all we can posture this man in a way that he can be appointed
> without hampering the judiciary, without doing anything to undermine
> the judiciary, I want to do it. I want to appoint this man.[151]

Despite the president's delay on the Lawrence appointment and the
strong opposition of the attorney general, Russell remained adamant. On
May 20, 1968, he wrote the president a lengthy letter repudiating the
charges made against Lawrence and noting he was "surprised, distressed,
and disappointed" upon learning Clark could not recommend the nomination.[152] Russell also advised the president more was at stake in the
Lawrence appointment than a federal judgeship. "It would be extremely
embarrassing to me," noted the Georgia Democrat, "if you turn down
the endorsement of Senator Talmadge and me of an outstanding lawyer
of unchallenged integrity after the fact that we had made such endorse-

ment has been publicized and discussed over the entire state." Russell left no doubt as to how deeply he felt about the appointment:

> I have never made a personal appeal to you for a Presidential appointment since you have occupied the exalted position of President of the United States. In this instance, however, where only a local appointment is concerned and a man of great competence and high character has been suggested, I feel justified in insisting most respectfully that you send Mr. Lawrence's nomination to the Senate.[153]

Continuing to do all in his power to secure the appointment, Russell supplied the White House with the names of more than one hundred prominent Georgians whom the FBI could contact in its background review of Lawrence.[154] He forwarded to the attorney general a recommendation of the Lawrence appointment signed by all of the former presidents of the Georgia Bar Association.[155] And he appeared to have been influential in getting Lawrence to repudiate, at least privately, the idea expressed in his 1958 speech that the *Brown* decision was an instance of judicial tyranny not worthy of being the law of the land.[156]

In a personal letter to a friend, a letter soon brought to the attention of the White House, Lawrence conceded he had drawn "too long a bow" in his 1958 speech and now, if appointed a federal judge, would "follow and respect the decisions of the U.S. Supreme Court."[157] So convincing were the sentiments expressed in the letter that upon reading it and being assured of Lawrence's commitment to equal justice under the law, no less a respected jurist and sometimes advisor to the president than Associate Justice Fortas concluded, "This is conclusive to me. I think we should go ahead on this now for sure."[158]

Russell used Lawrence's softened stance on racial matters to insist once again that the president nominate the Georgia attorney. The president relayed to the attorney general the information about Lawrence's professed changed stance on the integration issue and Russell's doggedness in seeing the nomination made. When Clark passed on this information to the groups in the South opposing the Lawrence nomination, they remained unmoved in their disapproval.[159]

Torn between his friendship with Russell and his desire not to impede desegregation in the South, the president once again elected to put off making a final decision on the Lawrence nomination. Even though Lawrence had already received the American Bar Association's highest possible rating of exceptionally well qualified, information not unknown to Russell, the president requested an additional investigation by the ABA.[160] Albert Jenner, the chairman of the ABA Committee on Judicial Selection, was directly solicited by Johnson to travel to Georgia and personally conduct a vigorous and intense investigation of the nominee.[161]

At this point, Russell was told a decision on the Lawrence nomination would not be forthcoming until the "final" ABA recommendation was forwarded to the president.[162] Already aware the ABA had given Lawrence its highest rating, Russell could not have been pleased with what he must have perceived as the stalling tactics of the White House. Nevertheless, he did not direct any of his indignation at the president.

The same could not be said in regard to his feelings toward Clark. Convinced the attorney general was behind the effort to derail the Lawrence nomination, Russell consistently heaped scorn upon Clark in private communications with Lawrence's supporters during this period. For example, after noting in regard to the Lawrence appointment "our trouble is the Attorney General," Russell went on to inform a constituent that Clark is the "most inept and poorly qualified AG in history [sic]."[163] To another Lawrence supporter inquiring of the status of the appointment, Russell confided, "we are continuing to work on this and we have everyone on our side here except the Attorney General."[164]

In June, 1968, when the president received word of Warren's intention to leave the Court, a final decision on the Lawrence nomination had still not been made. Russell's aides continued to press for a decision at the "earliest possible time."[165] Despite their efforts, both the president and the attorney general were purportedly still waiting for the Jenner report and the ABA's final recommendation on the merits of the Lawrence nomination before committing themselves.[166]

At about this time, mid-June, 1968, the president developed the strategy of gaining confirmation for Fortas and Thornberry by relying upon Dirksen to hold in check Republican opposition to the nominations and Russell to play the same critical role regarding southern Democrats.[167] This strategy, which suffered a severe blow when the administration lost the support of Dirksen, also was seriously undermined when the president let the backing of Russell slip away.

At the June meeting between Johnson and Russell at which the Georgia Democrat reportedly made a commitment to support Fortas and Thornberry, it is likely the Lawrence nomination also became part of the deliberations.[168] The meeting yielded at least a tacit understanding between the two old friends to the effect that Russell would support the Fortas and Thornberry nominations and Johnson would nominate

Lawrence upon the completion of Clark's screening of the nominee and receipt of a favorable recommendation from the ABA.

There is little doubt Russell indicated to the president at this meeting that he would support both the Fortas and Thornberry nominations. One White House aide has reported that for some time immediately after the Russell-Johnson meeting it was "fairly common knowledge" in the Senate that the Georgia Democrat was supporting both nominations.[169] No less an interested party than Thornberry has testified to Russell's intended support of the nominations. Thornberry noted that upon being telephoned by the president and informed Fortas was to be nominated as chief justice and he was being tapped to replace Fortas as associate justice, he expressed concern to Johnson as to whether the Senate would approve both nominations. Thornberry's description of the president's and Russell's response follows:

> He [Johnson] said, "I have a friend here," and it was Senator Russell from Georgia, whom I had known over the years and with whom I had gone hunting and had a rather high regard for as a friend. He told me Senator Russell had agreed to support both Mr. Justice Fortas and me. And then he put him on the phone. He [Russell] made some suggestions about a statement I should make, and then he said, "I'm for you all the way." I felt like from the discussions that the President had had with the leadership on both sides of the Senate and then, of course, Senator Russell with his influence with the southern senators, that probably there was a likelihood that both of us could be confirmed.[170]

After meeting with Russell and announcing the Fortas and Thornberry nominations, Johnson again conferred with his attorney general to ascertain the status of the Justice Department's screening of Lawrence and the ABA's recommendation. Clark informed the president once again that the final ABA investigation had not yet been completed but nevertheless insisted the nomination should not be made because of the impact Lawrence's appointment would have on desegregation efforts in the South. Obviously influenced by his meeting with Russell and angered by the attorney general's lack of support for the Lawrence nomination, the president obliquely conveyed to Clark the nature of his commitment to the Georgia Democrat:

> I told my friend Dick Russell that if there is a way to appoint that man [Lawrence], I want to do it. Now I know you don't want to appoint him. I know you're opposed to it, and I'm not telling you that I definitely am going to appoint him. I'm just telling you that I want to if there's any way

that I can. I don't think you want to nominate him, but I do; and if there's a way to posture him where we can nominate him, I want to do that. Now go get after it, and see if there's a way to do that.[171]

A short time later, after being advised by his aides of Russell's growing impatience,[172] the president again forwarded instructions to Clark to speed up the Justice Department's investigation. In the view of at least one White House insider, the attorney general, at this time, was deliberately "dragging his feet" on the Lawrence nomination.[173] According to this White House associate, Clark was aware that immediately upon the Justice Department's receipt of the anticipated positive report of the ABA, the president would be expecting a favorable recommendation from the Justice Department. Upon receiving this favorable recommendation, Clark anticipated the president would move quickly to satisfy Russell by forwarding the Lawrence nomination to the Senate. Consequently, the attorney general reportedly delayed the Justice Department's pre-nomination screening process deliberately in the hope something would happen in the meantime to persuade the president not to forward Lawrence's name to the Senate.[174]

As the Lawrence investigation dragged on, Russell showed signs of backing away from his support of Fortas. On the afternoon of July 1, 1968, two White House aides visited with the Georgia Democrat to assess his latest feelings regarding the Fortas nomination. Although the aides described the meeting as a "pleasant" one, they also noted Russell was "non-committal" in regard to supporting Fortas. Their report also indicated Russell had expressed strong support for Thornberry, cryptically proclaiming he "would like for him to be chief justice." However, in regard to the Fortas nomination, and despite his earlier tacit agreement with the president, the Georgia Democrat now reportedly intimated that he had not "formed a final view."[175]

On the very day of this "pleasant" meeting, Russell, his patience apparently worn thin by the seemingly interminable delay in receiving word of Lawrence's nomination, fired off an angry letter to the president. The extraordinary letter began with Russell's clearly conveying his indignation and frustration at the Justice Department's protracted delay in reporting the Lawrence nomination given the obvious pressing need of his services on the Georgia district court:

Without adding to the voluminous file or the record of the many conversations we have had on the subject, I remind you that on February 13th of this year—over four and a half months ago—my colleague, Senator

Talmadge, and I forwarded to you an urgent request based on public need for you to appoint Mr. Alexander A. Lawrence as United States District Judge for the Southern District of Georgia.[176]

Russell's letter then turned to the commitment he believed he had received from the president regarding the Lawrence nomination. In the Georgia Democrat's view, while he had been honest and straightforward in his dealings with the president on not only the Lawrence nomination but Fortas's and Thornberry's as well, the president had been guileful.

From our conversations, I had about become convinced that, despite the protests of the person who serves as your Attorney General, you would name Mr. Lawrence, and in addition, you stated to me on my visit with you on the evening of the 26th instant that you would appoint him as United States Circuit Court Judge if he, Senator Talmadge, and I desired that this be done.

To be perfectly frank, even after so many years in the Senate, I was so naive I had not even suspected that this man's nomination was being withheld from the Senate due to the changes expected on the Supreme Court of the United States until after you sent in the nominations of Fortas and Thornberry while still holding the recommendations for the nomination of Mr. Lawrence either in your office or in the Department of Justice.

Whether it is intended or not, this places me in the position where, if I support your nominees for the Supreme Court, it will appear that I have done so out of my fears that you would not nominate Mr. Lawrence.

Mr. Lawrence and I enjoy a close friendship that is the heritage of three generations, but for your information, when placed in a similar position by former President Truman when he nominated my own beloved brother to be a Judge of the United States Circuit Court, I told Mr. Truman that he had best withdraw that nomination as I did not intend to be blackmailed into voting for a District Judge in my own Federal Judicial District even to secure a Circuit Judgeship for a brother who was as close to me as two men could be. I still dislike being treated as a child or a patronage-seeking ward healer.

When I came to the United States Senate some thirty-odd years ago, I did not possess much except my self-respect. When I leave—either voluntarily, carried in a box, or at the request of the people of Georgia—I still intend to carry my self-respect back to Georgia.[177]

Russell's letter then addressed the critical consequences of what he perceived to be the president's failure to deal with him honestly on the Lawrence nomination.

This is, therefore, to advise you that, in view of the long delay in handling and the juggling of this nomination, I consider myself released from
any statements that I may have made to you with respect to your nominations, and you are at liberty to deal with the recommendations as to Mr.
Lawrence in any way you see fit. I shall undertake to deal objectively with
the nominations you have made to the Supreme Court, but however I
may vote, I want you to understand that it is not done with any expectation that I am buying or insuring the nomination of Mr. Lawrence to
either the District or the Circuit Court and that I do not propose to make
any future endorsements to you for judicial appointments even in my
own state.[178]

Additional insight as to the pique Russell felt at the time he fired
off his July 1 letter to the president is indicated by a communication the
Georgia Democrat sent to a Lawrence supporter the next day. After noting
he had "never been as disappointed in a man as I am in Johnson,"
Russell, obviously referring to the July 1 letter, concluded "I have
expressed my amazement and disappointment to the President as clearly
as I know how."[179] Despite these hostile remarks in the president's regard,
Russell aimed most of his wrath at Clark.

The business of this District [court] has been increasing substantially, but
the mystic and crystal ball operator who occupies the position of Attorney
General apparently does not think that the District needs even one new
judge. . . . I have never run into the position of any bureaucrat, however
fanatical and foolish, that is as incomprehensible to me as Ramsey Clark's
absolutely unwarranted and unjustified, but, nevertheless violent, opposition to Alex Lawrence.[180]

The president's immediate reaction upon receiving Russell's letter
on July 2 was one of outrage at Attorney General Clark. He telephoned
Clark, read the letter to him, and relayed the following message in language reportedly much stronger than what has been included in this
sanitized version:

Ramsey, I'm very unhappy. I think your foot-dragging on this has destroyed
one of the great friendships I've had with one of the great men that has
ever served this country. I'm unhappy about it.[181]

Johnson also told Clark that Russell was mistaken in his view the
White House was using the Lawrence nomination as part of a quid pro
quo deal to win his support for Fortas. The president insisted the Fortas

and Lawrence nominations were not and never had been linked together in any deal. Johnson and Clark both believed Russell's erroneous view was fueled by Fortas's opponents, who had concocted the story of a quid pro quo deal and managed to convince Russell of its veracity. The president ended his conversation with the attorney general by maintaining the White House still had a commitment to appoint Lawrence to the Georgia district court despite Russell's withdrawal of his pledge to support Fortas. Clark was instructed once again to forward a recommendation on the Lawrence nomination to the White House.[182]

Johnson then turned to saving the Fortas nomination and the friendship he believed had been shattered by the prolonged delay of the Lawrence appointment. On July 3, the president personally called the Georgia Democrat and reportedly made the following comments to him:

> Dick, I have your letter here in my hands. I don't think this letter reflects creditably upon you as a statesman. I don't think it reflects very well on our long friendship. I just don't think that it is the kind of letter that I want to have in my file for the historians to see. Now, I don't want it in my file. I just want you to know that I don't think that it reflects this kind of credit. I'm going to send it back to you. I'm not going to make a copy of it. I'm not going to keep it in my file. I'm not going to keep a copy in my file. I'm going to send the letter back to you. I hope you'll destroy it. Whatever you do with it is your decision, because it's your letter. It's not mine. I don't want it, and I don't want it in my file.
>
> I'm going to tell you . . . that I don't look upon you as having any sort of commitment to me with regard to Justice Fortas or Homer Thornberry. I know that you will do as you've done ever since I've known you, and that is make the decision your conscience and judgement dictates at the time that is right for the decision. I'm not going to ask you what that decision is. I'm not going to send anybody to you. I'm not going to have anybody else ask you. I'll know what your decision is when I see the vote tallied. That's as soon as I want to know. You do whatever you think the circumstances are, but do it in light—you say you don't feel like you have a commitment to me.
>
> I'm going to nominate your recommendation to be federal judge for the United States district court in Georgia, but it's not a quid pro quo. It wasn't when I first told you I was going to. It isn't now, and it isn't going to be. I never thought of the two together until you put them together in your letter. So I just want you to know I'm going to nominate your man, and I don't think you've got any commitment to me on Fortas. You do whatever you want to do on that, and I know it'll be the right decision.[183]

In a further attempt to mollify Russell, the president spent a significant amount of time preparing a written response to the July 1 letter. In a reply hand-delivered to the Georgia Democrat's office on July 3, the president reiterated his view that the delay in forwarding the Lawrence nomination to the Senate was designed not to assure Russell's support for Fortas but rather to await completion of the ABA investigation of Lawrence in order to build the best case for confirmation. This letter noted:

> The plain fact of the matter is . . . my [Johnson's] decision to nominate Mr. Lawrence was based entirely upon his qualifications and upon the recommendations of yourself and Senator Talmadge. It had and has no relationship to anything else. Certainly it had and has no possible relationship, direct or indirect, to the nominations of Mr. Justice Fortas as Chief Justice and of Judge Thornberry as Associate Justice of the Supreme Court.[184]

In the following days, the president, ignoring his pledge not to send anyone to see Russell, dispatched a bevy of subordinates to the Georgia Democrat's office to attempt to regain his support. However, the explanations proffered by these aides failed to budge Russell from the view expressed in his July 1 letter.[185]

Eventually, Attorney General Clark recommended the Lawrence nomination, although not without voicing misgivings about it. Shortly after receiving Clark's recommendation, Johnson personally informed Senator Russell on July 13 that the Lawrence nomination would be forwarded to the Senate.[186] On July 17, the nomination was indeed made.[187] Despite this presidential action and the Senate's subsequent confirmation of Lawrence with little opposition, Russell never fulfilled his reported pledge to work for Fortas's promotion to the chief justiceship. Indeed, as will be discussed below, the Georgia Democrat not only went on to vote against the cloture motion but also played an active and critical role in organizing and maintaining opposition to Fortas.[188]

Several observers of the White House's unsuccessful effort to appoint Warren's successor have concluded that the embittering events preceding the Lawrence appointment directly accounted for the withdrawal of Russell's support for Fortas and seriously undermined Johnson's strategy for gaining Senate approval of his chief justice designee. Russell's defection from the pro-Fortas side has been described as the pivotal factor ending all hopes the administration had of terminating the lethal filibuster launched against the nomination. In the opinion of one White House intimate, it was Russell's "pique over the delay in the Alexander [Lawrence] nomination . . . that really finished off Fortas."[189] Other sources have estimated Russell's opposition may have cost the pro-Fortas forces the votes of as many as twelve or more Southern Democrats.[190]

Several aspects of the events surrounding Russell's break with the pro-Fortas forces reflect unfavorably on Johnson's management of the nomination. Given the president's awareness of the key role Russell's continued support for the nomination was to have played in the confirmation strategy, and his apparent understanding of the Georgia Democrat's occasional inclination to act impulsively and dramatically when slighted or ignored,[191] Johnson's perceived complacency and acquiescence in Clark's obvious and prolonged holding up of the crucial Lawrence nomination is remarkable.

Contrary to the prevailing impression that Johnson would not tolerate unsubmissiveness, much less obstinacy, on the part of his subordinates, the president reportedly was most reluctant to overrule his attorney general in regard to judicial nominations. For example, one White House aide has reported that Johnson

> never nominated anyone that had not been recommended by the attorney general, and didn't think he could or would. People who don't understand Lyndon Johnson, or Ramsey Clark, or maybe a president and an attorney general probably wouldn't understand that.[192]

This aide's report goes on to note:

> The president didn't browbeat him [Ramsey Clark] into doing something that he didn't want to do. The thing that a lot of people never realized is that Ramsey was just as tough-minded and as obstinate a guy, in a nonderogatory sense, as the president was or as anybody else. And if he didn't want to do anything, if he didn't want to make a recommendation, the president couldn't force him to do it. . . . If the president ever said, "Now Ramsey, you either make a recommendation or I want another attorney general," and Ramsey didn't want to make a recommendation, he'd have sent his letter of resignation over.[193]

Even if it may have been Johnson's customary approach not to overrule his attorney general on judicial nominations, the selection of a chief justice, especially in the closing months of a president's term, is clearly an extraordinary event demanding atypical actions on the part of the chief executive. The president must or should have realized how essential Russell's support of Fortas was to favorable Senate action on the nomination. In addition, he was obviously aware of Russell's strong interest in having Lawrence appointed to the Georgia district court without delay. Nevertheless, during a critical time in the fight for Senate approval of his chief justice designee, the president needlessly placed the Fortas nomination in jeopardy by reticently permitting Clark to hold up the Lawrence appointment.

The president should have been more aggressive in attempting to persuade Clark to recommend Lawrence favorably and to do so with the utmost haste. Johnson either failed to inform or convince his attorney general of two essential facts. First, Russell's support of the Fortas nomination was indispensable to favorable Senate action. In addition, the Lawrence appointment was the price the White House would have to pay to maintain the Georgia Democrat's support of Fortas. Had Clark been so informed or convinced, he would likely have moved more quickly in reporting the Lawrence nomination favorably even though he had misgivings about the nominee's stand on racial matters. In the event this information did not persuade the attorney general to recommend Lawrence immediately, the president should have sent the nomination to the Senate without Clark's favorable recommendation. This surely would not have marked the first time a president and an attorney general had disagreed regarding a judicial appointment.

What made Johnson's subdued approach to Clark's stubbornness so crucial in this case was Russell's expectations. The Georgia Democrat fully expected that the president would overrule his attorney general in the event Clark did not favorably report the Lawrence nomination. For example, in April, 1968, Russell advised a Lawrence supporter he was prepared to "go over the head of the Attorney General to the President."[194] A few weeks later, the Georgia Democrat noted the following regarding the Lawrence nomination: "The President is in a peculiar position, but I believe that he will eventually over-ride the Attorney General if he does not change his mind."[195]

Johnson should have also anticipated that the long delay on the Lawrence nomination, in the face of insistent calls for action by Russell, was bound to upset the Georgia Democrat. Johnson understood that Russell was not likely to be placated for long, if ever, by delay and patronizing language. "One could not persuade Senator Russell by sweet talk, hard talk, or any kind of talk" remarked the president in an earlier assessment of the Georgia Democrat. "He respected action, not words."[196]

A firm and direct order from Johnson to send the Lawrence nomination immediately to the Senate may very well have upset Clark and other liberals.[197] But the reality of seeing Fortas installed as Warren's successor, especially when the anticipated Nixon victory in 1968 would likely lead to a more conservative chief justice, could be counted upon to lessen the disenchantment of liberals. No less a liberal spokesperson than Joseph L. Rauh, Jr., an activist lawyer with ties to the Leadership Conference on Civil Rights, confided there is not "a single liberal who is not for Abe's [Fortas] confirmation and who does not want to do everything he can do to accomplish it."[198] Given this sentiment, the president had the opportunity to convince the attorney general that the Lawrence appointment would be more than offset by Fortas's successful nomination as chief justice. That opportunity was never effectively seized.

Had President Johnson handled the Lawrence affair more adeptly, he might have been successful in preventing an irremediable act on the part of the Georgia Democrat, an act which reportedly doomed the Fortas nomination. At about the same time Russell's July 1 letter was forwarded to the White House, he decided to commit himself to opposing the Fortas nomination actively. Senator Griffin, the leader of the Republican opposition to the Fortas-Thornberry package, has reported he directly communicated with Russell sometime "right around the first of July." According to Griffin, the Georgia Democrat

> wanted to know whether I was serious in my opposition to the Fortas nomination. He asked whether I would stick to my guns, and be willing to carry the fight. Finally, after being satisfied with my answers, he said he wanted me to know he would be with me.[199]

Consequently, by the time President Johnson met with Russell on July 13 to inform the Georgia Democrat he was going to make the Lawrence nomination, it was already too late.[200] A more timely favorable response by Johnson to his old friend's repeated pleas to forward the Lawrence nomination to the Senate would very likely have solidified Russell's support of the Fortas-Thornberry package and deterred him from allying with the GOP forces in opposition to the nominations. Granting Russell's request for the Lawrence nomination in a more timely fashion would have at least provided a more fruitful opportunity to alter whatever inclination the Georgia Democrat had to join with Senator Griffin in opposing Fortas.

But Johnson's favorable response was not timely, and Russell went on to join forces with Griffin, sealing Fortas's defeat. No less an involved participant than Griffin has testified to the critical role Russell's switch to opposing the Fortas nomination had on the outcome:

> That was a turning point in the whole case, as far as I was concerned at that point, I felt there was a pretty good chance we could prevail . . .

because Dick Russell was the de facto leader of the southern bloc in the Senate.[201]

To summarize, President Johnson had devised a strategy to install Fortas as chief justice. A major element of the strategy was to maintain southern Democratic support of the nomination by securing the support of Senator Russell. While the strategy appeared sound, the president did not anticipate the loss of Russell's backing due to the Lawrence affair. Indeed, in neglecting to take adequate measures to prevent his subordinates, especially Attorney General Clark, from alienating Russell, the president played no minor role in undermining the strategy he had devised to gain Senate approval of Fortas. As a result, the support of southern Democrats was lost and these senators soon joined conservative Republicans in forming a coalition against Fortas that eventually succeeded in blocking Senate consideration of the nomination.

Presidential Management: Conclusion

Evidence presented in this chapter warrants the conclusion that President Johnson played a major role in the Senate's refusal to confirm Fortas as chief justice. The president's selection of a nominee vulnerable to non-ideological and non-partisan criticism, his following of a strategy and tactics destined to end in failure, and his forbearance of acts of subordinates undermining the confirmation effort all contributed significantly to the Senate's refusal to confirm Fortas.

Certainly the ideological opposition of Senate conservatives and the unpropitious timing of the nomination made the battle for confirmation difficult. Still, a majority of the Senate apparently favored the Fortas nomination, making confirmation a distinct possibility. The evidence strongly suggests that more effective and careful management of the confirmation process on the part of President Johnson would have led to Fortas's confirmation. To that extent, Abe Fortas's failure to become Chief Justice of the United States was also a failure in presidential management.

3. PRESIDENTIAL MANAGEMENT: THE HAYNSWORTH NOMINATION

> The Haynsworth appointment will
> be pointed to in the future as a prime
> example of stupid handling of a Su-
> preme Court appointment.
> —President's News Summary,
> October 10, 1969

THE ORDEAL OF Clement F. Haynsworth, Jr., began when the ordeal of Associate Justice Abe Fortas ended. After Fortas resigned from the Court on May 14, 1969, President Richard M. Nixon, on August 18, 1969, nominated Haynsworth, of the United States Court of Appeals for the Fourth Circuit, to fill the vacancy.

Senate Judiciary Committee hearings on the nomination were held from September 16 through September 26, 1969, with the nominee appearing on September 16, 17, and 23. Testimony at the hearings mainly focused on Haynsworth's sense of judicial propriety in participating, as a federal appeals court judge, in cases in which he had a financial interest. An additional focus was the nominee's judicial ideology as reflected in his previous decisions related to civil rights and labor-management relations. The Judiciary Committee voted 10-7 on October 9, 1969 to report the nomination favorably to the Senate. The Committee's majority report, along with the views of dissenting members, were filed with the Senate on November 12, 1969. Senate debate began on November 13, 1969, culminating in the rejection of the nomination by a 55-45 margin on November 21, 1969.

Nixon's management of the confirmation process contributed significantly to the Senate's negative action. This chapter focuses on two aspects of Nixon's counterproductive presidential management: (1) the selection of a nominee vulnerable to non-ideological and non-partisan criticism, and (2) the failure to oversee the Senate's consideration of the nomination in an effective and astute manner.

SELECTING A VULNERABLE NOMINEE

Nixon's selection of a nominee vulnerable on the non-ideological, non-partisan grounds of ethical insensitivity undermined the nomination in several significant ways. As discussed below, some senators employed the ethics issue as a cover to conceal their ideological and/or partisan opposition while others were moved to oppose Haynsworth from a genuine concern about the nominee's sense of propriety. Additionally, whether ethics was employed in a feigned or sincere manner, the propriety issue forged a link between the Haynsworth and Fortas cases that redounded unfavorably upon Nixon's quest for Senate confirmation of his nominee. While the nomination of an individual vulnerable to non-ideological, non-partisan criticism reflects unfavorably on a president's management of the screening process, the choosing of a nominee open to charges of ethical insensitivity a short time after similar concerns had been decisive in denying a sitting justice the chief justiceship and in eventually driving that justice from the Court appears to be an egregious instance of a mismanaged selection process. This review of President Nixon's management of the confirmation process begins with the Fortas-Haynsworth connection.

The Fortas-Haynsworth Connection

The unfavorable linking of the Fortas and Haynsworth cases stemmed from the Southern jurist's nomination's being forwarded to the Senate amid the bitter feelings generated by events involving Associate Justice Fortas. On May 15, 1969, Fortas became the first Supreme Court justice to resign under the threat of impeachment. Shortly after joining the Court in 1965, Fortas had accepted $20,000 from a charitable foundation controlled by multi-millionaire industrialist Louis E. Wolfson, who, at that time, was under investigation by the Justice Department for illegal stock manipulation. Based upon an arrangement in which Fortas was to serve as an advisor to the foundation in a life-long association, the $20,000 represented the first installment of an annual stipend which would continue to be paid to the associate justice's spouse in the event of his death. When Wolfson was indicted on these charges in 1966, Fortas returned the $20,000. Nevertheless, critics maintained the associate justice had unethically placed himself in a conflict of interest situation by accepting the fee in the first place.[1]

The Wolfson incident, coupled with the ethical issues raised in opposition to Fortas's nomination as chief justice in 1968, heightened public interest in the issue of judicial propriety. When Nixon was seeking a replacement for the retiring Chief Justice Warren, the rekindled public concern with the ethical sensitivity of jurists did not go unnoticed at the White House. While Fortas was under attack, Special Assistant to the President Patrick J. Buchanan warned Nixon of the link White House opponents would try to make between the Fortas case and future Supreme Court nominations. Buchanan noted that "because of the suspicion and skepticism about the Court's integrity in the wake of the Fortas thing, it seems almost equally important that the President's first choice not in any way be construed as 'Nixon's Fortas'."[2] After noting "Senate supporters of Fortas . . . are bound to be bitter over the harsh attacks," Warren E. Burger, hopeful but still unaware he was to be the chief justice nominee, cautioned Nixon that "when your first nomination goes to the Senate, this suppressed rage will likely assert itself and your nominee may become *their* 'whipping boy.' "[3] Nixon appeared to have been influenced by these warnings. He noted Burger's comments expressed "very good judgment"[4] and vowed "to put unquestioned integrity high on the list of any to be appointed to [the] Court."[5]

Nevertheless, in selecting Haynsworth, he chose a nominee vulnerable on grounds of ethical insensitivity. Given the intensity of the deliberations regarding Fortas's sense of propriety, the charges of ethical insensitivity leveled against Haynsworth had a telling influence on the Senate. Some estimation of the impact Fortas's demise had on the Haynsworth deliberations can be gleaned from the fact that no less than thirteen senators who voted against the Haynsworth publicly attributed their opposition directly to the events surrounding Fortas or strongly implied such was the case. These senators were Birch E. Bayh (D, Ind.), Thomas F. Eagleton (D, Mo.), Daniel K. Inouye (D, Hawaii) , Gale W. McGee (D, Wyo.), Stuart Symington (D, Mo.), Joseph D. Tydings (D, Md.), John Sherman Cooper (R, Ky.), Robert P. Griffin (R, Mich.), Mark O. Hatfield (R, Ore.), Charles McC. Mathias, Jr. (R, Md.), Jack Miller (R, Iowa), Hugh Scott (R, Pa.), and Margaret Chase Smith (R, Maine).[6]

The comments of some of these senators aptly reveal the crucial connection they perceived between the circumstances leading to Fortas's demise and their opposition to Haynsworth. Maryland's Tydings traced his disapproval of the Haynsworth nomination to the following:

> The Fortas affair cast over the entire Court a shadow of suspicion and mistrust from which the Court has not fully emerged. This aura hangs most noticeably over Mr. Fortas' vacant seat, the very one to which Judge Haynsworth has been nominated. We must recognize that the ultimate decision in the present matter cannot realistically be insulated from this specter.[7]

Senator McGee noted:

> Had there been no Fortas affair . . . a man of Justice Haynsworth's attainments . . . undoubtedly would have been confirmed. But, Mr. President, there was a Fortas affair . . . .[8]

Missouri's Eagleton simply stated he could not "in good conscience vote to replace Justice Fortas with Judge Haynsworth."[9]

From the GOP side of the aisle, Senator Hatfield noted the significant link between the Fortas and Haynsworth nominations.

> The doubt, discord, and polarization created by this [ethics] issue have destroyed the possibility of effective service by Judge Haynsworth on the Supreme Court.
>
> In the same matter, it became apparent that Justice Fortas no longer could function constructively after serious ethical questions had been raised, focusing public concern on the integrity of the Court.[10]

Maryland's Mathias maintained that Haynsworth had failed to meet the heightened ethical standard occasioned by the Fortas deliberations.

> The only conclusion to which I can bring myself is that his [Haynsworth's] confirmation would lower all judicial standards at a time when the public is anxious to see them raised.[11]

In addition to these public declarations, two other senators privately grounded their disapproval of Haynsworth on the Fortas connection. Senator Richard S. Schweiker (R, Pa.) was reportedly inclined to oppose Haynsworth because of "the Fortas background and the appearance that there is a legal and ethical double standard."[12] Senator Clinton P. Anderson (D, N.M.), shortly after announcing his opposition to the

Haynsworth nomination, privately confided to a White House official that "Fortas was close to me."[13]

The Fortas case had its most significant impact in undermining Haynsworth's support from the Republican leadership in the Senate. This is most evident when the motivation behind the critical opposition of the chairwoman of the Senate Republican Conference, Smith of Maine, and of GOP whip Griffin is examined. Senator Smith had opposed Fortas's confirmation as chief justice and supported the successful move to force him to resign from the Court. On both occasions, the Maine Republican based her decision on Fortas's alleged lack of ethical sensitivity.[14] In the Haynsworth deliberations, even though Smith's leadership position inclined her to approve the nominee of a Republican president, her sharp disapproval of Fortas's ethical insensitivity made it difficult for her to do so.

Smith attempted to resolve the dilemma the Haynsworth nomination posed for her, and for other GOP senators who had disapproved of Fortas's alleged unethical behavior by making a direct appeal to President Nixon. Early in the battle for Haynsworth's confirmation, she forwarded a private letter to the president confiding that she could not support the nomination and asking to have Haynsworth's name withdrawn. The letter, released to the public at a later date, clearly emphasized the link Smith made between the Fortas and Haynsworth cases. Because Haynsworth's reported ethical transgressions were, in her view, "very similar" to the infractions of Fortas, she could not vote for the South Carolina judge's confirmation.[15]

Despite Smith's private plea, Nixon refused to withdraw the nomination. Her behind-the-scene effort to resolve the dilemma rejected, Smith soon publicly announced her reasons for opposing the Haynsworth nomination. Once again, but this time in a widely-reported statement, she forcefully grounded her opposition to Haynsworth on an ethical standard heightened by the Fortas deliberations, noting:

> I agree with . . . opposition to the Haynsworth nomination for the same basic and fundamental reason that I agreed with Senator Griffin's opposition to the Fortas nomination a year ago.
>
> I do not believe in a double standard. . . .
>
> Let us not forget that Justice Fortas was forced to resign because of outside business transactions. And in remembering that so recent matter, let us recognize that the amount of evidence that should be necessary to justify refusing a confirmation is much less than the amount properly required to justify demanding his resignation after one has been confirmed and served.[16]

The Fortas case also cast its shadow over Senator Griffin. The Michigan Republican had been in the forefront of senators who strongly denounced Fortas's sense of judicial propriety. Indeed, Griffin's selection to the leadership position of minority whip could be traced in part to his key role in blocking the Fortas nomination. His involvement in the Fortas affair had earned him acclaim as a leader strongly committed to maintaining the integrity of the judiciary by insisting that those nominated to the Supreme Court be assessed under the strictest of ethical standards. Consequently, Haynsworth's alleged unethical behavior placed Griffin in a most uncomfortable position. His newly-won leadership position inclined him to support the Republican president on such an important matter as the Haynsworth nomination but his prominent role in the Fortas case pulled him in the opposite direction.

Not unlike his leadership colleague Smith, Minority Whip Griffin attempted to escape from the dilemma he faced by appealing privately to President Nixon. He reportedly joined fellow Republican senators Edward W. Brooke of Massachusetts, and John Tower of Texas in calling upon the president to avert embarrassment to the party by withdrawing the nomination.[17] After Nixon refused this request, Griffin was evidently left with no acceptable alternative but to oppose Haynsworth's nomination as vigorously as he had opposed Fortas's. In his public announcement of opposition on October 8, 1969, the Michigan Republican clearly admitted that the ethical charges developed against Haynsworth made it impossible for him to support the nomination.[18]

How instrumental were the defections of Republican leaders Smith and Griffin in bringing about Haynsworth's defeat? Since a switch of no more than five votes in favor of Haynsworth would have brought about a close but nevertheless successful confirmation, their defections were crucial to the outcome.

Many accounts confirm this conclusion. One report noted the anti-confirmation stance of Smith and Griffin had delivered a "severe setback" to Haynsworth's chances for success.[19] Another account described Griffin as the single most influential Republican in rounding up votes against Haynsworth.[20] An internal White House report on the prospects for confirmation concluded Senate leadership on the nomination was virtually "non-existent" because "Griffin [is] actively working against [the nomination]" and Smith is "openly opposed." This report also noted that in the critical early period in the battle for confirmation, October 1 to October 17, 1969, the attempt to organize Senate floor and whip action in support of the nomination had "collapsed with Griffin's defection."[21] This same report indicated two GOP senators, Cooper of Kentucky and

Len B. Jordan of Idaho, whose support was crucial to the outcome but who eventually would vote against the nomination, had been influenced by Griffin to oppose confirmation.[22] One additional White House report angrily noted that the failure of Griffin as well as of Minority Leader Scott to support Haynsworth had "doomed" the nomination and concluded that in retaliation for their costly disloyalty they "must go after the 1970 election."[23]

The most significant evidence of the impact Griffin's and Smith's defection had on Haynsworth's chances for success is provided by actions taken by White House officials attempting to offset the opposition of the two Republican leaders. Stung by Griffin's effectiveness in influencing other Republican senators to oppose Haynsworth's confirmation, Nixon fired off a memorandum to Bryce N. Harlow, Counselor to the President, in an attempt to control, if not terminate, the anti-nomination lobbying of the Michigan Republican. The president noted:

> Griffin apparently is lobbying quietly against Haynsworth behind the scenes. I think you should have a frank talk with him along these lines, that we understand his own position, but that as the Whip his attempting to work directly against the President will be very hard for most people to justify or understand.
>
> I do not intend to speak to him on this point; but I think you or someone else should.[24]

Harlow later reported, that he met with Griffin and the Michigan Republican said he would not work against the Haynsworth nomination.[25]

Nevertheless, at approximately this same time, another White House official also attempted to slow down Griffin's apparently effective anti-Haynsworth efforts. This official noted:

> I spent 45 minutes visiting with Senator Griffin in his whip office off the Senate floor. I appealed to him on a personal basis to pull in his horns and get on the team. He told me that he had gone too far down the road to turn around. I told him that the President was personally deeply involved and simply had to have this confirmation. He said he was sorry that the President was taking it so personally, that he had tried in the early days to get the President to withdraw the nomination.
>
> As a last resort, I told him that I hoped that since apparently he couldn't turn around that he would confine his activities to voting. He finally promised that he would do no more than absolutely necessary to protect his position. He said the papers in his State had editorialized on his position and were backing him.

I told him that for the good of the Party, the Administration, and himself, he ought not to fight this to the point of severing communications between himself and the President. He agreed that he did not want this to happen.[26]

In regard to Smith's defection, Clark Mollenhoff, Deputy Counsel to the President, was obviously aware of the influence the Maine Republican's opposition would have on other senators. Mollenhoff wrote a long memorandum to the president suggesting ways to offset Smith's disapproval. The deputy counsel advised it might be "beneficial to give some special Presidential attention to Mrs. Smith, for I am sure she would be moved by some direct Presidential opinion on the honesty of Judge Haynsworth." Mollenhoff's optimistic hope was that Smith could be convinced to change her mind and dramatically come out in support of Haynsworth. This failing, he suggested that even if the influential Maine Republican decided to vote against the nomination, she could be called upon to "set out the differences between the Fortas and Haynsworth cases." According to Mollenhoff, either of these actions by Smith "would give the force of her image of decency" to deflating the criticism raised against Haynsworth.[27] Evidently the White House was not successful in convincing Smith to carry out either of these actions and the force of her "image of decency" continued to be directed against the nomination.

Additional evidence of the impact the Fortas-Haynsworth connection had on Haynsworth's chances for confirmation is revealed by one other private comment made by White House officials. Notes of a White House staff meeting with Nixon during the Senate's deliberations suggest that Harlow, charged with rounding up support for the nomination in the Senate, had recommended Haynsworth be encouraged to withdraw his name. Harlow claimed the effort to gain support for the nomination was failing because of the difficulty in making a "credible" distinction between the Fortas and Haynsworth cases."[28]

In summary, the Fortas-Haynsworth connection appears significant for two reasons. It reinforced the inclination of Fortas's supporters in the Senate to vote against Haynsworth's confirmation. Bitter recollections of the derailed chief justice nomination and of the White House's role in Fortas's humiliating resignation from the Court made this opposition, especially on the part of Senate Democrats, more likely and more pronounced. In spotting this phenomenon, two conservative columnists concluded that a key ingredient in Haynsworth's rejection was the "post-Fortas lust for revenge among Democratic senators."[29]

The Fortas-Haynsworth connection also made it difficult for senators who had reportedly been offended by Fortas's sense of ethics to overlook similar changes when they were made against another nominee, even one who would have ordinarily received their strong support. Some senators such as Griffin, Smith, and others were likely to be, in the words of one insightful report, "so strongly on record against even the appearance of conflict of interest that they just may feel themselves prisoners of precedent when the vote on Haynsworth comes up."[30]

Awareness of this link between the Fortas and Haynsworth cases led Senator Barry Goldwater (R, Ariz.) to conclude that the Republican nominee suffered from the "historical fact that his appointment occurred shortly after the Fortas revelations."[31] Still, it must be remembered the damaging link between the Fortas and Haynsworth nominations could not have been credibly made had Nixon taken greater care in selecting a nominee free from charges of ethical insensitivity.

Ethics as a Cover Issue

President Nixon contributed to the Senate rejection of Haynsworth by providing senators with a cover issue to conceal the ideological and partisan nature of their opposition. And while the previous section focused on the specific link the ethics issue forged between the Fortas and Haynsworth nominations, this segment looks at the role of the ethical insensitivity charge raised against the Republican nominee independent of its relationship to the demise of Fortas. Had the Fortas case not occurred, senators inclined to oppose Haynsworth would still have been able to use the ethics issue to conceal the real motivation behind their opposition.

The role of ethics as a cover issue is clearly seen in the analysis of the roll call on the Haynsworth nomination presented earlier.[32] Close examination of Senate voting indicated that despite the widely-expressed concern about Haynsworth's sense of ethics, most senators assessed the seriousness of this issue with an ideological bias. This finding suggests that the clamor surrounding Haynsworth's sense of propriety was primarily employed to conceal ideological considerations as senators opposed to the nomination primarily, if not exclusively, on the contentious grounds of ideology or party were able to rest their disapproval on the less controversial and safer grounds of impropriety.

Several contemporary accounts of the Haynsworth confirmation struggle lend support to the conclusion the ethics issue was used primarily as a smokescreen to conceal ideological opposition. One report noted that

> the Haynsworth case . . . appears to have solidified a return of the Senate to an earlier policy of examining the ideology as well as the ethical fitness of nominees to the Supreme Court. One can say this even though the principal challenges were to Haynsworth's ethics rather than his Dixie attitudes on civil rights and labor. This was a surface thing; in many respects, liberals played the game conservatives did a year ago when they decried Abe Fortas's judicial conduct but stood their ground in opposition to his elevation to chief justice on the basis of Fortas's liberalism.[33]

Another account reached the conclusion that in the Senate's consideration of Haynsworth, the ethics issue was used by many senators "as a convenient cover for ideological or political opposition."[34]

Early on, Nixon recognized the potential of the ethics issue to generate opposition more as a cover than a legitimate issue. In preparing to meet the press before the Haynsworth nomination was even announced, the president noted in his own handwriting that in regard to conflict of interest, the prospective nominee must be "like Caesar's wife." Ironically, these presidential jottings indicate that under the heading "General Considerations," Nixon had crossed out the phrase "Because of Fortas case, emphasis on ethics."[35]

While the president's notes convey his awareness that the ethics issue could possibly be used as a cover issue, the testimony of White House aides and other Haynsworth supporters point to this as having become a reality. Nixon's chief political advisor, Murray Chotiner, concluded that for many senators the ethics issue raised against Haynsworth "was an excuse, not a reason."[36] Peter M. Flanigan, Assistant to the President, attributed Haynsworth's defeat in part to "the smoke surrounding the ethical issue."[37] In an attempt to draw some lessons from the Haynsworth rejection, Assistant Attorney General William H. Rehnquist concluded that the ideological opposition of civil rights and labor activists would not have been sufficient to defeat the nomination had these activists not been

> able to unfurl some banner other than their own under which they can enlist some of the more middle-of-the-road members of the Senate. In the Haynsworth debates, they used conflict of interest.[38]

Finally, William Loeb, of New Hampshire, publisher of the conservative *Manchester Union Leader*, testified not only to the use of the ethics issue as a cover but also to the president's careless approach to managing the selection process by privately scolding the White House for nominating an individual vulnerable to non-ideological, non-partisan criticism. In a letter to Senator Winston L. Prouty (R, Vt.) sent at the behest of the White House as part of the effort to drum up support for Haynsworth, the outspoken publisher noted:

> While there is nothing in his [Haynsworth's] background which really should disqualify him for a seat on the United States Supreme Court, I do think a more thorough investigation would have revealed that there were certain aspects about him which lent themselves to easy attack by demagogues inside the Senate and out.
>
> Any conservative, pro-American appointee will, of course, be attacked by the left-wingers, inside the Senate and out, and that is to be expected. Therefore, there is no sense in making such an attack easy by selecting individuals who are open to attack, even if improperly so.[39]

Ethics as a Legitimate Issue

While some senators employed Haynsworth's alleged lack of ethical sensitivity to conceal their ideological opposition to confirmation, this was not the case for other members of the Senate who failed to support the nomination. The Haynsworth deliberations revealed some senators who appear to have been genuinely influenced by ethical considerations in arriving at their decisions to oppose confirmation.

The first line of argument in support of this conclusion draws upon the roll call analysis of the vote on the nomination. While that analysis pointed to the dominant impact of ideology on Senate voting on the Haynsworth nomination, this factor failed to explain the roll call behavior of all senators. It will be recalled that at least seventeen senators voted in a way not consistent with their ideology and were accordingly classified as "deviant." Particularly important among this "deviant" group are the eight Republicans who were classified as "Conservatives" and who voted against Haynsworth: Cooper, Griffin, Jordan, Miller, and Smith of Maine, as well as Robert W. Packwood (Ore.), William B. Saxbe (Ohio), and John J. Williams (Del.). Because these senators were sympathetic to Haynsworth's perceived conservative ideology and shared the nominee's party affiliation, their votes against confirmation did not likely stem from considerations of ideology or party. It is highly credible that their negative votes emanated from genuine concern about the nominee's ethical insensitivity.

Specific evidence exists indicating that Williams, Cooper, Jordan, Miller, and Smith voted against the Haynsworth nomination out of a sincere concern about the nominee's lack of ethical sensitivity. The respective ideology indexes of eight for Williams and Miller and seventeen for Cooper, Jordan, and Smith decisively placed them among Senate "Conservatives." Consequently, there can be little doubt they enthusiastically embraced Haynsworth's perceived conservative ideology and would ordinarily have been counted upon to support confirmation actively.

The public statements of each of these five Republicans as well as private comments attributed to some of them attest to the ethics issue's being the dominant consideration leading to their opposition. Senator Williams informed his colleagues that had ideology been the only issue in the Senate deliberations he would have "enthusiastically endorsed the confirmation of Haynsworth."[40]

Senator Cooper later relayed the following reason for his negative vote on the Haynsworth nomination:

Although he [Haynsworth] hadn't personally profited from his decisions in the cases where he held stock in companies that were litigants before his court, he had violated the federal statute and judicial canons, both of which instruct judges to disqualify themselves in such cases. Since Haynsworth was a good lawyer, he must have known this, and yet he neither disqualified himself nor disclosed his violations during the Senate hearings on his nomination. That forced me to oppose him.[41]

At a time when the White House still had hopes of gaining Senator Jordan's vote on the Haynsworth nomination, the Idaho Republican was described as having "some difficulty" with the ethical charges raised against the nominee.[42] Jordan made his position on the nomination public a short time later, resting his opposition on the nominee's failure to appreciate how easily confidence in the judiciary "can be undermined by even the appearance of impropriety."[43]

Senator Miller proclaimed that "every senator should search his conscience to see whether the exercise of the confirmation power by the Senate is for the good of the country, not for the good of the White House, not for the good of the Senate but for the good of the people of this country." Employing this standard, the Iowa Republican concluded he must oppose Haynsworth's elevation to the Supreme Court because of the nominee's "careless approach to the Canons of Judicial Ethics."[44]

As indicated above, Senator Smith opposed Haynsworth in part to avoid giving the appearance of employing a double standard in assessing the ethical sensitivity of Democratic and Republican Supreme Court nominees. But she later implied the ethical charges raised against Haynsworth were sufficient in themselves, regardless of their link to the Fortas case, to merit rejection of the nomination. Years later, in recalling her early announcement of opposition to Haynsworth, Smith confided the following regarding her decision-making process on the nomination:

> I felt strongly that there were too many qualified people for the appointment to the Supreme Court, and the nominee should be without blemish.
>
> After the hearings were printed and I found that one of his [Haynsworth's] investments was questionable, I did not need to go beyond without returning to my first thought.
>
> I did not [usually] make early commitments on votes, feeling that there might be changes along the way and once pledged, I could not change; but with this one point against Mr. Haynsworth and the number of attorneys available for the appointment, I thought it was well to make the announcement. . . .[45]

The unexpected disapproval of the Haynsworth nomination by these five senators solidified their collective opposition as each of them could defend his/her actions by pointing to the opposition of other Republican conservatives. For example, Senator Smith consistently defended her vote against Haynsworth by citing the opposition of other conservative Republicans. To one constituent who accused the Maine Republican of deserting the conservative cause in voting against Haynsworth, she responded:

> The issue was not conservative versus liberal. For example, conservative Senator John Williams of Delaware, conservative Jack Miller of Iowa, and conservative Len Jordan of Idaho all voted against the Haynsworth nomination.[46]

To a charge her vote against Haynsworth represented both a hatred of the South and a slavish obligation to Negroes and labor unions, Smith responded by inquiring whether her accuser would also conclude

> that Senator John Williams hates the South or is under obligation to the Negroes or Labor unions since Senator Williams has announced his opposition to the Haynsworth nomination on the same grounds that I have.[47]

The opposition of these conservative Republicans reportedly accounted for far more than an additional five votes against confirmation. Their willingness to vote against the conservative nominee of a Republican president could not but bolster other GOP senators in their uncomfortable stand against the nomination. One report, specifically describing the impact of Senator Miller's opposition, very likely applied to the pivotal actions of each of the five conservative Republicans discussed above. According to this account, Miller's defection from the pro-Haynsworth camp involved "a good deal more than a single vote" as it would very likely encourage other undecided conservative senators to do the same.[48]

While the defections of all five of the conservative Republicans were bound to have an impact on other senators, Cooper's and Williams' opposition appears to have had been most influential in reducing support for Haynsworth. According to one report, Cooper's announcement he would vote against confirmation because of the nominee's ethical insensitivity created a "stampede of other Republicans to line up with him."[49] Senator Williams' announced opposition due to ethical considerations appears to have been even more damaging in undermining support for the nomination. The Delaware Republican's uncompromising concern for high standards of propriety in public service had earned him the sobriquet the "conscience of the Senate." Many senators respected and followed his judgment, especially in regard to assessing the ethical sensitivity of would-be public servants. Not surprisingly, Williams' decision to vote against the Haynsworth nomination for reasons linked to the nominee's improper sense of propriety would not go unnoticed by other senators.

Early in the battle for confirmation, Ehrlichman testified to the damaging multiplying effect Williams' defection would have on the Senate by noting "if Williams goes . . . it's lost."[50] In addition, White House memoranda consistently pointed to Williams' support as crucial because several senators reportedly confided they would follow his lead on the Haynsworth nomination. For example, one memorandum concluded that "on the Republican side the key vote is *Williams*. If he votes 'aye' he will influence Aiken, Boggs, Cooper, Dole, Jordan, and Prouty."[51]

White House predictions of the likelihood of specific senators' supporting Haynsworth consistently underlined the significant influence Williams' stand on the nomination could have on his colleagues. Senator George Aiken (R, Vt.) was described as "still uncommitted, inclined favorable. Will follow John Williams."[52] Even the venerable Senator Cooper was presented as one who is "likely to be swayed by John Williams."[53] Senator J. Caleb Boggs (R, Del.) was noted as wanting "to go with the President but will follow John Williams."[54] A few days after these White House reports, both Aiken and Cooper reportedly told administration staffers they "will vote with Williams."[55]

Ironically, White House concern about Williams' influence over colleagues Aiken, Boggs, Cooper, Dole, Prouty, and Jordan appears to have been exaggerated. Of the six senators, only Cooper and Jordan joined the Delaware Republican in voting against the Haynsworth nomination. Still, the opposition of Cooper and Jordan was critical to the outcome and it is highly possible that some of the remaining four senators may have been prepared to vote against the nomination were their votes needed to block Haynsworth's confirmation. In addition, given Williams' reputation within both wings of the GOP, it is very likely that some moderate-to-liberal senators like Saxbe of Ohio, Packwood of Oregon, and Scott of Pennsylvania, all of whom voted against the nomination, were strengthened in their opposition by the stand he took. This analysis draws support from one White House insider who estimated that Williams' opposition probably cost the pro-Haynsworth forces "a half dozen votes."[56]

Senator Griffin, who drew wide praise from many of his colleagues for courageously rounding up GOP votes against the nomination, has also testified to Williams' pivotal role. According to Griffin, the defeat of the nomination would not have been accomplished without Williams' strong stand against confirmation on the grounds of ethical insensitivity.[57]

An additional piece of evidence points to the critical impact a genuine concern with the nominee's ethical insensitivity had on some senators considering the Haynsworth nomination. Some five weeks before the confirmation roll call, White House staffers identified a "band of Republican Senators whose current indecision or opposition controls the fate of the Haynsworth nomination."[58] Included among this group of eleven key Republicans were Senators Cooper, Jordan, Miller, and Williams, all of whom eventually voted against confirmation, according to the evidence presented above, out of a sincere concern about Haynsworth's sense of propriety. Had the nominee not been vulnerable to the ethical charges, these four senators, as well as Senator Smith, would no doubt have supported the nomination and Haynsworth may have been spared rejection. Because a switch of five negative votes would have been sufficient to win Haynsworth's confirmation, the pivotal role of the ethics issue in leading these conservative Republicans to oppose Haynsworth becomes even more evident.

Finally, a private comment of a White House official provides still more testimony that some senators were sincerely moved by the ethics issue in deciding to oppose confirmation. Pat Buchanan's notes of a White House meeting in the middle of the confirmation struggle contain the frank assessment that the ethics issue "caused re-evaluation and some backing away by those [senators] pro or neutral before."[59] Buchanan's comment suggests that sincere concerns about the ethics issue cut into the support of senators who had been undecided or in favor of confirmation when the nominee's ideology and party were the only grounds upon which to oppose the nomination.

It is difficult to ascertain to what extent the non-ideological charges raised against Haynsworth sincerely figured in the negative votes of other senators beyond those discussed. There were more than likely additional senators who voted against or at least held back from supporting the nomination because of genuine concerns about the allegations of ethical insensitivity. For example, one White House report suggested the ethical allegations had caused at least one-quarter of the Senate to withhold support out of a "fear something new will pop up."[60]

While the full extent of the opposition stemming from an unfeigned concern about the nominee's ethics is uncertain, this is not the case regarding the negative impact of President Nixon's selection of an associate justice designee vulnerable to non-ideological and non-partisan criticism. This selection clearly increased Senate opposition to confirmation. And whether this opposition stemmed from a genuine concern about the nominee's lack of ethical sensitivity or served to mask more partisan motives, its presence could have been lessened, if not nullified, by more astute presidential oversight of the selection process.

OVERSEEING THE CONFIMATION PROCESS

After the nomination had been forwarded to the Senate, the president's management of the confirmation process also contributed significantly to Haynsworth's defeat. At least two aspects of Nixon's post-nomination management of the nomination are open to criticism. The president failed to make certain his subordinates cooperated with senators who were either seeking to win additional support for Haynsworth or who remained undecided on the nomination. Specifically, the White House failed to supply these senators with timely information useful for countering the charges made against Haynsworth. Additionally, Nixon either directly ordered or at least acquiesced in the undertaking of what were perceived to be heavy-handed and counterproductive tactics in attempting to pressure various senators to support Haynsworth.

The Failure to Cooperate

After the nomination was forwarded to the Senate, the White House reportedly failed to provide pro-Haynsworth and undecided senators with the necessary information they needed to counter the charges of ethical insensitivity raised against the nominee. In the opinion of Mollenhoff, a White House trouble-shooter belatedly given the assignment of assisting in steering the nomination through the Senate, it was the Nixon administration's "blundering that plunged the Haynsworth nomination into trouble in the first place."[61] According to Mollenhoff, a fatal mistake was the administration's stoic silence in the face of the charges raised against Haynsworth.

> When the first charges of conflicts of interest were raised in August [1969], they could and should have been answered fully and clearly to demonstrate the factual inaccuracies and distorted legal thinking behind charges stimulated by AFL-CIO lobbyists and their allies in the press. But the Nixon administration chose to remain aloof from the allegations, and Attorney General John N. Mitchell instructed Haynsworth not to discuss them.[62]

Mollenhoff's view is shared, among others, by Harry Dent, a former legislative aide to Senator Strom Thurmond (R, S.C.), and at the time of the Haynsworth nomination Special Counsel to the President charged with overseeing the administration's southern strategy. While the conflict of interest charges were being raised by opponents of the nomination, Dent criticized the administration for not dealing with the growing loss of support, noting "the liberals are beating Haynsworth's brains out and we can't even get the Justice Department to answer questions of Republican senators."[63] Dent's criticism reportedly stemmed from the Justice Department's policy of responding only to queries on the Haynsworth nomination made by Judiciary Committee Chairman James O. Eastland (D, Miss.) and Roman L. Hruska (R, Neb.) and no one else.[64] Ironically, this willingness to respond to Eastland's questions did not convince the conservative Mississippi Democrat of the Justice Department's effectiveness in supporting Haynsworth. According to Eastland:

> The folks . . . at the Justice Department don't know what they're doing. There's no real reason for the Haynsworth nomination to be in trouble, but they aren't explaining things and it is being bungled at every stage.[65]

Senator Marlow W. Cook (R, Ky.), Haynsworth's staunchest supporter in the Senate, also confided that he was "rather disappointed" at the lack of cooperation from the administration in his effort to win support for the nomination. When the attorney general's office finally got around to supplying Cook with the information he needed to build a case for Haynsworth, the exasperated Kentucky Republican noted that had the information been provided earlier, "there might not have been all this fuss."[66]

White House Communications Director Herb Klein lamented that for almost two months after Haynsworth's name was forwarded to the Senate, the Justice Department's silence had prevented him from providing satisfactory answers to questions raised by staunch Republicans who wanted to support the nomination. According to Klein, these senators initially thought the nomination was a good one but were beginning to have their doubts.[67]

The Nixon administration's reluctance to meet with and provide senators with information on the charges raised against Haynsworth clearly undermined the confirmation effort. The pro-Haynsworth forces' long period of silence created a situation in which allegations against the nominee were allowed to accumulate.[68] Consequently, some two months after the nomination was announced, the major problem in defending Haynsworth was seen as being posed not by any one allegation but rather by "the sheer number of charges that had not been explained."[69] For example, Senators Griffin and Williams reportedly told the White House that they were gravely concerned not about the nominee's alleged improprieties in any specific case but by "the overall impression that had been permitted to develop."[70]

The administration's silence about the charges raised against Haynsworth's sense of propriety also left the impression, whether warranted or not, that the allegations were true and could not be refuted. As one White House insider aptly put it:

> When a Nixon administration nominee for associate justice of the Supreme Court was being charged with specific improprieties, a 'no comment' from the White House press office was equivalent to Frank Costello pleading the Fifth before the Kefauver crime committee.[71]

For the most part, senators directed their criticism of the administration's silence not at Nixon but at the Justice Department and Attorney General Mitchell. However, there is at least one report that Nixon unwisely failed to make himself accessible to Republican senators who wanted to discuss the nomination with him in the critical months after Haynsworth was nominated. In faulting the president not only for denying these senators access but for not taking the initiative in discussing the nomination with them, this report concluded that early and complete refutation by the president of the allegations raised against Haynsworth might have won over "a significant number of Republican votes."[72]

Despite the inclination of senators to criticize only the Justice Department and Attorney General Mitchell for the crucial delay in responding to the charge against Haynsworth, this criticism must also be directed at the president. In the critical early stages of the confirmation battle, Nixon elected to take a detached stance and to delegate responsibility for seeing the nomination through the Senate.[73] In making that choice, the president, in effect, underwrote the actions of his subordinates if only because the Justice Department's initial policy of silence and its failure to cooperate with pro-Haynsworth and undecided senators could not have persisted in the face of a clear directive to the contrary from the president.

Antagonizing and Alienating the Senate

As the ethical case against Haynsworth developed, several key Republicans in addition to Minority Whip Griffin and Conference Chair Smith privately called upon the president to withdraw the nomination. Minority Leader Scott as well as conservative Republicans Tower and Goldwater and GOP liberal Brooke all besieged the president with petitions to retract the nomination.[74] For example, Brooke confided to the president that if the nomination were to go forward, it would be "extremely embarrassing to those of us who face a great conflict between our principles and our sense of obligation to you."[75]

These pleas apparently made an impact on Nixon but not the one intended by the worried Republican senators. Rather than assenting to their petitions, the president decided not only to go ahead with the nomination but to pursue more aggressive tactics in a renewed effort to drum up support for confirmation. Consequently, after having taken a relatively passive approach to gaining Haynsworth's confirmation, the White House, under the strong urging of the president, belatedly opted for a distinct change in tactics. It is not clear whether Nixon gave or simply acquiesced in the command to switch to a more combative approach in pressuring senators to support Haynsworth, but it is unlikely that so obvious and important a change would have been undertaken without his approval.

Nixon's endorsement of the change to more aggressive tactics in dealing with Haynsworth's detractors is evinced in comments he made to members of the Republican leadership shortly after deciding not to withdraw the nomination.

> All the liberals, the *Washington Post* and the *New York Times* would praise me highly if we withdraw him, but I don't intend to do that. I will stick by Haynesworth [sic] if there is one vote left for him in the U.S. Senate, and that's Agnew's. If we cave in on this one, they will think that if you kick Nixon you can get somewhere . . . I didn't get where I am today by running away from fights.[76]

A short time later, the president directly instructed Dent to signal the change in tactics by urging party chairmen throughout the South to "make statements praising R.N. [Richard Nixon] for coming out fighting in defense of Haynsworth."[77]

A more combative tone soon began to be sounded at White House strategy sessions on the Haynsworth nomination. Ehrlichman's notes of one session attended by the president on October 8, 1969, reflect the White House view that it was now time to "put the heat on" Republicans who were opposing Haynsworth because now "it's us or them."[78] Haldeman's notes of a similar strategy session attended by the president shortly after the one of October 8 contain the following terse and belligerent statements:

> On Haynsworth—need murderer's [sic] row in Senate.

> Need to kick Bayh [Senator Birch Bayh, leader of the anti-Haynsworth forces] around.

> Feel personal responsibility to whack on counterattack.

> Get people on Senate floor to speak up.

> Mitchell [Attorney General John Mitchell] move on some. Keep offensive going—esp. rip Bayh.[79]

Nixon's move to a more combative stance in gaining Haynsworth's confirmation was quickly picked up by White House subordinates. For example, shortly after the call for a more active White House effort on Haynsworth's behalf, Dent prepared memoranda succinctly outlining some of the tactics being undertaken by his office to implement the new approach. Included among Dent's undertakings were the following: the urging of state GOP chairpersons, Nixon federal appointees, and all who had been known to favor conservative causes, to contact their senators in Haynsworth's behalf; the encouraging of Southern newspapers to play up the "Southern angle" that Haynsworth was the victim of regional bias; the stepped up investigation of Senator Bayh's financial dealings and his contacts with organized labor in an attempt to uncover material to silence or discredit Haynsworth's sharpest critic; the compiling of a list of favors desired by senators from the administration, such as jobs, projects, and grants, in order to use this as leverage in seeking their support for Haynsworth; and the contacting of the "largest contributors" of campaign funds to the uncommitted senators of both parties in order to urge them to apply pressure in support of Haynsworth.[80]

Evidence that these tactics represented a distinct change in the White House's approach to seeking Haynsworth's confirmation is supplied by Haldeman's handwritten notation on one of Dent's memoranda. Haldeman testified to both his strong support of Dent's efforts as well as to the ordered turnaround in the administration's tactics by noting, "Darn good job! Glad someone is off his heels and running."[81] The implication of Haldeman's comment is that prior to October 27, the date of this memorandum, these tactics were not being used.

This distinct change in tactics and the effort to go all out in support of Haynsworth rather than withdraw the nomination were particularly disturbing to moderate Republicans. They believed that the White House had overseen a sloppy and incomplete pre-nomination screening of Haynsworth which had needlessly made the filling of the Supreme Court vacancy extremely controversial.[82] Additionally, these moderates were disturbed that after months of letting the charges against Haynsworth go unanswered, thereby severely undermining the hope for confirmation, the White House suddenly began to pressure them intensely to support the nomination. Not surprisingly, these moderate Republican as well as other GOP senators resented being unduly pressured to support a controversial nomination by a president they perceived to have done little to lessen their burden and who, in effect, had put them "on the spot."[83]

The argument here is not that the change in tactics represented poor presidential management. Indeed, given the White House's earlier more passive approach, which had reportedly not served Haynsworth well, a change in tactics may very well have been in order. Counterproductive presidential management was reflected not in the adoption of new tactics but rather in what those new tactics were. To many Republican senators, these tactics did little to help Haynsworth and much to undermine both the image of the GOP and the nominee's chances for confirmation.[84] An examination of the White House's handling of individual senators supports this assessment.

Even senators whom the White House successfully pressured into voting for Haynsworth expressed concern regarding the tactics employed. Conservative Republican James B. Pearson of Kansas, the focus of an intense White House campaign to win his support of Haynsworth, was one who publicly made known his dissatisfaction. As part of the effort to win the Kansas Republican's support, a private White House meeting between Pearson and Nixon was arranged shortly before the Haynsworth vote. Although it is not clear what occurred at this meeting, Pearson reportedly advised the president very soon after the conference began that he would support Haynsworth.[85] It was not until after the Senate had rejected the Haynsworth nomination that Pearson publicly revealed his opinion regarding the White House pressure directed his way. Offering an undetailed but nevertheless indicting comparison, Pearson charged that while the Johnson administration "used to twist arms and legs this [Nixon] administration twists throats."[86] While it is unclear whether Pearson was upset with pressure specifically applied by the president in their private meeting or by the aggressive effort to win his support, his remarks clearly reveal his strong dissatisfaction with the tactics employed by the White House.

Another Haynsworth supporter who expressed criticism of the White House's efforts to gain confirmation was Senator Ernest F. Hollings (D, S.C). One White House report confided that while Hollings had been "helping on the Haynsworth matter," he "has also been chopping up the President" and "contending the Administration has fallen down on the job."[87] After Haynsworth was rejected by the Senate, Hollings, according to a White House report, openly "blamed the Nixon administration for the defeat." In arriving at this conclusion, the South Carolina Democrat reportedly noted "there was no leadership from the White House, particularly early in the Haynsworth campaign and that later, Nixon aides used heavy-handed pressure tactics which backfired against the President's Court nominee."[88] In another analysis after the roll call, Hollings attributed Haynsworth's failure to gain confirmation to the White House's having played "too rough with members of the Senate."[89]

Other senators who voted for Haynsworth but nonetheless criticized the Nixon administration for its counterproductive tactics in presurring the Senate included Republicans Robert Dole of Kansas, and Goldwater. Reportedly frustrated by the White House's overseeing of the nomination, Dole confided to a trusted friend that he was "sick and tired of the way they are handling this."[90] Goldwater evidently spoke for other Republicans when he openly concluded that the move to more aggressive tactics by the administration only served further to discredit a nomination already seen as a distinct embarrassment to the GOP.[91]

Although Senators Pearson, Hollings, Dole, and Goldwater expressed dismay about the administration's tactics, their support of confirmation indicates that at least in their specific cases, the White House's efforts did not cost Haynsworth any votes. But the administration was not so fortunate in its dealings with other senators. Evidence clearly indicates that bitterness stemming from the White House's tactics played a contributing role in some senators' decisions to vote against confirmation.

Senator Jordan's determination to vote against Haynsworth apparently stemmed in part from his pique at White House pressure for his support. The conservative Idaho Republican, a consistent and loyal supporter of the administration, would ordinarily have been inclined to favor Haynsworth's confirmation. As indicated above, Jordan eventually voted against confirmation, citing the nominee's perceived lack of ethical sensitivity.

But in mid-October, 1969, Jordan was still undecided on the nomination. At about this time, the White House received a report describing Jordan as "hypersensitive to pressure." This same report noted that Senator Howard Baker, Jr., (R, Tenn.) advised the White House not to bear down in seeking Jordan's vote for Haynsworth because the senator "will react adversally [sic] to pressure."[92]

While still publicly uncommitted, Jordan wrote to the attorney general a short time later privately conveying his inclination to oppose Haynsworth.[93] The Idaho Republican later maintained that despite this letter, he had still not closed the door and continued to ponder the Haynsworth matter.[94] Ignoring Baker's advice, the White House apparently reacted to Jordan's letter to the attorney general by turning up the pressure. Several close friends and associates of Jordan's as well as representatives of the National Forest Products Association were contacted and urged to lobby the Idaho senator to support Haynsworth.[95] Further evidence the White House failed to heed Baker's recommendation is supplied by the report of a White House aide who confidently concluded on November 5, 1969, a few weeks before the crucial roll call vote, that a White House contact in Idaho would "work over" Jordan "within the next few days to bring him in." This same report advised against "backing off the pressure" on Jordan.[96]

The stepped-up White House pressure did not go unnoticed by Jordan. After noting that the White House pressure on him to support the nomination was greater than on any issue in his seven years of service in the Senate, the Idaho Republican added "the only way I can account for this unprecedented wave of interest is the fact that I decided I could not support Haynsworth and so notified the Attorney General." "Since that date," concluded Jordan, "calls to my state have been legion."[97] Jordan also complained that in regard to the Haynsworth nomination, "support of the president is urged as if it were a personal matter rather than an issue of grave constitutional importance."[98]

While it is difficult to ascertain whether this undue pressure on the reportedly hypersensitive Jordan caused his negative vote on the Haynsworth nomination, it clearly did not help win his support. Indeed, there is an additional report that the Idaho Republican was subsequently asked to vote for Haynsworth by a Department of Agriculture official who, almost in the same breath, mentioned an agriculture project the senator had been seeking for his state for several months. When Jordan was left with the impression that his vote on the Haynsworth nomination would determine whether he could expect much help from the Nixon administration in securing the project, he was reportedly "furious" at the White House for its bargaining tactics.[99]

There is an additional account indicating that another senator decided to vote against Haynsworth because of the White House's aggressive tactics. During the Senate's deliberations, GOP Senator Miller became a prime focus of the administration's belated mid-October effort to step up the pressure in order to gain the votes of uncommitted senators. A White House memorandum dated October 20, 1969, notes that "certain actions" have been initiated to "insure the vote of Senator Jack Miller in favor of the President's nominee for the Supreme Court."[100] Although it is not clear what actions were taken to insure Miller's support, an unidentified mid-western senator was reportedly threatened by a high official in the Department of Agriculture with a cutback in his state's agriculture subsidies if he did not support Haynsworth. According to this account, the mid-western senator, who was very likely Miller, became so incensed at this tactic that he voted against Haynsworth's confirmation even though he had been prepared "to back Shirley Temple if the president named her to the Court."[101]

One of the newly adopted tactics in the White House's more aggressive approach came to be described as the "fat cat" program, in which some of the major financial contributors to the campaigns of specific uncommitted senators were contacted by the administration and urged to lobby these senators to support Haynsworth. The program was coordinated by Assistant to the Secretary of Commerce Jack A. Gleason, described in one White House memorandum as a "man who looks after contributors," and by Kevin Phillips, Special Assistant to the Attorney General.[102] Evidence clearly indicates that this program represented a change in tactics. The contacting of key financial contributors apparently was not undertaken until mid-October, 1969, after Nixon had refused to withdraw the Haynsworth nomination and signaled the move to more aggressive tactics. The earliest mention of the "fat cat" program is in a White House memorandum of October 14, 1969, in which Gleason noted that he and Phillips "will coordinate approaches to fat cat types."[103]

Senator Saxbe was a prime target in this new program, and the contacting of his major campaign contributors began almost immediately. On October 15, 1969, at least nine major contributors in Ohio were contacted, including the highest ranking officials within Lubrizol Corporation, Republic Steel, General Tire and Rubber, L.M. Berry and Company, and Phelps Dodge Corporation.[104] Almost immediately after this effort began, the chairman of the Ohio Republican Party urged the White House to "stop the pressure on Saxbe."[105] Despite this request, Gleason advised a continuation of the pressure, expressing doubts whether "taking off the fat cat pressure now will be productive to our case."[106] Given this contrasting advice, the White House elected to heed Gleason's direction and in the following weeks the list of major contributors contacted to pressure Saxbe increased from nine to fifteen, now including General Telephone and Electronics and the Stouffer Foods Corporation.[107]

A White House report at this time noted that Saxbe was describing himself as "firmly uncommitted" on the Haynsworth nomination and concluded his vote could be gained so long as "he is properly handled."[108] Another White House report described Saxbe as "presently favorable to the President's position" on the Haynsworth nomination.[109] Even as late as November 4, a few weeks before the Haynsworth roll call, Saxbe reportedly had yet to commit himself on the nomination and his vote was still up for grabs.[110] Because the stepped-up pressure coincided with Saxbe's uncommitted position, his treatment by the White House had the potential to tip the scale in either direction.

And what was the effect of the increased pressure on the Ohio Republican? Saxbe reportedly became so incensed by the administration's effort to win his support by encouraging wealthy Ohio contributors to pressure him into supporting Haynsworth that he publicly labeled the White House arm-twisters "a bunch of amateurs."[111] What was most upsetting to Saxbe, however, was a report that a White House official had ordered Haynsworth's supporters in Ohio to check into his personal finances in order to gain some leverage in seeking his vote. Not even the hasty canceling of that order by the White House could deter the feisty Republican from openly reminding the administration that in attempting to win his support for confirmation by contacting his well-to-do constituents, it had "the wrong sow by the ear." Additionally, Saxbe remarked: "I don't fetch and carry when some fat cat calls up and tells me what to do."[112] Embittered by the White House pressure tactics, the Ohio Republican went on to vote against the Haynsworth nomination.

Reportedly, Nixon administration pressure on Minority Leader Scott also "backfired" thereby hardening his stance against the nomination. According to one account, Attorney General Mitchell and southern strategist Dent leaked the information Scott had promised the White House to support Haynsworth if his vote would make the difference. Scott denied ever having made such a pledge. Mitchell's and Dent's deliberate leaking of this false information was reportedly "designed to force Scott into making it come true."[113] The level of Scott's anger at the administration can be gauged from his reaction upon learning of the misrepresentation of his position. The Pennsylvania Republican was reportedly so furious that he told other senators at a private gathering, "Mitchell's a Goddamned liar."[114] This misguided tactic only served to solidify Scott's intention to vote against Haynsworth.

There is additional testimony from senators confirming the counterproductive impact of the administration's aggressive tactics in seeking support for the Haynsworth nomination. Senator Williams confided that while the ethics issue hurt the nominee, nothing in Haynsworth's past behavior troubled him about the nomination as much as the tactics used by the White House in its effort to force a united GOP front on the appointment.[115] Additionally, Senators Hatfield and Schweiker, who both voted against confirmation, were reportedly disturbed by the intensity of the White House pressure directed at them in the effort to gain their votes.[116] While one can only speculate whether the White House's bearing down contributed to their negative votes, it is likely the pressure only confirmed their resolve to vote against Haynsworth. Indeed, an individual described as Schweiker's "closest friend" reported to the White House during the Senate's deliberations that the Pennsylvania Republican was firmly against the nomination "and made more so by what he [Schweiker] alleged to be undue pressure from the White House."[117]

Presidential Management: Conclusion

The evidence presented in the preceding pages supports the conclusion Nixon's management of the confirmation process was a key factor in the Senate's refusal to confirm Haynsworth. In selecting a nominee vulnerable on ethical grounds, especially in the wake of Fortas's having been driven from the Court under similar circumstances, the president contributed to losing the support of senators who ordinarily would have enthusiastically supported Haynsworth. In addition, the selection of a nominee vulnerable on ethical grounds needlessly provided senators who were dissatisfied with Haynsworth's conservative ideology and/or party affiliation with a convenient cover issue behind which to conceal the partisan basis of their opposition. In failing to oversee effectively the post-selection phase of the confirmation process, Nixon further contributed to the Senate's rejection in two distinct ways. He did not make certain his subordinates cooperated productively both with pro-Haynsworth senators seeking to drum up support for the nomination and with undecided senators requesting information to assist them in their decisions. In addition, after signaling a change to a more aggressive approach to winning Senate support, Nixon failed to guard against the use of heavy-handed, counterproductive tactics by his subordinates.

In assessing the White House's management of the confirmation process even before some of the more damaging, counterproductive tactics were undertaken, a Nixon supporter concluded that the Haynsworth affair "will be pointed to in the future as a prime example of stupid handling of a Supreme Court appointment by an administration considered to be adept at big-time politics."[118] As indicated by the events described in this chapter, the administration's actions following this already unfavorable assessment of its handling of the nomination only served to reinforce the earlier appraisal of the White House's effort in Haynsworth's behalf. Without any doubt, President Nixon's management of the confirmation process was a significant factor in the Senate's refusal to confirm the nomination of Clement F. Haynsworth, Jr.

4. PRESIDENTIAL MANAGEMENT: THE CARSWELL NOMINATION

> The selection of Carswell was one of
> the most ill-advised public acts of the
> early Nixon Presidency.
> — Special Assistant to the President
> William L. Safire

THE BRUISING Haynsworth battle had left most senators physically drained and eager to support President Nixon's next nominee. Aptly summing up the highly receptive mood in the Senate at this time, Senator George Aiken (R, Vt.) whimsically opined, "anybody whose name will be sent up by the president will have no trouble getting confirmed unless he has committed murder—recently."[1] Although opponents of the ensuing nomination never uncovered evidence as serious as that alluded to by Aiken, there soon existed substantial grounds upon which to build a case against confirmation.

On January 19, 1970, President Nixon nominated G. Harrold Carswell, of the United States Court of Appeals for the Fifth Circuit, to the Supreme Court seat left vacant by the resignation of Fortas and the rejection of Haynsworth. Judiciary Committee hearings on the nomination were held from January 27, 1970, to February 3, with the nominee appearing on January 27 and 28. The hearings focused upon Carswell's ideology as reflected in his civil rights decisions as a federal judge. Additionally, testimony at the hearings addressed the question whether the nominee possessed both the competence and temperament demanded of a Supreme Court justice. On February 16, 1970, the Judiciary Committee voted 13-4 to report the nomination favorably. The majority and minority reports of the Committee were filed with the Senate on February 27.

The Senate formally commenced considering the Carswell nomination on March 13, 1970. During the ensuing debate, anti-Carswell senators sought to derail the nomination without a direct vote by moving, on March 26, 1970, to recommit it to the Judiciary Committee. The Senate subsequently agreed to vote on the motion to recommit on April 6, and, that motion failing, to vote directly on the Carswell nomination no later than April 8. After the motion to recommit was defeated by a 52-44 vote, the stage was set for a direct vote on the nomination. In a dramatic roll call on April 8, 1970, the Senate rejected the Carswell nomination by a 51-45 count.

Nixon contributed significantly to the Senate's refusal to grant confirmation first by selecting Carswell, who was vulnerable to criticism emanating from his purported lack of the legal ability and judicial temperament demanded of a Supreme Court justice. He further contributed to Carswell's defeat by falling short of the astute and effective presidential management required to gain confirmation once the nomination had been forwarded to the Senate.

SELECTING A VULNERABLE NOMINEE

Overseeing the Justice Department

According to White House aide Jeb Magruder, the only command from the president to the Justice Department in the wake of the Haynsworth defeat was immediately to find "almost any southerner" to fill the vacancy. Magruder notes that Justice Department officials were under such intense pressure from the White House to find a suitable nominee (i.e. southern, strict-constructionist, Republican) without delay that they acted with undue haste in recommending Carswell for the appointment.[2] The president, reportedly angry at Haynsworth's defeat and mistakingly trusting Attorney General John Mitchell's judgment, went forward with the nomination. This combination of anger, undue haste, and faith in the attorney general's appraisal led William L. Safire, Special Assistant to the President, to conclude later that "the selection of Carswell was one of the most ill-advised public acts of the early Nixon Presidency."[3]

Careless screening of Carswell failed to uncover incidents in the nominee's past which reflected unfavorably on his suitability to serve on the Supreme Court. Most notable among the undetected incidents were Carswell's 1948 speech in support of white supremacy; his participation, while serving as a United States attorney, in setting up a private corporation to take over an all white public country club under court order to desegregate; his signing of an affidavit, again while serving as United States attorney, chartering a booster club for the Florida State University football team limited in membership to "any white person"; his sale of property with a restrictive racial covenant in the deed; his reported rudeness and hostility to civil rights attorneys when he was a federal district judge; and his lackluster and undistinguished record in the lower courts.[4] The discovery and disclosure of these incidents by opponents of the nomination rather than by the Justice Department further embarrassed the White House and contributed to undermining the confirmation effort.

For example, shortly after the nomination was announced on January 19, 1970, a Jacksonville, Florida, television reporter found a copy of Carswell's pro-white supremacy speech in the records maintained by a county clerk in rural Georgia. The reporter uncovered what federal investigators had failed to find, even though the attorney general maintained that the Justice Department had undertaken "a most extensive background investigation."[5] According to Mitchell, federal investigators failed to discover the speech because the newspaper in which the speech was recorded was "no longer in existence."[6] Still, as the resourceful Jacksonville reporter understood and as the Justice Department officials knew or should have known, the newspaper in question was regarded as an official county record and preserved as such by the county clerk.[7]

A more careful pre-nomination investigation might have prevented a second embarrassing defeat for the president if only because Carswell would very likely not have been nominated had his complete background been known. For example, Mitchell has since maintained he never would have advised Nixon to nominate Carswell had he known the full extent of the Florida judge's background.[8] Additionally, Nixon's private reaction to the subsequent discovery of Carswell's role in the chartering of the all white Florida State University booster club suggests he would not have made this ill-fated nomination had he known of this incident and, no doubt, others in the nominee's past. When the president received a news summary setting out press reports of Carswell's involvement in chartering the club, he signaled his shock, anger, and displeasure by scrawling in the margin, "My God!"[9]

The incomplete Justice Department investigation of Carswell also made senators cautious and hesitant in supporting the nomination. Senate Republicans previously upset with Nixon for the controversial Haynsworth nomination were equally disturbed, if not more so, by the selection of a nominee assailable on the non-ideological grounds of lacking the required competence and judicial temperament. These senators apparently resented being urged to support a controversial nomination by an administration that had not carefully checked out the nominee's background. A glimpse of the resentment these senators felt toward what they perceived to be the White House's sloppy screening of the nominee is provided by the instructions they reportedly gave to then minority leader Senator Hugh Scott (R, Pa.) According to Scott, a number of Republican senators "of varied philosophical persuasion" urged him to "ask the Administration not to submit any new and controversial nominations for the balance of 1970."[10] The anger and frustration of these Republican senators is further reflected in Scott's reported "scolding" of the White House for failing to consult GOP senators prior to the nomination and in his chastisement of Mitchell for not having "done his homework on the Judge [Carswell]."[11]

The shoddy Justice Department investigation reportedly kept some senators from supporting confirmation out of fear there were still more potentially embarrassing incidents in the nominee's background.[12] These senators had lost so much confidence in the Justice Department that not even the president's personal assurances that there were no more damaging skeletons in Carswell's closet could convince them to support the nomination emphatically, if at all.

Columnist Tom Wicker joined others in concluding that one of the major factors accounting for the defeat of the Carswell nomination was the Justice Department's "abject failure to investigate his past record." Wicker nevertheless implied that the blame for the shoddy investigation must rest with President Nixon. Attributing the Justice Department's careless investigation to Nixon's failure to control subordinates within his administration, Wicker went on to describe the management of the Carswell nomination as about "as miserably botched an operation as any president has mounted since the Bay of Pigs"[13]

A Vulnerable Nominee

The selection of a nominee vulnerable on the grounds of competence and judicial temperament generated additional opposition against confirmation in two distinct ways. As with ethical considerations in the Fortas and Haynsworth cases, some opposing senators used the competency and/or temperament issues to conceal their ideological or partisan objections to the nominations, while others appear to have been genuinely moved by them.

Competence and Temperament as Cover Issues. Evidence pointing to the use of competence and temperament as cover issues can be seen in the previous analysis of Senate voting on the Carswell nomination revealing that many senators were influenced by ideology in assessing the seriousness of these charges,[14] The inclination of "Liberal" and "Conservative" senators to divide so sharply in their assessments of Carswell's competence and judicial temperament strongly suggests that these issues were employed in large part to mask ideological opposition. Senators opposed to the Carswell nomination on the controversial grounds of ideology or partisanship were provided the opportunity to defend their negative votes on the less quarrelsome, safer grounds of competence and/or temperament.

There is additional evidence of the use of competence and temperament as cover issues. A Senate staffer who actively assisted Senator Birch E. Bayh (D, Ind.) in leading the fight against Carswell has conceded that the Carswell nomination could not have been derailed solely on ideological grounds.

> We couldn't win if we made it strictly a civil rights fight. We had to have a "cover" issue. In Haynsworth's case, it was conflict of interest. In Carswell's case, it was lack of qualifications.[15]

Additionally, William H. Rehnquist, then an assistant attorney general, has testified that civil rights and labor groups could not have succeeded in blocking confirmation had ideology been the only issue in these cases. According to Rehnquist,

> Our experience with past nominees shows that these groups together cannot successfully defeat a nominee unless they are able to unfurl some banner other than their own under which they can enlist some of the more middle-of-the-road members of the Senate. In the Haynsworth debates, they used conflict of interest, and with Carswell the combination of "mediocrity," some rather thin evidence of personal hostility to blacks, and a claimed contradiction in his own testimony about an earlier transaction [the country club incorporation].[16]

Furthermore, the impact of the competency issue raised against Carswell was unexpectedly and notably increased when a staunch supporter and floor manager of the nomination conceded that the nominee possessed only mediocre legal talents. In a sincere but misguided effort to win support for the nomination, Senator Roman Hruska (R, Neb.)

provided a more extensive cover behind which opponents could conceal their ideological opposition by making a plea for pedestrianism on the Court. Hruska told reporters Carswell should be confirmed "even if he were mediocre," adding,

> There are a lot of mediocre judges and people and lawyers, and they are entitled to a little representation, aren't they? We can't have all Brandeises, Frankfurters, and Cardozos.[17]

In the ten-day period following the Hruska statement, nine Democratic senators announced their opposition to the nomination. All nine based their disapproval at least in part on Carswell's alleged mediocre legal ability.[18] In addition, three senators previously reported in favor of the nomination switched to "leaning against" within three days after Hruska's damaging defense of Carswell.[19] During this same period, four other senators moved from being in favor of confirmation to "uncommitted."[20]

Evidence exists suggesting that some of these senators seized the opportunity presented by the Hruska statement to conceal the real motivation behind their disapproval. For example, *The Washington Post* concluded the Hruska statement provided Senator Vance Hartke (D, Ind.) "with an excuse for opposing the President."[21] Hartke's ideology index of one hundred clearly placed him among Senate "Liberals," indicating he may very well have employed the competence issue to mask ideological objections to the nomination. At least two other Senate Democrats, Albert Gore (D, Tenn.) and J. William Fulbright (D, Ark.), with respective ideology indexes of seventy-five and sixty-seven placing them among Senate "Liberals," reportedly employed the Hruska statement to their advantage.[22] These two senators evidently told their disappointed constituents that while they shared their desire to see a Southern strict constructionist on the bench, they wanted one "smart enough to deal with the damn Yankees."[23]

Competence and Temperament as Legitimate Issues. Some indication of the number of senators sincerely moved to oppose the nomination by the competence and temperament issues is provided by the roll call analysis of the confirmation vote. Although the voting analysis revealed that most senators were primarily influenced by ideology in assessing Carswell's suitability for the Supreme Court, this was not the case for all roll call participants. The ideology factor failed to explain the votes of the seven so-called "deviant" senators, those who voted in a way not consistent with their ideologies. Of particular note here are the five "Conservatives," four Republicans and one Democrat, who voted against the Carswell nomination. The four Republicans were Marlow Cook (Ky.), Hiram L. Fong (Hawaii), Robert W. Packwood (Ore.), and Margaret Chase Smith (Maine); the lone Democrat was Howard W. Cannon (Nev.). The respective ideology indexes of these five senators which placed them among Senate "Conservatives" were fifty-eight for Cook, forty-two for Fong, fifty for Packwood, seventeen for Smith, and fifty for Cannon.

Because these indexes place some of these senators on the fringe of the "Conservative" category, it is more precise to describe this group as being moderate to conservative in ideology. Employing that terminology, one would still assume that these five moderate to conservative senators would have been favorably impressed by Carswell's perceived conservative ideology and inclined to support confirmation. That they all voted against confirmation suggests their actions were triggered not by considerations of ideology or partisanship but rather by a genuine concern about Carswell's alleged lack of competence and/or judicial temperament. The following analysis, focusing specifically on the motivations behind the votes of four of these senators, provides further support for this conclusion.

Senator Cook had fought valiantly, if unsuccessfully, for the confirmation of the conservative Haynsworth, so it could hardly be argued he would be opposed to the Carswell nomination on ideological grounds. Indeed, as a member of the Judiciary Committee, Cook had voted in favor of the Carswell nomination when it was favorably reported to the floor of the Senate in February, 1970. At that time, Carswell's conservative ideology had already been well publicized.[24]

It would appear, therefore, that Cook's eventual switch to opposing Carswell was primarily due to charges raised after the Judiciary Committee's report. In this regard, it should be noted that although there had been some testimony before the Judiciary Committee critical of Carswell's competence, some of the major information reflecting unfavorably on the nominee's legal ability was not broadly publicized until after the committee report had been issued. For example, Hruska's devastating statement conceding Carswell's mediocre legal talents was not made until March 16, 1970. In addition, the Ripon Society and Law Students Concerned for the Courts did not make public the results of their study until March 25, 1970. This study, it will be recalled, indicated Carswell's reversal rate by the court of appeals was ten percentage points higher than the average reversal vote for all federal district judges in the fifth circuit.[25]

Cook's publicly stated reasons for opposing Carswell, as well as White House reports of the Kentucky Republican's motivations, all point to the singular influence of the competency issue. One White House report conceded that Cook's concern about the nominee's competence was genuine by noting the Kentucky Republican "sincerely believes Carswell to be inferior, without qualifications for the High Bench."[26] Another White House report, indicating the impact of the study prepared by the Ripon Society and Law Students Concerned for the Courts, concluded that Cook's opposition stemmed from his concern about the "reversals of Carswell's decisions."[27]

Additionally, Cook's public statements directly spoke to his concern about the competency issue. In explaining his negative vote on the nomination, the Kentucky Republican recounted how on April 7, 1970, the day before the Carswell roll call, he was the president's guest at a posthumous Medal of Honor ceremony for several United States military personnel who had served in Vietnam. According to Cook, this ceremony convinced him to oppose Carswell.

> Those were men who did their best and lost their lives and all of a sudden I thought that we're going to vote for someone who did not fulfill the degree of excellence in the legal field that I thought these men deserved.[28]

Cook further expressed his doubts about Carswell's competence by complaining that the Florida judge "could not carry Clement Haynsworth's briefcase."[29]

Additional evidence of how strongly Cook felt about Carswell's perceived lack of competence is provided by examining the extensive but vain efforts by the White House to win the Kentucky Republican's support. During Senate deliberations on the nomination, White House staffers were aware Cook had recommended candidates for a United States marshal's position and for a federal district judgeship in Kentucky. Early in the confirmation battle, the administration delivered on the Kentucky Republican's marshal candidate in seeking to gain the senator's support for Carswell.[30] Despite this action, Cook continued to withhold a pledge to support confirmation.

As the roll call on Carswell neared, the White House stepped up efforts to win Cook's support. Ignoring Justice Department concerns the Kentucky Republican's candidate for the judgeship was unqualified, Nixon evidently passed the order at a White House meeting to "give Cook his judge" and "do the things that get us the votes."[31] After this meeting and two days before the Carswell roll call, Nixon had a thirty-minute private session with Cook in a direct bid to gain his vote. Briefing papers prepared immediately before this meeting encouraged the president to solicit Cook's support for Carswell by offering him the right to select still another federal judge.[32] Despite this apparent offer, Cook did not agree to support Carswell.

Finally, the day before the Carswell vote, Nixon directly instructed Bryce Harlow, Counselor to the President, to seek Cook's vote for confirmation by offering him a prestigious and potentially powerful position. According to Harlow, the president ordered him to do the following:

> Contact Senator Cook before the Carswell vote to let him know of the President's hope to use Cook as part of a special group of presidential lieutenants in the Senate, and that the President was hopeful that the Carswell vote would reinforce this possibility.[33]

Despite this extensive wooing, Senator Cook went on to vote against the Carswell nomination.

Senator Fong also appears to have been sincerely influenced by the competency issue to oppose Carswell. The Hawaii Republican had testified to his support of conservative judicial nominees by his vote for Haynsworth and his endorsement of the Carswell nomination in the Judiciary Committee. However, Fong's favorable reaction to Carswell began to waver once the events reflecting on the nominee's competence and judicial temperament became more widely known.

Unlike Cook, Fong did not make any public statements of his reasons for opposing Carswell which could provide evidence of his motivations. His public silence regarding Carswell stemmed from his having privately confided to the White House in March, 1970, that he was strongly inclined to vote against confirmation but would support Carswell if his vote were absolutely needed.[34] Not knowing how close the Carswell roll call would be, Fong cautiously avoided making any public statements on the nomination.

He did, however, privately express concerns about Carswell that testify to the impact of the competence and temperament issues on his vote. One White House report implied that charges reflecting unfavorably on the Carswell's judicial temperament had taken their toll on Fong's desire to support confirmation. According to this report, "claims of Carswell's racism [are] widely publicized in Hawaii" making the confirmation roll call an "extremely difficult political vote for Hiram [Fong] who seeks re-election this year."[35] Additionally, Fong signaled his opinion of Carswell's legal expertise by privately labeling the nominee a "jackass."[36]

Maine's Senator Smith, whose ideology index of seventeen clearly identifies her as a "Conservative," also appears to have been genuinely moved by Carswell's temperament to oppose confirmation. Evidence indicates the temperament issue, specifically Carswell's lack of candor in testifying before the Judiciary Committee, was, among other considerations, a contributing factor in Smith's decision to vote against confirmation.[37] Shortly after voting against Carswell, Smith confirmed that ideology was not a factor in her decision and offered the following explanation for her action.

> I could not resolve in my own mind the conflict of his testimony before the [Judiciary] committee with the established and documented facts on the incorporation of the club.
> I dislike saying it, but I do not think he was truthful before the committee.[38]

Senator Smith's strong conservative leanings give her statement of opposition a clear ring of truth.

Senator Cannon, of Nevada, initially favored the Carswell nomination because he wanted to "see the Court more conservative."[39] However, he voted against confirmation because in his view Carswell "wasn't an outstanding jurist."[40] Given Cannon's moderate ideology and desire for a more conservative Court, there is little reason to doubt the veracity of his statement of opposition.

Two southern Democrats also appear to have been motivated to oppose confirmation to some extent by non-ideological concerns about Carswell's competency and temperament. Senators Fulbright of Arkansas and William B. Spong, Jr., of Virginia were no doubt desirous of seeing a southerner appointed to the Court. And even though both senators had an ideology index of sixty-seven, categorizing them as "Liberals," their relatively low rating marked them more as moderates than as members of the liberal wing of the Democratic party.[41] Because it is unlikely they would employ the factors of competency and/or temperament to mask ideological opposition to the nomination, statements from them basing their opposition on these factors have increased credibility. Spong openly declared that his vote against confirmation stemmed from concerns of "competence and temperament rather than philosophy."[42] Fulbright was described as having reached the conclusion that Carswell lacked the requisite degree of competence to serve on the Supreme Court.[43]

No doubt there were other moderate senators within each party who were genuinely moved by non-ideological considerations in voting against confirmation. At the least, these considerations likely nudged into the anti-Carswell camp those senators disenchanted with the nominee's conservative ideology but still undecided as to how they would vote.[44]

The finding that sincere concerns about the non-ideological factors of competence and/or temperament moved at least seven senators, and likely more, to oppose Carswell is significant. Given the slim six-vote margin by which the Senate turned down the nomination, a switch of no more than three ballots in favor of Carswell would have led to a roll call deadlock and Vice President Spiro T. Agnew would have provided the favorable vote breaking the tie. Accordingly, had Carswell been free from non-ideological criticism, he would have been confirmed.

Additional evidence indicating that some senators were moved to oppose Carswell out of sincere concerns about his competence and temperament is provided by the doubts expressed by the nominee's supporters as to whether he possessed the temperament and legal ability ordinarily demanded of a Supreme Court justice. What is remarkable about the Carswell case is how frequently these supporters lent legitimacy to the competence and temperament charges by disparaging the nominee's qualifications to serve on the Court. There is the Hruska mediocrity statement noted previously. However, Hruska was not alone among Carswell's supporters in damning the nomination by faint praise as Senator Russell Long (D, La.) offered an almost equally devastating, if less publicized, defense of Carswell:

> It might be well to take a B student or a C student who was able to think straight, compared to one of those A students who are capable of the kind of thinking that winds up getting us a one-hundred-percent increase in crime in this country.[45]

Other supporters expressed less than glowing assessments of Carswell's qualifications. Senator Robert Dole (R, Kan.) voted for Carswell but nonetheless felt compelled to answer charges that the defeat of the Florida judge's nomination was an act of regional discrimination against the south by northern liberals. The Kansas Republican remarked that with Carswell's "thin qualifications, he would have had a hard time making it [confirmation] even if he had come from Maine."[46] Senator Ernest Hollings (D, S.C.) supported Carswell but offered the view the Florida jurist "was not qualified to carry Judge Haynsworth's law books."[47]

Even White House officials most intimately involved in the selection of Carswell privately admitted he "simply did not possess the quality required for a Supreme Court Justice."[48] Additionally, White House Director of Communications Herbert G. Klein has testified to both his and his staff's view of Carswell's qualifications to serve on the Court.

> We had a few individual doubts on the Haynsworth nomination and many more on Carswell. But our duty was to defend them. And we did. I would defend Haynsworth again. Carswell was a bad choice.[49]

Furthermore, notes made by John D. Ehrlichman, Assistant to the President, of meetings attended by Nixon, suggest that White House officials held a decidedly low opinion of Carswell's legal ability. Included among the comments noted by Ehrlichman which were evidently expressed by administration officials at White House meetings discussing Carswell were the following:

Undistinguished legal training.

If you're only "above average" at Mercer Law School, what does this make you.

No great prestigious lawyer.

No national reputation. No great figure.

Boob. Dummy. What counter?[50]

OVERSEEING THE CONFIRMATION PROCESS

If the Haynsworth rejection showed President Nixon likely pitfalls to avoid on the road to confirmation, it was not evident in his handling of the Carswell nomination. Nixon's management of the post-selection phase of the Carswell nomination can be faulted on several accounts. The president chose to ignore the advice of most of his close associates and released a letter written to Senator William B. Saxbe (R, Ohio) that only served to antagonize and alienate members of the Senate. In addition, the White House adopted a costly and counterproductive strategy in an ill-conceived effort to defeat a motion to recommit the Carswell nomination to the Senate Judiciary Committee, and further undermined support for confirmation by choosing not to make the nominee available for private meetings with senators who wished to query him. Finally,

Nixon can be faulted additionally for failing to make certain that the White House staff's handling of senators did not generate additional opposition against confirmation.

The Saxbe Letter

In late January, 1970, the White House remained confident Carswell would be confirmed by the Senate, and Senator Bayh conceded there was little hope of defeating the nomination.[51] As the attacks on the nominee intensified through February and several liberal Democrats announced their opposition, administration officials became concerned but continued to be confident.

In March, however, several incidents occurred which reflected unfavorably on the nomination and undermined its support. The early days of March saw the legal community stepping up its publicity campaign drawing attention to Carswell's alleged mediocre legal ability. Hruska's plea for mediocrity was made on March 16. And finally, on March 25, *The Washington Post* published a memorandum written by the ABA representatives who had met with Carswell the night before he had appeared before the Judiciary Committee.[52] The memorandum appeared to contradict several statements Carswell had made in testimony before the Committee and consequently reflected unfavorably on his candor.[53]

With confirmation still likely but with Carswell under attack and losing support, Nixon decided to take action. In doing so, he made one of the more damaging tactical errors undermining support for confirmation: the release of the Saxbe letter.

The idea for the Saxbe letter had originated with Special Counsel to the President Charles W. Colson. As support for Carswell began slipping in mid-March, 1970, Colson drew up a plan designed to gain additional support for confirmation. He proposed that in a hard-hitting letter to an uncommitted senator, the president describe his view of the Senate's proper constitutional role in reviewing Supreme Court nominations. As conceived, this description would maintain that while the Senate could legitimately reject the nomination of an individual who had transgressed the bounds of judicial propriety, it could not properly deny confirmation to a nominee subjectively judged by senators to be too conservative or possessed of too meager legal expertise.[54] Colson believed release of this letter would put additional pressure on undecided or opposed senators and force them into the pro-Carswell camp.

Colson's plan drew little support from other White House advisors charged with coordinating the effort to win Senate approval of Carswell. Magruder has noted that every one of these advisors "rejected Colson's proposal as both bad law and bad politics."[55] Colson persisted, however, and took his plan directly to the oval office where Nixon apparently gave his approval.

Colson then contacted Saxbe who agreed to participate in the plan by requesting a letter from the president in which Nixon would have the occasion to express his view as to the Senate's proper role in the confirmation process and to reiterate his unqualified support of Carswell. The plan then called for Saxbe, who was publicly uncommitted on the nomination but who had privately promised his vote to the White House, to announce his support of Carswell upon receiving the letter.[56] Nixon and Colson evidently believed the arguments presented in the presidential letter would not only be well received by the Senate, but would also be perceived as influential in moving Saxbe from uncommitted to favorable on the nomination, thereby encouraging other senators to support confirmation. In furtherance of these objectives, Saxbe was to disclose the contents of the presidential communiqué not only at a news conference in order to "attract maximum press attention" to its arguments but also at a weekly GOP luncheon attended by a dozen or so moderate-to-liberal Republican senators in an attempt to persuade some of them to support Carswell.[57]

Saxbe apparently agreed to take these two additional steps without being fully apprised of the views the president would express in the letter. However, upon receiving the letter and being disturbed and disappointed by its contents, he neither called the press conference nor used the letter to attempt to persuade other GOP senators.

On April 1, 1970, in an apparent change of plans evidently occasioned by Saxbe's reluctance to participate further, Nixon released the letter. In it, he not only reaffirmed his complete support of Carswell but, more significantly, warned senators that a negative vote on confirmation would be taken as a direct challenge to his executive prerogative to appoint justices of the Supreme Court. The letter noted:

> What is centrally at issue in this nomination is the constitutional responsibility of the president to appoint members of the Court—and whether this responsibility can be frustrated by those who wish to substitute their own philosophy or their own subjective judgment for that of the one person entrusted by the Constitution with the power of appointment. The question arises whether I, as president of the United States, shall be

accorded the same right of choice in naming Supreme Court justices which has been fully accorded to my predecessors of both parties.[58]

Release of the letter was met by outrage in the Senate. The prevailing view was that the arguments presented in the letter represented a degrading and dangerous attack by the president upon the Senate's cherished power of advice and consent. With evident institutional loyalty, senators of both parties criticized Nixon's narrow view of the Senate's role in the confirmation process. Bayh spoke for the Democrats by asserting Nixon's arguments were simply "wrong as a matter of constitutional law, wrong as a matter of history, and wrong as a matter of public policy."[59] Minority Leader Scott, alert to the disastrous impact a perceived presidential attack on the Senate's power of advice and consent would have on Carswell's hopes for confirmation, bluntly advised the White House that "one more stunt like that and Carswell will get two votes."[60] Republican Senator Packwood recalled later that the Saxbe letter generated extensive and uniform indignation among his colleagues primarily because the president failed to realize how protective the Senate is of its power. "The Senate doesn't like to do very much" mused Packwood, "[but] it doesn't like to be told it doesn't have the right to do very much."[61]

While the Saxbe letter was testily received in the Senate, it is difficult to trace any negative votes on the nomination directly to this tactic. Nevertheless, Bayh was convinced that Senator Smith of Maine decided to vote against confirmation because she was angered by the views expressed in the letter.[62] Smith lent support to this conclusion by confiding to a constituent who sought her opinion of the letter, "I thought the Saxbe letter was less than convincing, was poorly stated and very badly timed. My reaction to it was negative."[63]

At the least, it is clear this tactic failed to meet the optimistic goals envisioned by Nixon and Colson. Not only did the letter not succeed in convincing any undecided senators to join the pro-Carswell forces, it may have had just the opposite impact. For example, no less an involved participant than Saxbe concluded that if the letter had any impact on his Senate colleagues, it was an adverse one.[64] And while the Ohio Republican delivered on his promise to announce for Carswell shortly after release of the letter, he did so in a manner leaving little doubt as to his opinion of the nominee and the misguided White House tactic. According to one account, when Saxbe declared his support for the nomination at a press conference, he "pointedly held his nose as he did."[65]

Additionally, Magruder saw release of the letter as "the final straw, the one that caused Carswell's nomination to be defeated by a slender margin."[66] Another report concluded the Saxbe letter undermined support for confirmation because it was done with "typical heavy-handed over-kill."[67] Columnist Tom Wicker attributed Carswell's defeat in part to the "boomeranging claims" of the Saxbe letter and the "faulty staff work" that produced it.[68] A detailed study of the Carswell rejection concluded the release of the Saxbe letter may very well have been the fatal factor which doomed the nomination.[69] Finally, an astute observer of the performance of presidents has noted that the Saxbe letter was an obvious error in presidential discretion, because after its release "Carswell's opponents froze solid, doubters drifted toward opposition, [and] proponents turned mushy."[70]

Counterproductive Strategy on Recommittal

On March 28, 1970, in an effort to defeat the nomination by preventing it from coming to the Senate floor, anti-Carswell senators moved to recommit the nomination to the Judiciary Committee. The recommittal motion was generally viewed as a "graceful solution," not only enabling Republican senators to block Carswell's confirmation without voting directly against the GOP nominee but also tactfully allowing southern Democrats to avoid directly opposing the nomination of a fellow southerner. It was widely assumed that Senate acceptance of the recommittal motion would doom the nomination.[71]

Evidence indicates that President Nixon oversaw the adoption of a strategy on recommittal which brought momentary success but eventual failure. Apparently under direct orders from the White House, pro-Carswell forces in the Senate undertook an all-out effort to defeat the recommittal motion. On April 6, 1970, these forces succeeded as the Senate voted down the motion to recommit by a 52-44 count.

While defeat of the motion was indispensable to Carswell's confirmation, the roll call on recommittal was still but a prelude to the more important final and direct vote on the nomination. In contrast to the administration's exhaustive effort to defeat the motion, anti-Carswell forces in the Senate had elected not to push for victory on recommittal, silently conceded victory to the administration on the recommittal motion, and concentrated their efforts on winning the crucial direct vote on confirmation.

According to Senator Bayh, this critical switch in strategy on the part of the anti-Carswell forces went undetected by the nomination's supporters. As a direct result of the failure to recognize the change in strategy, the White House ordered a total but eventually counterproductive effort to drum up support against the recommittal motion. In Bayh's view, this order was a serious blunder because the administration's call for a maximum effort to defeat recommittal allowed Carswell's opponents to undercut support for the nomination when it later came before the Senate two days later for the crucial direct vote.[72]

The administration's exhaustive effort on the recommittal motion worked against the nomination in several ways. Those Republican senators inclined to oppose confirmation but uneasy about voting against a GOP nominee were given an opportunity to resolve their dilemma by the recommittal roll call. For example, Senator Charles H. Percy, of Illinois, as well as his GOP colleagues Fong, Cook, Packwood, and Smith of Maine, all sided with the White House on recommittal and voted against the motion. Consequently, these senators were later able to vote directly against Carswell's confirmation absent the onus of having opposed a Republican president twice in succession on key roll calls. They could counter claims of their disloyalty to the GOP by pointing to their vote on recommittal as at least some evidence of their loyalty.

A damaging aspect of the administration's maximum effort on recommittal stemmed from the fact that some of the votes it so eagerly sought to secure were not really needed. The eight-vote margin by which recommittal was defeated indicates there were at least three or four votes the administration could have sacrificed and still have succeeded in blocking the move to recommit the nomination. This aspect of the recommittal effort was to prove costly two days later when the Carswell nomination came directly before the Senate.

Indeed, by the time the Senate went on to reject the nomination, the pro-Carswell forces realized that by pulling out all stops to win by the largest margin possible on recommittal, needed votes for confirmation were lost. An elated Senator Bayh pointed to the significant role the White House's misguided strategy on recommittal played in the defeat: "The White House had shot its wad on recommittal. They cranked up for the wrong vote."[73] According to a more neutral observer than Bayh, the failure of the White House either to detect or to realize the significance of the anti-Carswell forces' shift in strategy was a costly mistake, forcing the pro-Carswell forces to stumble blindly into the trap that opponents of the nomination had rigged.[74]

It is still uncertain whether Nixon's decision to go all out on recommittal directly cost the administration votes on the confirmation roll call. What is certain, however, is that had the president been alerted to the switch, he would have had the opportunity to consider adopting a strategy to offset the move of the anti-Carswell forces. Consideration of this strategy might have propelled the White House to distinguish more carefully between the votes that were absolutely needed to defeat recommittal and those that were expendable.

The attractiveness of this strategy from the administration's standpoint becomes more evident on closer inspection. Given the margin of victory on recommittal, the White House could have encouraged three or four senators, whose constituents were pressuring them to oppose Carswell, to vote in favor of recommitting the nomination. This perceived anti-Carswell action might have mollified a sufficient number of the constituents pressuring these senators to enable them more freedom to vote in favor of the nomination on the confirmation roll call. These senators could have claimed they would have preferred returning the nomination to the Judiciary Committee for further deliberations and, indeed, had voted to that effect, but after unsuccessfully opposing the White House on recommittal, they now felt obligated to defer to the president out of a sense of balance and fairness and support confirmation.

The potential existed for this strategy to be successful. There were seven senators who voted with the administration on recommittal but then went on to vote against confirmation. Two of these senators, Republicans Percy and Packwood, were steadfastly opposed to confirmation and unlikely to retreat from that position. However, five other senators, including Republicans Fong, Cook, and Smith of Maine, and Democrats Quentin N. Burdick (N.D.) and Thomas J. Dodd (Ct.) were, at the time of the recommittal vote, uncommitted on confirmation. At least three of the members of this group could have been prevailed upon to appease their constituents by voting for recommittal so that they could more easily support the administration on the confirmation roll call.

Despite the merit of this strategy, it was never suggested, much less given serious consideration, by the president and the White House staff. This was so in large part because administration officials failed to realize until it was far too late that they lacked the votes to win on the confirmation roll call. In this regard, White House Press Secretary Ronald L. Ziegler later maintained that at no time during the Carswell deliberations did anyone inform the president that the votes were not there for confirmation.[75] What confused the pro-Carswell forces as well as the president was the mistaken view the Senate tally on recommittal would be an accurate reflection of the confirmation vote. For example, Senate Republican Whip Robert Griffin, believing the vote count on the recommittal and confirmation roll calls "would be about the same," openly anticipated Senate approval of the nomination.[76] Obviously,

Nixon was not well served by those aides who failed to maintain an accurate head count in the Senate; but because the president has ultimate responsibility for managing all aspects of the confirmation process, their failure became his as well.

Making Carswell Unavailable to Senators

As the Senate moved toward making a decision on the nomination, the White House, again apparently under orders from President Nixon, made another strategic move lessening the chances for confirmation. It was decided Carswell would not be made accessible to several undecided senators who had expressed an interest in meeting with the nominee.

Two factors apparently motivated the White House to deny these senators access. The prevailing view of White House staffers was that any personal contacts between the nominee and undecided senators would only tend to damage Carswell's chances for confirmation.[77] Accordingly, the administration's reluctance to make Carswell available may have stemmed from its genuine lack of confidence in the nominee's ability to dispel the doubts that some senators had about his qualifications. In addition, Nixon appears to have been generally upset with some senators for their lack of support for the administration, especially their refusals to back enthusiastically either Haynsworth or Carswell. In a retaliatory move aimed at those viewed as disloyal, Nixon passed the word to cut off all communications with these senators. For example, the president gave the command to "put the full freeze" on a group of senators including Republicans Percy, Charles McC. Mathias, Jr. (Md.), Richard S. Schweiker (Pa.), Clifford P. Case (N.J.), Charles E. Goodell (N.Y.), and very likely others.[78] Consequently, the decision to make Carswell unavailable likely represented a specific application of the president's order to ignore all requests from certain disaffected senators.

Evidence exists suggesting that denying senators access to Carswell did not help the confirmation effort. For example, Senators William B. Spong (D, Va.) and Mike Gravel (D, Alaska) strongly implied that they would have supported confirmation had they been able to meet with the nominee, and had he been able to satisfy their doubts of his fitness to serve on the Court. Spong maintained that if Carswell had "cleared up the questions" reflecting on his fitness to be an associate justice, he would have been "delighted" to vote in favor of confirmation.[79] One of Gravel's greatest concerns was Carswell's apparent willingness to retire into silence while the White House attempted to push the nomination through the Senate. According to the Alaska Democrat, a Supreme Court nominee who in effect took the Fifth Amendment to valid Senate inquiries was not fit to serve on the Court.[80] Denied access to the nominee, both Spong and Gravel eventually voted against confirmation.

Additionally, Senator Mathias reported that as far back as March 10, 1970, he had begun requesting that the Justice Department arrange for him to meet with Carswell. Despite his repeated urgings, Mathias noted, his requests had gone unacknowledged until the night before the confirmation roll call when the White House realized the nomination was in trouble and apparently decided to end the "full freeze" in a belated, desperate effort to gain his vote. While Mathias had sincerely been undecided at the time of his requests to meet with Carswell, he maintained that the administration's offer to arrange a post-midnight meeting in a motel with the nominee the night before the confirmation roll call appeared indelicate if not unseemly. Besides, by the time the White House finally got around to responding to his requests, Mathias had already decided to vote against the nomination.[81]

Several considerations indicate that the White House failure to arrange these meetings with undecided senators hindered Carswell's chances for confirmation.[82] Contrary to what may have been the prevailing view at the White House, the senators requesting personal meetings with Carswell had not unalterably made up their minds to vote against confirmation. For example, Mathias contended that if he had been unequivocally committed to opposing Carswell, he would never have requested a meeting which was bound to be, in the Maryland Republican's words, "painfully embarrassing."[83] Furthermore, while Mathias, Spong, Gravel and perhaps others were not inflexibly opposed to confirmation, they would likely vote against the nomination if the meetings were not arranged. Accordingly, the White House had very little to lose by setting up the meetings.[84] Finally, the administration's reluctance to make Carswell available allowed the anti-confirmation forces to hint more convincingly that there was still more unfavorable information lurking in the nominee's background.[85]

Mishandling the Senate

President Nixon did not oversee the handling of relations with the Senate in such a way that a favorable atmosphere for confirmation was established. On the contrary, the president's management of dealings with the Senate very likely increased opposition against the nomination. The case for drawing this conclusion involves examining the White House's general approach to the Senate as well as its specific handling of individual senators.

The Atmosphere of Hostility. In the wake of Haynsworth's rejection but before the Carswell nomination was even announced, relations between the Senate and the administration were less than amicable. Several liberal Republicans correctly discerned that the president had deliberately chosen to exclude them from any role in shaping administration policy and in sharing in any largesse controlled by the White House. According to the press secretary to Senator Goodell, one of the aware recipients of the presidential cold shoulder, the ostracizing of GOP liberals represented a lost opportunity to build Senate support for White House programs.

> If the president had these men over to the White House occasionally or called now and then to get their opinions, he would create an atmosphere that would make it difficult for them to oppose him. It's utterly stupid not to do it. The president and his staff simply don't understand the Senate— most of all, they don't understand how seducible it is.[86]

The announcement of the Carswell nomination did little to lessen the feelings of hostility toward the White House already simmering in the Senate.[87] The choice of the mediocre Florida judge deeply offended at least one GOP senator who saw it as Nixon's attempt to belittle the Court and to "rub the Senate's nose in the mess it had made of the Haynsworth nomination." The unidentified senator offered the following in defense of his interpretation of the administration's motives:

> I learned that the Justice Department had rated Carswell way down below Haynsworth and a couple of other candidates . . . . That made it clear that the choice of Carswell was vengeance—to make us sorry we hadn't accepted Haynsworth—and, at the same time, it was an attempt to downgrade the Supreme Court and implement the southern strategy. The attorney general obviously believed that we had no stomach for another fight after Haynsworth, and that we would accept any dog, so he took this opportunity to show his disdain for the Senate.[88]

President Nixon further contributed to the hostile atmosphere in the Senate by electing to set a confrontational tone throughout the deliberations on the Carswell nomination. Nixon or his chief lieutenants consistently signaled aides to be belligerent with senators failing to endorse Carswell. And while no single instance on its own demonstrates that the White House generally adopted a confrontational approach toward the Senate, a review of the messages being sent to subordinates indicates the style most encouraged by the president and his top assistants was one emphasizing conflict rather than cooperation—witness the following illustrations.

At a White House meeting attended by the president shortly after the nomination was announced, the pro-Carswell forces were urged to strike back aggressively at those attacking the nominee. Chief of Staff H. R. Haldeman's notes reflect the signal being sent: "Keep cracking back—don't just lie low. Put investigators to work. Rip the hypocrisy off these people."[89] A few days later, Haldeman's jottings again reveal the White House pressing Carswell's supporters to "get into the fight" because the effort to gain confirmation has become a "real battle."[90]

Other illustrations of the vindictiveness if not downright meanness encouraged by the White House abound. When ABC News had the temerity to predict that the Senate would vote to recommit the Carswell nomination and thereby kill it, Nixon was furious. He ordered White House Communications Director Herbert Klein to "ram this down their [ABC's] throat" if recommittal was defeated, as it was.[91] Similarly when reports surfaced in Indiana indicating that Senator Bayh, who was highly critical of Carswell's legal ability, had failed a bar exam in 1960, it was the president who pressed to give the report wider exposure. Nixon directly ordered aides to distribute the report of Bayh's failure to newspapers and television stations throughout the nation.[92] Cooler heads eventually prevailed as Magruder was able to parry the order by patiently explaining to the president why the administration should not exploit the information regarding Bayh, noting "senators will usually not attack one another on such a personal basis, and lawyers—who have taken bar exams and know how rough they are—seldom attack on this basis."[93] It is both ironic and revealing that a young aide had to remind Nixon, a lawyer himself, that some blows against opponents, no matter how tempting, can be counterproductive if not perceived as fair. One would expect the roles to have been reversed with an astute and cool president calming the more aggressive instincts of a youthful true believer.

Another vivid example of the confrontational approach Nixon conveyed occurred three weeks before the confirmation roll call of April 8, 1970. Attorney General Mitchell, who had been assigned prime responsibility for the Carswell campaign, was ordered by his doctor to take two weeks off after months of nonstop twelve-hour days.[94] At a subsequent

White House meeting, the president and his aides considered who would do the best job as Mitchell's replacement in overseeing the Carswell nomination. According to Ehrlichman's notes, the scholarly and affable Rehnquist was recommended but Nixon forcefully rejected this suggestion because, in the president's words, the assistant attorney general was "not a nutcutter." Mitchell's duties were then passed on to Deputy Attorney General Richard G. Kleindienst who presumably possessed the surgical talents demanded by the president.[95]

The confrontational style fostered by the White House can also be glimpsed in the administration's reaction to senators who conveyed that they would not support confirmation. When Republicans Mathias, Schweiker, Case, Goodell, and Percy came out against Carswell, Nixon apparently ordered subordinates to punish these senators by never inviting them to the White House again.[96] In addition, Schweiker was singled out for further retribution as aides were reminded to continue "screwing" the Pennsylvania Republican on appointments and other patronage.[97] When Democrats Cannon and Burdick failed to support the nomination, a White House directive, evidently sanctioned by Nixon, signaled subordinates that they were now free to "dump on" these senators.[98] And when Margaret Chase Smith refused to come out in support of Carswell, the sophomoric, macho, and mean-spirited reaction of administration officials was privately to ridicule the distinguished senator from Maine, crudely referring to her at White House meetings as "Margaret Chaste Smith."[99]

Several accounts of Carswell's demise indicate that Nixon's promoting of a climate of confrontation in the Senate, and the resultant use of heavy-handed tactics to gain support, significantly worked against confirmation. One report concluded that Nixon contributed to the defeat of Carswell because "the methods he used to win confirmation antagonized senators from both parties and from all regions."[100] Another noted that participants in the confirmation fight cited the "White House staff's failing incompetence" as the "central cause" of Carswell's downfall.[101] Reflecting on the overbearing, counterproductive tactics employed by the administration, Bayh and other members of the anti-Carswell forces referred to the White House as their "staunchest ally" in the confirmation battle.[102] Even Senator Dole, who drew high praise as a strong defender of Carswell, later concluded the defeat of the nomination could be attributed in part to "those idiots downtown."[103]

Dealing with Individual Senators. Motivated by the contentious tone set by Nixon, if not by his direct orders, White House aides made a series of tactical moves which appear to have led several senators to oppose confirmation. The most dramatic instance of this effect occurred in the attempt to win the support of Senator Smith of Maine.

As the roll call on the nomination approached, the votes of three undecided Republicans—Smith, Cook, and Winston Prouty of Vermont—became crucial. The anti-Carswell forces were confident that five senators who had previously supported the administration's position on recommittal would vote against confirmation on April 8. These five were Republicans Percy, Packwood, and Fong, and Democrats Dodd and Burdick.[104] Because forty-four senators favored recommittal, the anti-Carswell forces counted on at least forty-nine votes against confirmation, a number sufficient to reject the nomination because it was generally recognized that only ninety-six senators would participate in the roll call.[105]

The White House soon became aware of this unfavorable head count and took steps to turn it around. A few days before the April 8 roll call, Nixon met with Prouty to seek his support. The stakes were high and the president spared little in the largesse he offered the Vermont Republican. Nixon promised the worried Prouty unlimited backing in his upcoming re-election bid, including professional assistance and use of the administration's staff to investigate his opponent's background in order to develop useful campaign fodder. To further allay Prouty's fear of being unable to raise sufficient money to wage a vigorous campaign, Nixon promised "we will not allow you to lose on account of lack of money."[106] Concerned about the negative impact a vote for Carswell would have in Vermont, where the legal community was strongly against confirmation, but enticed by the president's offer of assistance, Prouty cautiously accepted Nixon's offer. He agreed to vote in favor of confirmation only if his support were absolutely needed. Were the expected margin of victory or defeat more than one vote, he remained free to vote against confirmation.[107]

Because Prouty had voted for recommittal and had been counted upon to oppose confirmation by the anti-Carswell forces, his qualified and unannounced defection reduced the prospective votes against confirmation from forty-nine to forty-eight. White House officials soon realized that Smith's and Cook's votes would determine the fate of the nomination.[108] Were they both to support Carswell, the vote would be deadlocked at forty-eight, with the vice-president prepared to break the tie in favor of confirmation.

According to several reports, Smith and Cook had anticipated that their votes would be crucial to the outcome. Realizing they would be put under enormous pressure to support the administration, but still undecided about endorsing the controversial Carswell, the two senators privately agreed to stand together in opposition to the nomination in the event either of them decided to vote against confirmation. This commitment assured them that so long as they both voted against Carswell, neither of them could be placed in the uncomfortable and unenviable position of having cast the decisive vote defeating the Republican nominee of a Republican president.[109]

As noted above, Cook decided on April 7, one day before the roll call, to vote against confirmation. While he did not so inform the president and was still considered to be undecided by White House head counters, he did alert Smith to his decision. Because Cook believed there were now more than enough votes to reject the nomination and his sole vote would not constitute the margin of defeat, he conditionally released Smith from her commitment to join him in voting against confirmation so long as no other senators switched to the pro-confirmation side at the last minute.[110]

There is some dispute whether Smith, after hearing from Cook, informed the White House that she would now vote in favor of the nomination. Several reports indicate that either the Maine Republican or one of her assistants confided to the White House that she would support confirmation.[111] However, Smith has vehemently denied that she or any one on her staff ever informed the administration how she intended to vote on the nomination.[112]

There is little doubt, however, that Smith did not want her intentions on the nomination disclosed to other senators. Throughout her years in public life, Smith had long followed a tradition of withholding her position on a controversial roll call until the time came to cast her ballot. One advantage of this for the proud and independent senator from Maine was that it avoided what she perceived as the inappropriate use of her name by those attempting to pressure her Senate colleagues.[113] Mindful of this tradition as well as of her conditional but nevertheless binding commitment to Cook, Smith sought to be perceived as undecided on the nomination until she absolutely had to cast her vote. Additionally, she fully expected others to honor this approach by refraining from using her name in attempting to influence other senators.

A few hours before the scheduled roll call on April 8, White House aides privately informed several Republican senators announced or leaning against the nomination that Smith had pledged to vote in favor of confirmation.[114] These senators were reminded that the addition of Smith's support put the White House within one or two votes of winning on the confirmation roll call. The aides further emphasized the narrowness of the margin separating victory from defeat by pointing to several other senators, notably Prouty and Dodd,[115] who were inclined to support the nomination in the event the administration needed their votes. Each of these GOP senators was evidently informed that he could cast the decisive ballot spelling victory for Carswell thereby winning the president's deepest gratitude and promise of support for future state projects or federal appointments.

The unauthorized use of Smith's name to pressure her GOP colleagues immediately backfired on the White House.[116] Alerted to the White House move, Senator Edward W. Brooke (R, Mass.) approached Smith on the Senate floor, tactfully reminded his New England colleague of her tradition of not prematurely making known her position on controversial roll calls, and asked whether it was true, as White House aides were so informing other senators, that she intended to vote for Carswell. Smith reportedly colored. Brooke, sensing her anger, hastily added that while it was not his intention to try to influence her in anyway, he believed she should be made aware of the reports emanating from the White House just in case she had neither made up her mind nor authorized the use of her name.

Infuriated by Brooke's information, Smith immediately telephoned White House aide Harlow and demanded to know whether he had indeed told other senators she would vote in favor of Carswell. While there is no available record of Harlow's response, his evasive reply evidently only heightened Smith's anger. Quite uncharacteristically, the incensed Smith reportedly cursed Harlow, informed him under no condition would she now vote for Carswell, and slammed down the receiver.

Arriving in the Senate chamber, Smith immediately asked Schweiker and Mathias whether the White House had indicated to them that she had pledged to vote in favor of confirmation. When both senators confirmed Brooke's report, Smith reportedly retreated to her desk on the Senate floor and sat, tight-lipped, waiting for the roll call to begin. So infuriated was Smith by what she perceived as the White House's unauthorized use of her name, if not the outright distortion of her position, that she went on to vote against the Carswell nomination.

The profound impact the White House ploy had on Smith can be gauged from the fact that more than twelve years after Carswell's rejection, she still expressed anger at Harlow, the apparent architect of the tactic. In a 1983 interview, Smith complained that although Harlow had apologized immediately after the Carswell vote for misrepresenting her position, he later continued to maintain that she had indeed promised the White House she would vote for Carswell. Insisting she had never made such a pledge to the White House, Smith went on to describe Harlow as "despicable."[117]

The loss of Smith's vote, and the manner in which her potential support was squandered, should not be minimized. Several accounts concluded that Smith's vote against Carswell, abetted as it was by clumsy liaison work on the part of the White House, sounded the death knell for the nomination.[118] Nor should the counterproductive handling of Smith be viewed simply as the irresponsible act of an overzealous White House aide. In encouraging subordinates to adopt an aggressive approach toward the Senate and then failing to control their misguided tactics, the president bears responsibility for the counterproductive handling of Senator Smith.

The White House lost other opportunities to gain key additional votes for Carswell. The inability to gain these votes was critical to the outcome because the six-vote margin by which the nomination was rejected was actually slimmer than it appeared. As indicated above, and as is so often the case on controversial Senate roll calls, several senators had promised to vote in favor of confirmation in the event the White House needed their support to snatch victory from defeat. When it became apparent the Carswell nomination was lost, the White House let these senators off the hook. However, had the White House been able to turn around no more than one or two senators counted among the anti-Carswell camp in the days or hours prior to the roll call, these additional votes coupled with the backing of those who had promised their support, if needed, would very likely have been sufficient to gain confirmation.

Why was the White House unable to gain these key additional votes? In part, the earlier vindictive treatment of senators by White House officials came back to haunt the administration. It will be recalled that there were several liberal Republicans, including Percy and Schweiker, whom Nixon ordered ostracized from the White House because of their perceived disloyalty.[119] In giving the cold shoulder treatment to these senators and thereby exacerbating an already unfriendly situation, Nixon made it very unlikely these senators would want to help the White House out of any difficulties—witness the following examples.

Hours before the Carswell roll call, Nixon ordered his Senate liaison staff to try to get Senator Percy to agree to a "live pair" with the ailing Senator Mundt of South Dakota.[120] Because Mundt would be absent from the roll call, the pairing action sought by the president would, in effect, erase Percy's negative vote and help Carswell's cause.

Even though this arrangement afforded Percy the opportunity to be on record as opposing Carswell and, at the same time, enabled him to help the president, he refused to go along. Had Percy's friendship and cooperation been cultivated in the weeks leading up to the roll call, he might have responded favorably to the president's request. As it was, the ostracized senator went on to vote against the Carswell nomination and Mundt remained unpaired.

Senator Schweiker was another who appeared influenced to vote against confirmation by the atmosphere of hostility and the misguided tactics fostered by the White House. Not only did Nixon order Schweiker banned from the White House and deprived of all patronage controlled by the administration, the Pennsylvania Republican was specifically singled out as one senator with whom the president would not meet to discuss any aspect of the Carswell case.[121] Despite the hostility directed at Schweiker, the administration still endeavored to win his vote. In fact, the tactic of releasing the Saxbe letter was undertaken in part to attempt to persuade Schweiker to support Carswell.[122] All hope was lost in gaining his vote, however, when the White House managed to worsen its already fractured relationship with Schweiker by publicizing the names of several prominent Pennsylvanians it had requested to put the heat on Schweiker to support Carswell. Schweiker was reportedly furious at this tactic, confiding, "if they [the White House officials] knew anything at all about me, they wouldn't have been so stupid, because it was bound to boomerang."[123]

Finally, the inclination of Senator Fong to vote against Carswell was reportedly solidified by still another unsound tactic by the White House. Fong's vote on the Haynsworth nomination had been won in part by Nixon's promise to appoint one of the Hawaii Republican's intimates to a judicial vacancy on the Court of Appeals for the Ninth Circuit.[124] When the White House sought to pressure Fong into supporting Carswell by holding out the same unfulfilled promise, he was understandably upset, maintaining his friend was already entitled to the federal judgeship because of his (Fong's) vote in support of Haynsworth.[125] While Fong had an additional reason for opposing the nomination, notably the racism issue raised against Carswell that was well-publicized in Hawaii and likely to be a factor in the senator's upcoming re-election campaign, it is likely Nixon's perceived reneging on the judicial vacancy hardened Fong's resolve to oppose confirmation.

The foregoing analysis of presidential management of the post-selection phase of the confirmation process indicates that Nixon contributed to undermining the Carswell nomination in several ways. The

Saxbe letter, the counterproductive strategy on recommittal, the decision not to make Carswell available to key undecided senators, the fostering of an atmosphere of hostility in the Senate, and the failure to deal effectively and wisely with specific members, all point to missed opportunities to gain additional support for the nomination. Indeed, a convincing case exists that these events reveal that Nixon's management of the post-selection phase of the process actually served to generate additional opposition against the nomination.

Presidential Management: Conclusion

The evidence presented in this chapter justifies the conclusion that President Nixon's management of the confirmation process played a significant role in the Senate's rejection of the Carswell nomination. From selecting a nominee vulnerable to serious non-ideological, non-partisan criticism to failing to oversee the development and implementation of a sound strategy and appropriate tactics conducive to gaining confirmation, the president contributed to generating additional opposition against the nomination.

Nixon's actions may not have been fatal to the Carswell nomination had other conditions unfavorable to confirmation not been present. The Democrats' control of the Senate augured the possibility that ideological considerations would lead some liberal and moderate senators to oppose the conservative nominee regardless of what Nixon did. Nevertheless, Carswell's conservative ideology made confirmation more difficult but not impossible. Given the slim margin by which Carswell was rejected, the conclusion is inescapable that a more astute effort at overseeing the confirmation process would have brought about Senate approval of the nomination.

By way of a postscript, a final fragment of evidence supporting the conclusion that the Carswell case represented a failure of presidential management lies in Nixon's reaction to the defeat. The day after the Carswell rejection, Nixon angrily denounced those senators who had voted against one or both of his Southern nominees, accusing them of hypocrisy, vicious character assassination, sectional bias, and an egregious disregard of the president's right and power of appointment.[126] While this display of anger represented the president's public reaction, the private response reflected another view. Evidently dissatisfied with the results of the Haynsworth and Carswell nominations, Nixon quietly ordered a full-scale review of his administration's handling of the confirmation process in regard to Supreme Court nominations.[127] When eventually completed, the review clearly identified significant weaknesses in White House management of the process and went on to recommend important changes in overseeing future nominations to the Court. The review's unflattering appraisal of the White House's handling of the two unsuccessful nominations confirmed what Nixon must have already suspected: Haynsworth and Carswell were rejected in part because of his own failure in presidential management.

5. EXPLAINING UNSUCCESSFUL SUPREME COURT NOMINATIONS

WHY DID THE Senate, after a long period of acquiescence, refuse to confirm the Fortas, Haynsworth, and Carswell nominations? Are these three cases separate, idiosyncratic events sharing little in common, or do they reveal a discernible pattern? Before providing answers to these and related questions, a review of the key factors leading to the Senate's refusals to confirm the Fortas, Haynsworth, and Carswell nominations is in order.

The major factor in all three of these unsuccessful nominations was the perceived ideology of the nominees. Despite the presence of non-ideological, non-partisan grounds upon which to base opposition to confirmation, senators generally responded to the nominations on the basis of whether they approved of the basic philosophy they anticipated the nominees would bring to the Supreme Court.

Analysis of the Fortas, Haynsworth, and Carswell nominations further suggests that ideological opposition alone would very likely not have been sufficient to bring about the Senate's unfavorable actions. Unpropitious timing played a pivotal contributory role in the withholding of the chief justiceship from Fortas. More importantly, failures in presidential management contributed significantly to bringing about the Senate's negative actions in all three cases. And while presidential management always loomed less influential than the nominees' perceived ideology, it was decisive in all three instances in generating the additional votes changing victory into defeat.

A PATTERN OF UNSUCCESSFUL NOMINATIONS

The Fortas, Haynsworth, and Carswell nominations were all forwarded to the Senate amid one of the two adverse conditions strongly associated with unsuccessful Supreme Court nominations. It will be recalled that the rate at which the Senate turns down Supreme Court nominations increases sharply when two unfavorable conditions are present: (1) a majority of the senators considering the nomination do not share the same party affiliation as the president, and (2) the nomination is forwarded to the Senate in the last full year of a president's term or in the interregnum period after a new chief executive has been elected. Table 8 provides comparative data on the Senate's refusal rates for nominations made when neither party composition nor timing were unfavorable, when one of these conditions was unfavorable, and when both conditions were unfavorable.[1]

Table 8
Senate's Rate of Refusals to Confirm, 1789-1988

Presence of Unfavorable Conditions of Senate or Timing	Nominations Made	Nominations Refused	Rate of Refusal
Neither condition present	92	9	10%
One condition present	36	7	19%
Both conditions present	14	10	71%
Total	142	26	18%

Between 1789 and 1988, the refusal rate for all Supreme Court nominations is slightly more than eighteen percent (twenty-six of 142). However, the refusal rate increases significantly when one and especially when two of the adverse conditions are present. When neither unfavorable condition is present, the refusal rate is less than ten percent (nine of ninety-two). But it increases to more than nineteen percent (seven of thirty-six) when one unfavorable condition is present and to a resounding seventy-one percent (ten of fourteen) when two unfavorable conditions exist. Notably, almost half (ten of twenty-one) of all refusals to confirm Supreme Court nominations before 1968 occurred when both of these adverse conditions were present.

The data of table 8 suggest that the failures of the Fortas, Haynsworth, and Carswell nominations can be attributed in part to their having been forwarded to the Senate under one of the two unfavorable conditions. While Fortas's nomination was acted upon by a Senate controlled by his fellow Democrats, it was forwarded to the upper house late in Johnson's last year in office. And while the Haynsworth and Carswell nominations were made early in Nixon's term, they were acted upon by a Senate in which the Republican party was in the minority.

Still, the history of unsuccessful Supreme Court nominations suggests that the presence of one of the two adverse conditions taken alone cannot account for the Senate's refusals to confirm. Before 1968, twenty-five nominations were forwarded to the Senate amid one of the two adverse conditions and only two failed to gain confirmation.[2] Because many presidents succeeded in winning confirmation for their Supreme Court nominations under conditions similar to those confronting Johnson and Nixon, the presence of one of the adverse conditions in each of the Fortas, Haynsworth, and Carswell cases can provide, at best, only a partial explanation of the Senate's negative action in these three instances.

The success of previous presidents suggests further that a more thorough understanding of the Senate's refusals to confirm demands an examination not only of the structure confronting the nominations but also of the management of the confirmation process. Indeed, some support for the influential role of presidental management in previous unsuccessful Supreme Court nominations is provided by one review indicating that instances of counterproductive presidential management have appeared in at least twelve of the twenty-one failed nominations occurring before the Fortas, Haynsworth, and Carswell cases.[3] More significantly, this review disclosed that no less than seven of the nine unsuccessful nominations occurring when both party composition and timing were favorable, and confirmation would ordinarily be expected, involved reported instances of counterproductive presidential management. The subjective nature of the review necessitates caution in accepting its conclusions regarding the frequency of counterproductive presidential management in previous unsuccessful nominations. Nevertheless, the review's findings hint that an understanding of the factor of presidential management is essential in explaining unsuccessful Supreme Court nominations.

IDEOLOGY, TIMING, AND PRESIDENTIAL MANAGEMENT: AN EXPLANATION

Drawing upon the pattern established by the Senate's refusal to confirm Supreme Court nominees and the analysis of the Fortas, Haynsworth, and Carswell cases, one can explain more fully the roles of ideology, timing, and presidential management in unsuccessful Supreme Court nominations.

The Role of Ideology

The inclination of the Senate to refuse to confirm Supreme Court nominations when the president's party is in the minority is not difficult to understand. Presidents and senators know that justices of the Supreme Court play a crucial role in shaping public policy through the decisions promulgated by the Court.[4] They are also aware that the most significant element influencing these decisions is the ideology of the justices. Consequently, in furthering his/her policy goals, a president generally seeks to appoint to the Court individuals sympathetic to his/her own ideology. Given the link between party affiliation and ideology, the nominees, not suprisingly, are usually selected from the ranks of the chief executive's party.[5] Because some senators do not share the president's policy goals and/or ideology, there will likely always be some potential ideological opposition to confirmation every time a Supreme Court nomination is made.

What is most important is not simply the presence of latent ideological opposition but the extent of that potential resistance and the likelihood it will be activated. The analysis of unsuccessful Supreme Court nominations, especially those of Fortas, Haynsworth, and Carswell, suggests that both the timing of the vacancy and presidential management can increase the extent of the opposition and provide the occasion for its activation. Accordingly, a key to explaining unsuccessful Supreme Court nominations lies in understanding not only the impact of the party composition in the Senate on the outcome but also the influence of other factors such as timing and presidential management.

The extent of the potential ideological opposition confronting a nomination can be approximated by assessing the party composition of the Senate. While party affiliation is not a perfect proxy for ideology, it does provide an accurate enough reflection of the ideological composition of the Senate to permit the drawing of some helpful generalizations. Not unexpectedly, a president whose party holds a majority in the Senate will generally face less potential ideological opposition than one whose party is in the minority.

This generalization helps explain why Supreme Court nominations forwarded to Senates in which the president's party is in the minority are turned down at a higher rate than those acted upon by Senates in which the chief executive's party is in control. Because dissatisfaction with a nominee's ideology is more likely to come from opposition party members, there will usually be more extensive potential ideological opposition confronting a nomination in which the president's party is in the minority than when his/her party is in control of the Senate. Consequently, nominations forwarded to Senates in which the president's party is in the minority are more likely to be denied confirmation.

The fact that over eighty-one percent (116 of 142) of all previous Supreme Court nominations have gained Senate approval suggests that in most cases the ideological opposition has either been insufficient or has remained dormant. What appears to be a necessary ingredient for activating latent ideological opposition is the presence of at least one other unfavorable factor beyond the initial negative perception of the nominee's ideology on the part of some senators.

The Role of Timing

A nomination made during the last full year of a president's term or in the interregnum period after a new chief executive has been elected presents an additional factor upon which to base opposition to confirmation. The unfavorable timing of the vacancy can generate opposition of its own as well as activate the otherwise dormant ideological resistance, significantly increasing the likelihood of the Senate's refusal to confirm. This is readily seen in the remarkably high refusal rate of seventy-one percent (ten of fourteen) for such nominations when they are also forwarded to a Senate in which the chief executive's party is in the minority.

The Fortas case suggests several reasons why the unfavorable timing of the vacancy can directly generate opposition and activate otherwise latent ideological opposition. When a Supreme Court nomination is sent to the Senate late in a president's term, senators opposed to confirmation for ideological reasons tend to become more optimistic and emboldened in their opposition because of the increased likelihood of derailing the nomination. Opposition to confirmation is seen as something more than tilting at windmills as senators opposed to the nomination realize that any delay in considering the nomination will work against confirmation. As the Fortas case clearly demonstrates, vacancies occurring at unpropitious times can enable a mere handful of senators, steadfastly opposed to the nomination on ideological grounds, effectively to block Senate consideration through a filibuster or other delaying tactics.

The unfavorable timing of the nomination also enables senators opposing the nomination for ideological reasons, but reluctant to do so publicly, to conceal the real basis for their disapproval. Because of the disadvantageous timing of the nomination, senators can publicly base their opposition not on the nominee's ideology but on the loftier principle that the filling of any vacancy on the Supreme Court should await the election of the next president. As in the initial GOP opposition to Fortas, disapproving senators can argue that it would be more democratic and more in the public interest to enable the appointment to be made by the incoming president. And while the timing of the vacancy can be employed as a cover issue to conceal more factious motives, it can also generate opposition on the part of senators sincerely concerned about the more sublime issues of democracy and the public interest.

Finally, the Fortas case indicates that the unfavorable timing of the nomination can directly lessen the reluctance of senators to oppose confirmation for ideological reasons. The disinclination of most senators to oppose a Supreme Court nomination solely and openly on the more politically controversial grounds of ideology or party appears to wane as the president's term draws to a close. What is ordinarily perceived as a legitimate presidential prerogative early in the term is generally not so viewed in the sunset of a presidency. This would especially appear to be the case when a president attempts during the last months in office to appoint an individual to the Court whose ideology is not viewed favorably by many in the Senate. The realization that a departing and in some cases recently defeated president is attempting to influence the ideological composition of the Supreme Court can free even the most deferential senators to oppose the nomination openly for reasons of ideology and, perhaps, even party.[6]

The Role of Presidential Management

The Fortas, Haynsworth, and Carswell cases provide insights into how and why presidential management of the selection phase of the confirmation process can have a significant impact on the Senate's deliberations. As previously noted, presidents generally seek to shape the Court to their own ideological likeness, and consequently some ideological opposition to their Supreme Court nominations is inevitable. This opposition, however, is needlessly increased when presidents nominate individuals who are vulnerable to non-ideological, non-partisan charges. This is so for several reasons.

Selecting a nominee vulnerable on non-ideological and non-partisan grounds gives senators an additional and sometimes decisive basis for opposing the nomination. Senators who are sympathetic to the nominee's ideology and party and who would ordinarily support confirmation can be led to vote against the nomination because of these additional non-ideological and non-partisan charges. This phenomenon was readily seen in the critical votes cast by liberal Democrats against Fortas and by conservative Republicans against Haynsworth and Carswell.

More importantly, the ethics issues used against Fortas and Haynsworth as well as the competence and judicial temperament charges raised in opposition to Carswell testify to the devastating results to be expected following the nomination of an individual vulnerable on such grounds. These three cases suggest that the most significant impact of these non-ideological, non-partisan factors in increasing opposition lies in their use as cover issues masking antagonism toward the nomination stemming from ideological or partisan concerns. The use of non-ideological, non-partisan factors as a pretext is consistent with the aforementioned reluctance of senators to base their opposition to a Supreme Court nomination on ideological grounds when there exist more widely accepted, legitimate bases upon which to rest their disapproval.[7] Were senators publicly to base their opposition on ideological and/or partisan grounds, they would run the risk of alienating constituents sympathetic to the nominee's ideology and/or party if only because every senator's constituency is divided to some extent along ideological and party lines. On the other hand, because there is generally unanimous agreement within each senator's constituency that a future Supreme Court justice should possess sufficient ethical sensitivity and competence, opposing a nomination on these more acceptable grounds will offend fewer, if any, constituents.

The selection of a nominee vulnerable to non-ideological, non-partisan criticism can work against confirmation in other ways. Senators inclined to support the nomination might become reluctant to do so out of fear that more damaging information reflecting on the nominee's suitability to serve on the Court will still be uncovered. All senators understandably guard against being placed in the embarrassing position of publicly coming out in favor of a nomination only to have highly unfavorable facts about the nominee surface a short time later. For example, the piecemeal disclosure of instances reflecting unfavorably on Carswell's judicial temperament appears to have made some senators wary about coming out in support of confirmation.

Additionally, some senators feel less inclined to come to the aid of a president and support his/her beleaguered nominee when they remain convinced that the chief executive's sloppy management of the screening process made the fight for confirmation more controversial than it had to be. For example, the Nixon White House's failure to be sensitive to Haynsworth's alleged ethical infractions, especially in the wake of Fortas's having been driven from the Court for similar considerations, and its subsequent shortcomings in investigating Carswell's background, left some senators stoically unmoved by requests to rally around the nominees.

The Fortas, Haynsworth, and Carswell cases also indicate that presidential management in the post-selection phase of the confirmation process can also be critical in generating sufficient opposition to defeat the nomination. A key aspect of the post-selection stage is the president's overseeing of the adoption and execution of tactics designed to carry out successfully the strategy for confirmation. No matter how well-conceived the original strategy, poor implementation through the use of tactics inconsistent with and counterproductive to the overall plan can needlessly generate opposition against the nomination. For example, Johnson's strategy of relying upon Russell's support in securing southern Democrats' approval of the Fortas-Thornberry package was derailed by his tactical mishandling of the Lawrence nomination. Likewise, Johnson's plan to seek speedy confirmation of Fortas was undercut by the delay occasioned by the flak surrounding Warren's contingent retirement.

The Fortas, Haynsworth, and Carswell confirmation battles further suggest that effective presidential management must entail taking care to ensure that positive relationships with senators are maintained. In overseeing his administration's numerous dealings with senators, especially in seeking to build support for confirmation, the president must avoid unduly alienating key members of the Senate and thereby causing or convincing them to withhold crucial support for the nomination. A senator miffed about not being adequately consulted on the nomination, or one upset about not being provided sufficient information on the nominee, or one disturbed by the heavy-handed pressure of the president or his lieutenants, or even one personally offended by actions not directly related to the nomination, can be led to oppose confirmation because of these considerations. Johnson's misguided decision to consult with only a few senators before devising the Fortas-Thornberry package, and the resultant anger of some who were not solicited, notably McClellan, illustrate this point. Likewise, the Nixon administration's tardiness in providing GOP senators with information to answer the charges raised against Haynsworth, as well as its clumsiness and insensitivity in pressuring senators in both the Haynsworth and Carswell battles, testify to the negative impact careless presidential management of the post-selection phase can have on the outcome.

EXPLAINING THE FORTAS, HAYNSWORTH, AND CARSWELL CASES

A focus upon the integration of the three key factors, ideology, timing, and presidential management, can help provide an explanation of the unsuccessful Fortas, Haynsworth, and Carswell nominations. But this explanation necessitates an understanding of the controllable and non-controllable considerations that contributed to the unfavorable Senate action in each case. Non-controllable considerations can be described as those elements confronting the nomination which the president can do little or nothing to change and which thereby set the framework in which he/she is forced to operate. Conversely, there are other aspects of the confirmation process subject to the president's discretion and through which he/she can significantly influence the Senate's deliberations on the nomination. These latter considerations can be described as controllable.

Non-Controllable Considerations

One obvious non-controllable consideration goes a long way toward explaining the unsuccessful Fortas, Haynsworth, and Carswell nominations. Each nomination was forwarded to either a Senate in which the president's party was in the minority or at a time late in the president's term. And while the presence of one of these adverse, non-controllable considerations contributed to the Senate's negative action, it did not preordain the unfavorable result. It should be recalled that while the Senate's nineteen percent refusal rate for nominations made amid one of these two adverse considerations is greater than the ten percent rate when no unfavorable conditions are present, the former is still far below the seventy-one percent ratio when both negative elements are present. Accordingly, the presence of only one of the adverse conditions in the Fortas, Haynsworth, and Carswell instances did not preclude positive Senate action. Indeed, a review of each case suggests the probability of favorable action had the only negative aspect remained the presence of one of the adverse conditions.

Controllable Considerations

The Fortas, Haynsworth, and Carswell nominations indicate that in each instance controllable, discretionary actions of the presidents contributed to increasing the opposition against confirmation. Notable among these actions were the selection of nominees vulnerable to non-ideological, non-partisan criticism; the devising and implementation of ill-conceived strategies and tactics; and the lapses in effectively oversee-ing relationships with senators so as to provide a favorable atmosphere in the Senate for considering the nominations.

These failures in presidential management contributed to under-mining the Fortas, Haynsworth, and Carswell nominations in several distinct but related ways. They increased the level of opposition raised against the nomination by providing a convenient cover behind which some senators, opposed to the nominations for ideological reasons but reluctant to do so solely on this ground, could conceal the real basis for their disapproval. The presence of a cover issue in each instance helped to trigger and intensify the pre-existing but generally latent ideological and/or partisan opposition confronting each nomination. These fail-ures in presidential management also directly contributed to generating a few additional votes against each nomination which could not be attributed solely, if at all, to ideological or party considerations. These unanticipated negative votes were crucial to the outcome.

This last point deserves some elaboration. As this study and others have indicated, ideology accounts for most of the votes cast against Supreme Court nominations.[8] Nevertheless, the comparatively fewer votes directly traceable to presidential management, timing, or other factors have been crucial to the outcome in large part because unlike successful Supreme Court nominations, unsuccessful ones have usually been denied confirmation by narrow margins.[9] For example, one study has revealed successful Supreme Court nominations have been approved by an average margin of forty-five votes while unsuccessful ones have been rejected by an average margin of less than eight.[10] Because, on average, a switch of only four of five votes would have turned the unsuc-cessful nominations into successful ones, each negative vote can be viewed as crucial.

Having all turned upon narrow margins, the key roll calls on the Fortas, Haynsworth, and Carswell nominations are not exceptions to this general rule. Haynsworth was denied confirmation by a 55-45 margin, indicating that the switch of a mere five or six votes would have turned defeat into victory. Carswell was rejected by an even slimmer 51-45 count in which no more than three votes decided the nominee's fate. And while there was not a direct vote on the Fortas nomination, the cloture roll call requiring a two-thirds vote of par-ticipating senators to terminate debate was 45-43 in favor of so doing.

Indeed, a switch of fourteen votes in favor of cloture would have been sufficient to terminate debate and force a direct vote on the Fortas nomination which would very likely have been favorable. In this context, each negative vote traced to timing in the Fortas case and to presidential management in all three cases was critical in determining the result.

Drawing upon the factors of ideology, timing, and presidential management, an explanation of the unsuccessful Fortas, Haynsworth, and Carswell nominations can now be summarized. Ideological opposition latent primarily among senators of the opposition party but also among members of distinct wings of the president's own party confronted each nomination at the time they were forwarded to the Senate. An estimate of the extent of this opposition is provided by the number of senators who did not share the president's ideological inclinations which in turn is approximated by the count of senators who did not share the president's party affiliation. This ideological opposition would generally have remained passive and limited had it not been activated and expanded by the unfavorable timing of the Fortas nomination and by mismanagement of the confirmation process by Johnson and Nixon. The activation of significant ideological opposition behind the covers provided by the unfavorable timing of the Fortas nomination, and by all three nominees' vulnerability to serious non-ideological, non-partisan criticism, joined with the genuine opposition directly generated by these considerations in bringing about the defeats of Fortas, Haynsworth, and Carswell.

A related question is why did these three unsuccessful nominations occur at this specific time? To a great extent the particular convergence of the factors of ideology, as reflected in party composition in the Senate, timing, and presidential management have already explained this occurrence. Because the latter factor is the only controllable one of the three, it is interesting to speculate why Johnson and Nixon fell victim to their own failures in presidential management.

The answer may well lie in James David Barber's categorizing of both Johnson and Nixon as "active-negative" presidents. According to Barber, active-negative presidents are identified by the following characteristics. They are "ambitious," and "power-seeking."[11] Their approach to life is combative and they have a persistent problem managing their aggressive feelings. Life is viewed by them as a "hard struggle to achieve and hold power."[12] Active-negative presidents are further described as having a strong tendency to adhere rigidly to a line of policy or a plan even if it is destined to end in failure.

They disdain compromise and seek to crush any enemies who have scoffed at them.[13]

Several aspects of Johnson's and Nixon's management of these ill-fated nominations reflect the active-negative character type. Notable among these in Johnson's case are the following. The failure to compromise seems evident in Johnson's refusal to back away even slightly from the contingent retirement scheme by setting a definite date for Warren's retirement, as well as in his insistence upon coupling the Fortas nomination with that of Thornberry rather than one more agreeable to conservatives and/or Republicans. In the power-seeking manner suggested by the active-negative typology, he sought to have it all by attempting to place not just one but two old friends on the Supreme Court. Johnson's aggressiveness is glimpsed in his calculated attempt to use the inflammatory anti-Semitism issue to further his goal of winning confirmation for Fortas and Thornberry. The tendency to adhere rigidly to a line of policy is reflected in his attempt to push the nominations through the Senate by pursuing a strategy that had worked in the past, one involving extensive reliance upon old buddies Dirksen and Russell to keep other senators in line. And when this strategy appeared destined to fail, Johnson seemed locked into it, unable to alter his course and move toward a workable compromise.

Some of Nixon's actions in the Haynsworth and Carswell cases also evince the active-negative character type. His rigid adherence to a policy, as well as his aggressiveness and disdain for compromise, are indicated by his refusal to withdraw the Haynsworth and Carswell nominations even when so advised by Republican leaders in the Senate. These traits are also revealed in his vindictive, non-yielding decision to follow the Haynsworth rejection with the nomination of the second-rate Carswell, a choice viewed by many as a deliberate attempt to get even with the Senate for disapproving Haynsworth.[14] The active-negative type's combativeness and desire to crush his enemies is glimpsed in the numerous instances of heavy-handed tactics as well as in the hostile rhetoric and name-calling that peppered White House conversations between the president and aides regarding both nominations. Finally, Nixon's active-negative preoccupation with seeking and holding on to power is revealed in his ill-advised decision to draft and release the Saxbe letter during the Carswell deliberations. This letter clearly placed emphasis not on the salient issues confronting the nomination but rather on how the Senate's rejection of Carswell would represent an unconstitutional and unprecedented attack on presidential power.[15]

IMPLICATIONS

Beyond explaining the Senate's refusals to confirm Fortas, Haynsworth, and Carswell, the factors and general pattern of unsuccessful Supreme Court nominations presented above hold some important implications for the three major components of the United States political system. A discussion of these significant implications follows.

Implications for the President

One of the more important implications that this explanation of unsuccessful nominations has for the presidency relates to confirmation strategies. Given the mix of favorable and unfavorable conditions under which a Supreme Court nomination can be made, a president intent on avoiding a rebuff by the Senate must remain flexible on the choice of a nominee. The president cannot blindly proceed as if his/her party is in substantial control of the Senate, as if the time at which the nomination occurred is favorable, and as if his/her own actions and decisions in overseeing the confirmation process are incapable of generating additional opposition. The review of unsuccessful Supreme Court nominations, especially the Fortas, Haynsworth, and Carswell cases, suggest that to do so is to court disaster.

While there is little a president can do to change the party composition in the Senate and the timing of the vacancy on the Court, he/she can control the designing of a strategy for confirmation. This control over strategy, stemming in large part from the president's exclusive authority over selecting the specific individual whose nomination is forwarded to the Senate, can be used not only to offset potentially damaging opposition occasioned by an unfavorable setting but also to increase support for confirmation. And while the designing of an effective strategy can take many forms, the president, appreciating the difference between the ideal and the possible, must understand that the individual he/she would nominate under optimally favorable conditions is not the one he/she should nominate under less favorable conditions.

More specifically, a president must always be concerned about nominating an individual to the Court who is vulnerable on non-ideological, non-partisan grounds. Given the latent ideological opposition confronting all Supreme Court nominations, the presence of serious non-ideological, non-partisan grounds for opposing confirmation can be critical in activating this opposition. Such a vulnerable nomination, even when made early in a president's term and forwarded to a Senate controlled by his/her own party, may generate enough opposition to bring about a failure to gain confirmation. Of course, in this otherwise favorable setting, the non-ideological, non-partisan charges must usually be serious enough not only to trigger the dormant ideological opposition of senators and provide them with an effective shield to conceal the real basis of their censure but also to stimulate the sincere non-ideological, non-partisan disapproval of senators who ordinarily would have supported the nomination on ideological and/or partisan grounds.

While a president must always guard against presenting a nominee vulnerable on non-ideological, non-partisan grounds to the Senate, this becomes essential when one or both of the two conditions usually associated with past unsuccessful nominations are present. When only one adverse condition is present, i.e., when party composition or timing is not favorable, the Fortas, Haynsworth, and Carswell cases suggest that the president must carefully oversee the pre-nomination screening of the candidates to make certain the nominee selected is free from serious non-ideological, non-partisan criticism. With this precaution taken, the president stands an excellent chance of gaining confirmation from the Senate because in most previous instances the presence of only one of the unfavorable conditions was not sufficient on its own to generate enough opposition to bring down the nomination.

The presence of both unfavorable conditions calls for more extraordinary measures on the part of the president because the discovery of an issue which raises even the slightest non-ideological, non-partisan criticism will in all probability erase any chance of confirmation. Consequently, a president forced to make a Supreme Court nomination when both party composition and timing are unfavorable must make certain his/her nominee is free from the slightest trace of criticism. The chances for success will still be marginal, but such an approach will at least enable the president to make the strongest case possible for confirmation.

In addition, a president in his/her last year in office and with the Senate controlled by the opposition party would be wise to take other steps designed to increase significantly the chances for confirmation. For example, a decidedly liberal president confronting a Senate controlled by conservatives at any time, but especially in his/her last year in office, must realize that these adverse considerations raise the real possibility that his/her preferred choice of a liberal nominee may not be confirmed. Consequently, prudent presidential management calls for the adoption of a strategy anticipating compromising with the Senate on ideology by selecting a moderate or a conservative who will be enthusiastically received by more senators.

An alternate strategy would be for the president to nominate a liberal but to offset the anticipated opposition by selecting the nominee from the ranks of the Senate. This would increase the likelihood of confirmation because "the Senate almost invariably treats as a *cas d' honneur* the presidential designation of a sitting member and normally, although not so predictably, of a past colleague in good standing."[16] The designation of a present or former senator would also lessen the chances that a minority of senators would resort to delaying tactics in order to prevent direct consideration of the nomination. Most senators would not tolerate such a move, holding to the belief that a former or present senator is at least entitled to a direct review by his present or former colleagues.

Still another strategy would entail the selection of a liberal whose reputation and qualifications to serve on the Court are widely perceived as outstanding. The designation of a nominee who is universally acclaimed as possessing a brilliant legal mind would make it more difficult for moderate and perhaps even conservative senators to vote against confirmation.[17]

Finally, the presence of both adverse conditions may necessitate the president's consulting with a bipartisan panel of Senate leaders and actively involving the members of this group in the search for a suitable nominee. While this maneuver lessens the president's discretion in choosing a nominee, it would increase the chances for confirmation by producing a candidate acceptable to most members of the different ideological groups and parties in the Senate. In addition, this procedure would enable the president to offset any partisan attacks on the nomination by proclaiming his/her neutral approach to staffing the Court and pointing to the bipartisan panel as evidence of this neutrality. Finally, the inclusion of Senate leaders from both parties in the choice of a nominee may very well serve to guarantee their support of the nomination throughout the confirmation struggle.[18]

Astute management of the pre-nomination screening process offers additional advantages to a president seeking Senate approval of his Supreme Court nominee. A thorough and complete pre-nomination screening of the candidates provides the president with a clearer perspective on the strengths and weaknesses of each potential nominee and increases the likelihood of an intelligent and confirmable choice. The screening can not only alert the president that a particular candidate will be seriously vulnerable on certain non-ideological, non-partisan grounds, but, if trouble arises, can also provide the opportunity for the chief executive to switch confidently to another nominee with a similar ideology but free from any threatening non-ideological, non-partisan criticism. Even in the event that the president elects to go ahead with his/her original vulnerable choice, foreknowledge of the issues reflecting unfavorably on his/her selection permits the chief executive to plan a more effective strategy for confirmation and to begin immediately to defuse opposition stemming from the charges raised against the nominee. Additionally, the willingness of senators to come to the aid of a beleaguered nominee can be affected by the extent to which the president is perceived as having actively sought to avoid making a controversial nomination, and a thorough pre-nomination screening can help establish this favorable perception.

A key aspect of the post-selection phase of the confirmation process involves the president's overseeing the adoption and implementation of tactics designed to carry out successfully the strategy for confirmation. No matter how well-conceived and potentially effective the original strategy, the use of tactics inconsistent with and counterproductive to the overall plan can needlessly generate opposition against the nomination. Counsel regarding the use of specific tactics consistent with the strategy for confirmation must admittedly be vague and generalized. Given the various strategies available for adoption within the unique setting of each vacancy, a president seeking confirmation of his/her nominee will be called upon to make a series of tactical moves; and given neither the singular details pertinent to the nomination nor the overall plan adopted, one can only advise prudence and astuteness in devising and implementing them.

In summary, the essence of prudent and astute management involves presidential actions that increase or at least maintain the initial level of support for the nomination. And while a president cannot be expected to gain the approval of all senators considering the nomination, he/she must employ the considerable power he/she has to provide a setting as conducive as possible to confirmation. How the president accomplishes this will not always be clear because the pursuit of a counterproductive strategy and the use of damaging tactics will often not readily be grasped until after serious and sometimes irreparable harm has been done to the nomination. Therein lies the heavy burden of presidential management. Accordingly, the challenge confronting any president seeking Senate approval of a Supreme Court nomination is to anticipate and avoid these pitfalls in the oftentimes dim light of the confirmation process.

Implications for the Senate

In United States legal history, two views of the nature of law have vied for general acceptance.[19] Adherents of the traditional view contend there exists a body of objective maxims that judges can understand through the application of sound legal reasonings and that will lead to the finding of the "right" law. Consistent with this view, the traditionalists maintain that competent and ethical judges will agree in interpreting these maxims and in finding the right law despite distinct differences in their backgrounds and ideologies. To followers of the modern view, a body of objective maxims does not exist and, consequently, the application of sound legal reasoning to a difficult question of law seldom produces a clear and unambiguous answer. Because there are innumerable zones of genuine doubt as to "right" law, modernists expect that competent and ethical judges interpreting the same precedents, statutes, or constitution can and will disagree. Consequently, there exists ample opportunity for the ideologies of judges to enter into their purportedly objective decisions.

The primary role of ideology evident in the pattern of previous unsuccessful nominations suggests most senators have accepted the modern view of law. From the early days of the republic, senators have generally reacted to Supreme Court nominations on the basis of whether or not they were in agreement with the ideology of the nominee. Equally competent and ethical nominees have simply not been treated the same. Senators have been inclined to favor, and overlook the criticisms of, those potential justices whose ideology they supported, while denying similar treatment to those whose ideology they opposed. This ideologically oriented behavior makes sense only if these senators have rejected the traditional view of the law and embraced the modern view. Furthermore, it can be expected that as the modern view of law continues to gain wider acceptance,[20] the number of senators inclined to base their confirmation votes on ideological criteria will continue to grow. Verbal behavior to the contrary, most senators will continue to make a Supreme Court nominee's ideology the major consideration in their decisions to grant or withhold consent to the nomination.

The pattern of unsuccessful Supreme Court nominations culminating in the Fortas, Haynsworth, and Carswell cases also sheds some light on the long-debated question of what criteria senators should apply in assessing the qualifications of individuals nominated to the Court. As noted above, some have argued that senators should completely defer to the president regarding the nominee's ideology and consider only the prospective justice's objective qualifications, while others have maintained that senators should carefully assess each nominee's basic philosophy. While the debate will no doubt continue, the latter, more expansive view of Senate powers is bolstered by the review of unsuccessful nominations if only because many senators in the past have consistently scrutinized the ideology of Supreme Court nominees. Indeed, in grounding their confirmation votes on an assessment of the ideology of Fortas, Haynsworth, and Carswell, modern senators were following a long tradition of Senate behavior fostered if not directly endorsed by the founding fathers.

Implications for the Court

While the Supreme Court has been noted for protecting the rights of the minority,[21] its continuing significant role in the United States political system has been directly linked to its having remained responsive to popular sentiment.[22] And whether the sentiments of the majority have pointed toward or away from justice, the inclination of senators to assess the ideology of prospective justices assists in keeping the Court in step with the prevailing public mood. When the Senate refuses to confirm a Supreme Court nominee on ideological grounds, it reaffirms that the appointment of justices is a shared power in which the president maintains substantial discretion but not without limits. When the president seeks to appoint individuals whose ideological views are perceived as not reflecting the prevailing view of the people, or when this mood is unclear or as yet unexpressed pending an upcoming election, the Senate can and indeed has refused to confirm Supreme Court nominations. Certainly not all senators have applied ideological criteria in assessing Supreme Court nominees, and no doubt some senators have been concerned about matters less weighty than philosophy, but on the whole there has been a sufficient concern with each potential justice's ideology to keep the Court in step with popular sentiment.[23]

The Senate's occasional concern with objective criteria such as ethics, competence, and temperament also holds an important implication for the Court. Most assuredly when these criteria are sincerely used, but perhaps even when they are employed as cover issues, the Senate conveys an ideal model of what a Supreme Court justice should be. Surely the aforementioned ideological concerns of most senators indicate a strong interest in shaping the policy results of the Supreme Court. But concerns about ethics, competence, and temperament emphasize not so much the final outcome of a decision but rather the process through which a decision is made. In employing these objective criteria at least some of the time, the Senate conveys the desire for justices who are ethical, learned, and fair.

Finally, the review of unsuccessful nominations confirms that the Supreme Court is a political institution engaged in shaping public policy. Two aspects of the process through which prospective justices have been denied confirmation clearly point to the political nature of the Court. The nominees' ideology, the very attribute most likely to influence the future policies enunciated by the Court, has played the dominant role in determining the final action of the Senate. In what can best be described as a politically motivated act, nominees have generally been denied confirmation because a sufficient number of senators disagreed with the policies likely to be supported by the prospective justices. In addition, and as the Fortas, Haynsworth, and Carswell cases indicate, the Senate's refusals to confirm Supreme Court nominations can be traced in part to counterproductive presidential management of the confirmation process. Consequently, the vital question of who shall assume a seat on the Court turns upon the political skills of the president. Put simply, the Court is a political institution because the process through which justices are confirmed or rejected has always been political.

BLACKMUN TO BORK

In the fifteen years following the rejection of the Carswell nomination in 1970, the Senate went on to confirm seven Supreme Court nominations in succession. Because the focus of this study is on unsuccessful Supreme Court nominations, an extensive analysis of these successful cases will not be presented. Instead, a brief review drawing upon insights gained from the analysis of the Fortas, Haynsworth, and Carswell cases will speculate why these nominations gained confirmation.

On May 12, 1970, the Senate overwhelmingly confirmed President Nixon's nomination of Harry A. Blackmun, of Minnesota, Judge of the United States Court of Appeals for the Eighth Circuit, to be an associate justice of the Supreme Court. The vacancy on the Court created by Fortas's resignation and sustained by the rejections of Haynsworth and Carswell was finally filled after more than a year. As the Democrats still controlled the Senate at the time Nixon nominated Blackmun, the nomination had to confront one of the adverse conditions associated with previous unsuccessful Supreme Court nominations. However, Nixon avoided the pitfalls he failed to dodge in the Haynsworth and Carswell deliberations, and wisely undercut ideological opposition in the Senate, by selecting a compromise nominee perceived as more liberal than the two previous unsuccessful nominees.

It appears Nixon was very aware that his selection of Blackmun represented a compromise on ideology. But because he was concerned that compromising in this instance would give the appearance of caving in to Senate liberals, Nixon attempted to discredit any suggestion Blackmun was less conservative than Haynsworth and Carswell. As was often the case with the complex and evasive Nixon, he ironically testified to the ideological compromise evident in the Blackmun nomination by denying that it represented any concession at all. Witness the classic instance of protesting too much in the following directive from Nixon shortly before the Blackmun nomination was announced:

> When the Blackmun nomination is sent down it is vitally important that somebody like Hruska praise the nomination as being that of a man who has the same philosophy on the Constitution as Haynsworth and Carswell. This case must be . . . the highest priority with our whole Congressional and PR staff. The attempt of liberals will be to find shades of difference between Blackmun and Haynsworth and Carswell. As a matter of fact, Blackmun is to the right of both Haynsworth and Carswell on law and order and perhaps slightly to their left, but very slightly to the left only in the field of civil rights. I know the argument will be made that we ought to give the liberals a chance to save face, but there are much higher stakes—my pledge to name strict constructionists to the Court and the inevitable charge that I was forced to back down by the Senate and name a liberal or even quasi liberal.[24]

The selection of Blackmun served to keep dormant any potential ideological or other opposition on the part of liberal and moderate senators. Indeed, when it was disclosed that Blackmun had participated in cases in which he had a financial interest, a charge fatal to Haynsworth, little was made of the issue. Apparently, the sheer exhaustion of the Senate after two draining rejections of prospective justices, and the perceived ideological compromise evident in the choice of Blackmun, had paved the way for his unanimous confirmation.

In September, 1971, Associate Justices Hugo Black and John Marshall Harlan, II, announced their retirements from the Court.[25] Nixon still faced a Senate controlled by the Democrats and had to be careful not to propose nominees vulnerable on non-ideological, non-partisan grounds. After flirting with disaster by suggesting that Republican Representative Richard H. Poff, of Virginia, an anti-civil rights conservative with slender judicial credentials, might be one of the nominees, Nixon wisely avoided needless controversy and perhaps another Senate rejection by withdrawing Poff from consideration. But the president then submitted for the American Bar Association's appraisal a remarkably undistinguished list of six potential nominees. Included in the list were Sylvia Bacon, a judge on the Superior Court of the District of Columbia who had less than a year's judicial experience and had authored the illiberal no-knock search and preventive-detention provisions of the District of Columbia's crime bill of 1967-1968; Senator Robert C. Byrd, a longtime opponent of civil rights legislation and former Ku Klux Klan member who had never practiced law nor been admitted to the bar; and Charles Clark of Mississippi, and Paul H. Roney of Florida, two conservative Nixon appointees to the federal court of appeals for the Fifth Circuit who had a combined total of three years of judicial experience. Nixon's preferred choices on the list, however, were an undistinguished California appellate court judge, Mildred Lillie, and an Arkansas municipal-bond lawyer, Herschel H. Friday, a good friend of Attorney General and Mrs. Mitchell.

The ABA eventually rated Judge Lillie as "unqualified" by an 11-1 margin and unenthusiastically deemed Friday "not opposed" by a 6-6 count. In forwarding its recommendations to the White House, the ABA tellingly urged the president to expand the list of nominees to include individuals with more stature than those presently under consideration. After the Justice Department and the ABA accused each other of leaking the names on the list to the media, Nixon angrily withdrew the slate of six and vowed no longer to submit the names of potential Supreme Court nominees to the ABA.

Despite his pique at the ABA, Nixon wisely, if begrudgingly, passed over all the nominees among the original six and nominated two individuals with outstanding credentials, Lewis F. Powell, Jr., of Richmond, Virginia, and William H. Rehnquist of Arizona. Powell, a past president of the ABA and distinguished member of the legal profession, easily won confirmation by an 89-1 margin. Rehnquist, a United States assistant attorney general, respected if not revered as a brilliant conservative, had a more difficult time but still breezed through the Senate by a margin of forty-two votes. In pragmatically turning to nominees of distinctly higher quality after considering mediocre candidates vulnerable to non-ideological, non-partisan criticism, Nixon avoided the serious pitfall that he failed to steer clear of in the Haynsworth and Carswell deliberations.[26]

One of the more interesting instances of effective presidential management is Gerald R. Ford's successful nomination of John Paul Stevens, Judge of the United States Court of Appeals for the Seventh Circuit, to assume Associate Justice William O. Douglas's seat on the Court. The odds were stacked heavily against the Republican president's winning confirmation for any Supreme Court nominee as the Democrats controlled the Senate and the Douglas vacancy had occurred only weeks before Ford would begin his last year in office, increasing the likelihood that time would become a serious consideration. Consequently, Ford came within weeks of having to face the two unfavorable conditions associated with the highest rate of refusals to confirm by the Senate. Additionally, Ford had no direct elective claim to the White House, having been named vice-president after Agnew's resignation and having succeeded to the presidency upon Nixon's stepping down in 1974. As if this were not enough, while a member of Congress Ford had led the bitter effort to impeach Justice Douglas and now the conservative president was ironically called upon to name the liberal justice's replacement.

Given these considerations, especially the critical timing of the vacancy, a small group of senators offended by anything in the nominee's background could have filibustered and permanently derailed the nomination. But Ford's effort in gaining the Senate's consent under these bleak circumstances appears to have been a model of caution and compromise. In selecting the "moderate"[27] Stevens, Ford not only guarded against offending GOP conservatives who would have balked at a liberal nominee but also managed to satisfy liberal senators who likely would have sought to block a decidedly conservative candidate. In addition, Ford was determined to avoid any non-ideological, non-partisan criticism that may have provided a basis for opposition by seeking a nominee with an outstanding and unimpeachable reputation.[28] Not surprisingly, the ABA granted Stevens its top evaluation, stating he met "the highest standards of professional competence, judicial temperament and integrity."

President Ford's strategy of excellence worked exceedingly well. While presidents in similar circumstances had often seen their nominees go down to defeat, Stevens was overwhelmingly confirmed by a 98-0 margin just sixteen days after his nomination was submitted to the Senate.

Unlike his immediate Republican predecessors, Nixon and Ford, President Reagan's first three nominations to the Supreme Court were made amid favorable circumstances. The 1981 nomination of an Arizona court of appeals judge, Sandra Day O'Connor, to replace the retiring Potter Stewart as associate justice, was forwarded to a Senate controlled by the Republican party and early in Reagan's first term. Likewise, the nominations of Associate Justice Rehnquist to succeed Warren E. Burger as chief justice, and of Judge Antonin Scalia, of the District of Columbia Court of Appeals, to assume Rehnquist's position, were received by the GOP-controlled Senate in 1986, early in Reagan's second term.[29] Accordingly, Reagan did not have to confront either of the conditions associated with unsuccessful nominations in seeking to gain Senate confirmation of his first three nominees to the Supreme Court.

Additionally, O'Connor, Rehnquist, and Scalia remained generally free of any serious non-ideological, non-partisan criticism during the Senate deliberations on their nominations. Not surprisingly, and despite Reagan's lack of ideological compromise especially in nominating the conservative duo of Rehnquist and Scalia, the three nominations were acted upon favorably by the Senate. O'Connor's nomination was confirmed by a convincing 99-0 vote and Scalia gained the Senate's assent by a 98-0 count. And while Rehnquist had to weather a filibuster designed to block his promotion to the chief justiceship, he was eventually confirmed by a 65-33 margin.

In November, 1986, however, the Democrats recaptured the Senate, indicating that any future Reagan nominees to the Supreme Court would have to face at least one of the conditions associated with unsuccessful nominations. In addition, each passing day signaled that Reagan was entering the twilight of his presidency, raising the possibility that any prospective justice of the Supreme Court designated by him might have to confront the additional opposition threatened by an end-of-the term nomination. The likelihood existed that any future Reagan nominees to the Supreme Court would have to face the usually lethal combination of a Senate controlled by the opposition party and a nomination made during the last full year of a president's term.

On June 26, 1987, less than seven months before Reagan began his last full year in office, Justice Powell announced his resignation from the Court. Amid the ominous setting presented by the disadvantageous party composition in the Senate and the relatively unfavorable timing of the vacancy, Reagan sought to find a confirmable replacement for Powell. The final chapter focuses upon the president's effort to win Senate confirmation of Powell's successor.

6. THE BORK AND GINSBURG NOMINATIONS

> It's just real ineptitude to have picked
> him [Bork]. He was done before he
> started.
> —Senator J. Bennett Johnston

ROBERT H. BORK'S nightmare began on July 1, 1987, after Justice Lewis F. Powell, Jr., announced his resignation from the Court, and President Ronald Reagan nominated the District of Columbia Circuit Court of Appeals Judge to fill the vacancy.[1] After a protracted and heated debate focusing on the nominee's judicial philosophy, the Senate rejected the nomination by a vote of 58-42 on October 23, 1987.

On October 29, 1987, Reagan tried again, nominating Judge Douglas Ginsburg, also of the District of Columbia Circuit Court, to succeed to Powell's position.[2] But this nomination was withdrawn on November 7, 1987, after it was revealed that Ginsburg had smoked marijuana both as a student at Cornell and as a law school professor at Harvard. Ginsburg was also faulted for a possible conflict of interest violation stemming from his 1986 handling of a case involving the cable television industry when he was head of the antitrust division of the Justice Department. At the time Ginsburg was participating in this case, he owned stock in a cable television company likely to be affected by the outcome.

On November 11, 1987, in a third attempt to fill the vacancy, Reagan nominated Judge Anthony M. Kennedy of the United States Court of Appeals for the Ninth Circuit.[3] The Kennedy nomination was confirmed by the Senate on February 3, 1988, by a 99-0 count.

The goal of this chapter is to provide an explanation of the Senate's refusals to confirm Bork and Ginsburg by drawing upon the background provided by the Fortas, Haynsworth, and Carswell cases and other unsuccessful nominations.

IDEOLOGY AND THE BORK NOMINATION

The dominant factor leading the Senate to reject the Bork nomination was the nominee's perceived ideology. The case for the primacy of ideology rests upon two considerations: a review of the extensive debate in the Senate and an analysis of the roll call vote on the nomination.

The Bork Debate

Unlike the Fortas, Haynsworth, and Carswell cases, where much of the Senate debate focused on non-ideological considerations such as ethics and competence, the deliberations on Bork centered on the nominee's ideology. Debate on Bork's fitness to serve on the Supreme Court focused on two related ideological considerations: the nominee's general judicial philosophy of original intent, and its specific application to a host of policy areas including the right of privacy, civil rights, gender discrimination, criminal procedure, separation of powers, antitrust law, and labor relations. The following discussion will focus on Bork's philosophy of original intent and its application to two policy areas which seemed to draw the most attention, the right to privacy and civil rights.[4]

Original Intent. Judge Bork was recognized as one of the leading advocates of the doctrine of original intent. In Bork's view, the original intent approach necessitates that in deciding cases judges closely adhere to the intentions of those who framed the Constitution or the specific legislative act in question. Failure to heed the intention of the framers is seen by supporters of original intent as an ill-conceived repudiation of judicial restraint leaving judges with no clear guidelines in reaching a decision other than their own subjective policy preferences. In turn, one of the prime dangers of judges' relying upon subjective policy preferences lies in its impact on judicial legitimacy.[5] According to Bork:

> The judge's authority derives entirely from the fact that he is applying law and not his own personal values . . . . How should a judge go about finding the law? The only legitimate way is by attempting to discern what those who made the law intended.[6]

In Bork's view, the original intent approach is compatible with democracy because judges who fail to base their decisions on principles specifically rooted "in the Constitution or in the statutes being interpreted . . .

engage in judicial legislation . . . inconsistent with the democratic form of government that we have."[7] Accordingly, at the core of the original intent approach to judicial decision making is the principle that popular majorities, through their elected representatives, rather than non-elected judges, should decide most policy issues.[8] Original intent, however, is not completely majoritarian. When the elected representatives of the people infringe upon a freedom which the Constitution's framers clearly intended to protect, the judge must assert the rights of the minority. This careful assertion of minority rights is also a key part of the Court's legitimacy. As one observer has noted:

> The Supreme Court draws its legitimacy from the need—in a democratic system predicated on majority rule but also on minority rights—for a nonelective branch, insulated from majoritarianism, to patrol the boundaries and determine the areas in which majority preferences may not determine policy.[9]

To some critics, original intent requires judges to rely on too narrow a source for constitutional interpretation, especially in light of the framers' inability to foresee future developments threatening individual liberties. These critics maintain that judges must be willing to go beyond the original intention of the framers, and draw from the Constitution general principles consonant with modern concepts of justice. For example, Associate Justice William J. Brennan has concluded:

> The genius of the Constitution rests not in any static message it may have had in a world that is dead and gone, but in the adaptability of its great principles to cope with current problems and current needs.[10]

Original intent has also been attacked because its adherents generally reject the concept of unenumerated rights. Critics of original intent argue that the Constitution not only provides protection for an exhaustive list of expressed enumerated rights but for certain unenumerated rights as well. Bork's critic, Harvard professor of law Laurence H. Tribe, has maintained that the Constitution was not designed to "threaten the individual liberty that the people retained and did not cede to any level of government."[11] Tribe's approach, suggesting that the people possess rights beyond those expressly included in the Constitution, stands in contrast to the view attributed to adherents of original intent recognizing an individual right only when it can be found in a specific provision of the founding document.

Bork's original intent stance drew sharp criticism from those opposed to his confirmation. Tribe concluded that if Bork were confirmed he would be the first justice to interpret the Constitution as though it contained an exhaustive description of individual rights.[12] Law professor Herman Schwartz asserted that Bork's cramped view of a judiciary tightly restricted by the framers' original intent "would keep the Constitution in knee breeches and livery."[13]

The Right to Privacy. Bork's philosophy of original intent, when applied to the right to privacy issue, drew considerable attention in the confirmation debate. Of particular note was Bork's apparent rejection of the view that the Constitution contained a general right to privacy. The debate in this regard generally focused upon Bork's disagreement with the Supreme Court's decision in *Griswold* v. *Connecticut*, 381 U.S. 479 (1965), declaring unconstitutional a Connecticut birth control statute banning the sale and use of contraceptives and prohibiting physicians from counseling on birth control.

In striking down the Connecticut law, the Court held that certain fundamental rights are protected even if they are not expressly enumerated in the Constitution. Writing for the majority, Associate Justice William O. Douglas argued the "specific guarantees in the Bill of Rights have penumbras, formed by emanations from those guarantees that help give them life and substance."[14] In Douglas's view, the Connecticut statute unconstitutionally restricted the intimate marital relationship that while unexpressed in the Constitution was nonetheless protected by the general right to privacy emanating from other specified provisions.

The general right to privacy endorsed by the majority in *Griswold* has become the legal underpinning for a series of Supreme Court opinions protecting specific privacy rights absent an expressed provision in the Constitution. Notable among these is the pro-abortion judgment in *Roe* v. *Wade*, 410 U.S. 113 (1973), that was most conspiciously denounced by Judge Bork.[15] Following his original intent approach, Bork maintained that the majority's reasoning in *Griswold* was fundamentally flawed, arguing there was no general right to privacy prohibiting Connecticut's actions because there exists no specific provision to that effect in the Constitution. In Bork's view, the majority's establishment of this general right was a shocking instance of judicial law-making contrary to the intent of the framers.

At the hearings on his nomination, Bork backed ever so slightly away from his often stated position rejecting the view that the Constitution contains a general right to privacy. He suggested that while he did not agree with the Court's reasoning in *Griswold* finding a general right to privacy in the penumbras of other specific provisions, he would not rule out the possibility that a more acceptable rationale supporting a general right to privacy could be found in the Constitution.[16]

Civil Rights. Bork's record regarding civil rights also drew severe criticism from those opposed to the nomination. Opponents cited his opposition, while an associate professor at Yale Law School, to legislation banning discrimination in employment and public accommodations which ultimately became Titles II and VII of the Civil Rights Act of 1964. For example, in 1963, Bork noted that the principle underlying the proposed ban on discrimination in public accommodations was one of "unsurpassed ugliness."[17] In 1964, he described the legislation outlawing discrimination in public accommodations and employment as an ill-conceived attempt to "compel association even where it is not desired."[18]

Bork's opposition to the provisions of the Civil Rights Act of 1964 was the focus of Nicholas deB. Katzenbach's testimony before the Judiciary Committee considering the Bork nomination to the Supreme Court. Katzenbach, who served as attorney general from 1964 to 1966, pronounced it "inconceivable that a man of intelligence and perception and feeling could have opposed that legislation on the grounds that it deprived people of freedom of association." According to Katzenbach, Bork's opposition could only mean he had "valued the right of people in public situations to discriminate against blacks if that is what they chose to do."[19]

Bork's commitment to protecting minority rights was also called into question by his criticism of the Supreme Court decision striking down the poll tax, a device primarily used to keep poor blacks from exercising their right to vote. In *Harper* v. *Virginia Board of Elections*, 383 U.S. 666 (1964), the Supreme Court held "a state violates the equal protection clause of the Fourteenth Amendment whenever it makes the affluence of the voter or payment of any fee an electoral standard."[20] Bork maintained that the Court was wrong to hold poll taxes unconstitutional in *Harper* because there existed no expressed intention of racial discrimination on the part of the state election board. His critics countered, however, that the history of the poll tax in Virginia clearly indicated that it was intended to discriminate against blacks and that this fact was correctly recognized by the Supreme Court in *Harper*.[21] In the view of these critics, Bork's refusal to appreciate the discriminatory intent of the poll tax, evident in his criticism of *Harper*, reflected "a pronounced lack of sensitivity to how the law affects real persons."[22]

While Bork's criticism of individual cases in the civil rights area continued to concern opponents of the nomination, they were most troubled by his overall lack of commitment to promoting equal justice under the law.[23] For example, Burke Marshall, a former assistant attorney general in charge of the Justice Department's Civil Rights Division, testified before the Judiciary Committee considering the Bork nomination and expressed grave concern about the nominee's fitness to serve on the Court:

> It is not my purpose to criticize Judge Bork for his views about any single one of these decisions. No doubt there is something to his views in each case, considered separately. No doubt there is indeed some arguably valid ground on which any Supreme Court decision can be described as incompletely or wrongly reasoned. The real concern is with the tenor, the tone and the substance of Judge Bork's discussion of these matters. It seems to show no awareness, no understanding of the enormity and the scope of the system of racial injustice that was implemented by law in this country.[24]

Confirmation Conversion? Senators' attempts to deduce Bork's ideology from his record were made more difficult by the nominee's reputed inconsistencies in what he had said or written in the past and the views he expressed in testimony for the Judiciary Committee in 1987. For example, Bork had long held the position that the equal protection clause of the Fourteenth Amendment was never intended to protect the rights of women and should not have been so used by the Supreme Court, as it had been at least since 1964. In Bork's view, because the Court had no principled way of determining which non-racial groups were purportedly protected under the equal protection clause, it could not legitimately employ it to construct substantive individual rights for women or other non-racial categories.[25] However, in testimony before the Judiciary Committee, Bork stated for the first time his belief that the equal protection clause should be extended beyond race and should apply to classifications based on gender.[26]

Some critics accused Bork of belatedly changing his stand on controversial legal questions in order to improve his confirmation chances. Criticism of the nominee's so-called "confirmation conversion" is typified by the Judiciary Committee testimony of Harvard law professor Tribe:

> The point is not that some of Professor Bork's academic writings or speeches were provocative, or that his positions changed from time to time: Academics are expected both to provoke and to evolve. The point is, rather,

that positions Judge Bork has consistently taken over a long period, lasting well beyond his becoming a federal judge, seem to have shifted in the brief time since his nomination . . . . Even on the most charitable view, the noteworthy shifts . . . cannot escape attention.[27]

The Views of Bork's Supporters. Supporters of the nomination sharply disagreed with Bork's critics' conclusions regarding his qualifications to serve on the Supreme Court. His supporters noted that opponents failed to appreciate the difference between the role of a professor and that of a judge.[28] They argued that while a professor is free to criticize and oppose a court's decision and reasoning, a judge must always allow great weight to precedents established by higher courts. Accordingly, a judge can disagree with the supporting rationale behind a decision and yet continue to abide by it as a matter of "settled law." Consequently, while Bork's supporters conceded that the nominee had often criticized landmark Supreme Court decisions, they carefully noted that

that is what law professors do. But as a judge [Circuit Court for the District of Columbia] he has faithfully applied the legal precedents of both the Supreme Court and his own Circuit Court . . . . Judge Bork understands that in the American legal system, which places a premium on the orderly development of the law, the mere fact that one may disagree with a prior decision does not mean that the decision ought to be overruled.[29]

Bork's supporters also criticized opponents for misrepresenting the nominee's position on many substantive issues, and for attempting to depict him as an extremist undeserving of a seat on the Supreme Court. These supporters maintained that Bork's position on the major legal issues placed him "well within the judicial mainstream."[30] Taking what they proclaimed to be an objective view of the nominee's record, Bork's supporters concluded that he was "eminently qualified by ability, integrity, and experience, to serve as an Associate Justice of the Supreme Court."[31]

Ideology: Negative Impact in the Senate. Despite the case made for confirmation by Bork's supporters, senators consistently cited his basic approach of original intent, as well as his more specific views on the right to privacy, civil rights, and other areas in arriving at their decisions to oppose confirmation.

Original intent. Bork's philosophy of original intent clearly entered into the judgement of those senators who opposed confirmation. The Judiciary Committee majority report on the nomination, which was highly critical of Bork's original intent approach and concluded he should not be confirmed, won the endorsement of nine of the fourteen committee members. Numbered among the nine opposing senators were Joseph Biden (D, Del.), Edward M. Kennedy (D, Mass.), Robert C. Byrd (D, W. Va.), Howard M. Metzenbaum (D, Ohio), Dennis DeConcini (D, Ariz.), Patrick J. Leahy (D, Vt.), Howell T. Heflin (D, Ala.), Paul Simon (D, Ill.), and Arlen Specter (R, Pa.). The majority report noted that Bork's alleged respect for settled law and precedent

> does not alleviate the concern that the nominee would pursue his particular theory of original intent. It does not remove the risk that important precedents preserving individual liberties and human dignity would be robbed of their generative force.[32]

Committee member Senator Kennedy offered a particularly unfavorable and, according to the nominee's supporters, exaggerated assessment of the dire consequences latent in Bork's philosophy of original intent:

> Robert Bork's America is a land in which women would be forced into back-alley abortions, blacks would sit at segregated lunch counters, rogue police could break down citizens' doors in midnight raids, school children could not be taught evolution, writers and artists would be censored at the whim of government, and the doors of the Federal courts would be shut on the fingers of millions of citizens for whom the judiciary is often the only protector of the individual rights that are at the heart of our democracy.[33]

The right of privacy. Bork's perceived rejection of a general right to privacy left many senators disturbed. The nine-member Judiciary Committee majority endorsed the testimony of Harvard law professor Kathleen Sullivan regarding the nominee's views on the Constitution's guarantee of a general right to privacy:

> On the scope and right to privacy, good and reasonable, fair-minded men and women differ greatly, and in good faith, and that has happened and is happening now, and I expect it to continue as long as there is a right of privacy to argue about.
>
> But there has been no disagreement on the Supreme Court, for 75 years, that there exists some right to privacy and it is that disagreement of Judge Bork's that we are focussing on.
>
> There are two sides to the issue on its scope, but there have not been, in our jurisprudence, two sides of the issue as to its existence, and that is what puts Judge Bork outside the mainstream.[34]

In addition, the senators joining in the Judiciary Committee's majority view emphatically concurred in Chairman Biden's view regarding Bork's disinclination to interpret the Constitution so as to include a general right to privacy. In foretelling the threat Bork's interpretation held for the protection of individual rights, Biden concluded:

> Will [Judge Bork] be part of the progression of 200 years of history of every generation enhancing the right of privacy and reading more firmly into the Constitution protection for individual privacy? Or will he come down on the side of government intrusion? I am left without any doubt in my mind that he intellectually must come down for government intrusion and against expansion of individual rights.[35]

Bork's position on the general right to privacy apparently influenced senators other than those serving on the Judiciary Committee to oppose confirmation. Senator Bob Packwood (R, Ore.) broke ranks with his party and came out against confirmation primarily on the basis of the nominee's stand on the right to privacy and the resulting likelihood that he would vote to overrule the expanded right to abortion established in *Roe* v. *Wade*:

> I am convinced that Judge Bork feels so strongly opposed to the right of privacy that he will do everything possible to cut and trim, and eliminate if possible, the liberties that the right to privacy protects.[36]

Because Packwood was respected by other senators as an authority on privacy issues and was committed to lobbying his colleagues to vote against confirmation, his defection from the pro-Bork camp reportedly was destined to have an impact beyond his single vote.[37]

Civil rights. Senators opposed to confirmation concluded that Bork's criticism of and opposition to positive steps furthering civil rights disclosed a troubling pattern. In the view of at least the nine members joining in the Judiciary Committee's majority report, the nominee's

> persistent pattern of criticism of civil rights advances, coupled with a conspicuous failure to suggest alternative methods for achieving these critical objectives, reflects a certain hostility on Judge Bork's part to the role of the courts in insuring our civil rights.[38]

These members concluded that Bork's confirmation "would reopen debate on the country's proudest achievements in the area of civil rights and return our country to more troubled times."[39]

Opposition to Bork's confirmation due to the nominee's perceived lack of support for civil rights also spread beyond senators who were members of the Judiciary Committee. Senator Bill Bradley (D, N.J.) noted that he was "not prepared to take the chance" the nominee no longer held the views he had expressed as a law professor when he criticized the 1964 Civil Rights Act and landmark pro-civil rights decisions of the Supreme Court.[40]

Perhaps the most crucial impact Bork's perceived anti-civil rights stance was to have in generating votes against confirmation occurred among the several moderate-to-conservative southern Democrats who opposed the nomination. And while the opposition of these Dixie senators will be analyzed later in this chapter, it should be noted that these southern Democrats became a focal point of much of the pressure generated by those opposed to Bork's confirmation. For example, former president Jimmy Carter vehemently denounced Bork's civil rights views and urged his southern colleagues to reject the nomination, noting:

> As a Southerner who has observed personally the long and difficult years of the struggle for civil rights for black and other minority people, I find Judge Bork's impressively consistent opinions to be particularly obnoxious.[41]

External Views of the Senate Debate. Further testifying to the key role of ideology in the Senate's rejection of the Bork nomination are the comments of those who observed the struggle for confirmation from outside the Senate. Shortly after the announcement of the Bork nomination, one report concluded that the controversial judge's selection "portends the biggest ideological battle of President Reagan's second term."[42] A short time later, Howard H. Baker Jr., White House chief of staff, anticipated a difficult ideological struggle but optimistically predicted winning Senate approval of Powell's successor:

> We're at a crossroads in the philosophical direction of government in the country. And the Bork nomination will help decide which path the government takes.[43]

Tom Wicker testified to the ideological nature of the struggle and succinctly summarized the logic underlying the participants' preoccupation with ideology:

> The reason Mr. Reagan chose Judge Bork, and that conservatives are happy about the choice, is that they believe this nominee, if confirmed, will tip the Court solidly to the right for many years to come.

> The reason Judge Bork is opposed by so many liberals, and so many beneficiaries of liberal legislation and rulings, is that they believe the conservatives are exactly right about the nominee's effect on the Court.[44]

David Broder echoed his fellow columnist's estimation of the ideological considerations extant in the Senate's deliberations:

> The Bork appointment looks like a last-minute effort to cement into the judicial branch a philosophy which may be losing its voter appeal. Each senator will have to judge the consequences in his or her own constituency.
> It should offend no one that the battle has this intensely political coloration. The pope's visit reminds us that even those who have a higher calling are chosen through a political mechanism. The Senate will be no holier than the College of Cardinals.[45]

Ideology, Party, and the Roll Call Vote

If party and/or ideology were significant factors in Bork's defeat, there should be indications that senators voted along party or ideological lines in turning down the nomination by a decisive 58-42 count. The data presented in table 9 indicate that senators did indeed generally vote along party lines, as almost eighty-seven percent (forty of forty-seven) of the Republicans voted in favor of confirming the GOP nominee while less than four percent (two of fifty-four) of Democrats did the same. The wide divergence between Republicans and Democrats initially suggests that the vote on the Bork nomination was affected by party considerations.

Table 9
Party Affiliation and the Vote on the Bork Nomination

	Votes For Confirmation	Votes Against Confirmation	Total	Percent in Favor
Democrats	2	52	54	4%
Republicans	40	6	46	87%
Total	42	58	100	42%

For table 10, the Senate is divided in half as before, on ideological lines, using *Congressional Quarterly's* 1987 Conservative Coalition Opposition scores for each senator.[46] These scores can be employed as a measure of a senator's ideology, the higher the score indicating the more liberal the senator.[47] For table 10, the fifty senators with the highest scores are classified as "Liberals," and the fifty with the lowest as "Conservatives."[48] (See appendix 3.)

Table 10 suggests that the Senate also generally followed ideological lines in voting on the Bork nomination. While only eight percent (four of fifty) of the "Liberals" favored confirmation, seventy-six percent (thirty-eight of fifty) of the "Conservatives" were so inclined. Additional evidence of the impact of ideology on Senate voting on the nomination is seen in comparing the average Conservative Coalition Opposition scores of senators who voted against confirmation with those who supported the nomination. This comparison reflects a mean score of 58.7 for opponents of the nomination and a relatively more conservative 15.4 average for Bork's supporters.

Table 10
Ideology and the Vote on the Bork Nomination

	Votes For Confirmation	Votes Against Confirmation	Total	Percent in Favor
Liberals	4	46	50	8%
Conservatives	38	12	50	76%
Total	42	58	100	42%

Ideology or Party? It will be recalled that in the analysis of the Fortas, Haynsworth, and Carswell roll calls, some preliminary difficulty was encountered in determining whether ideology or party was the dominant factor explaining Senate voting. This difficulty, which occurred in large part because of the strong correlation between party affiliation and ideology, necessitated additional steps in the analysis before it could be determined which of the two intertwined factors was dominant. One of these additional steps involved focusing upon the number of deviants (i.e., senators who voted in a way inconsistent with their ideology or party) generated by each of these factors in explaining the Senate vote. Ideology clearly produced the fewer number of deviants in all three cases to demonstrate convincingly its greater strength as a factor when compared with party.

The additional step of examining the deviant votes on the Bork roll call must be taken in order to begin to determine whether ideology or party was the dominant factor. Table 11 indicates the number of deviants produced by party and ideology in the Bork roll call as well as in the Fortas, Haynsworth, and Carswell cases and the extent to which the overall number of deviants was reduced or increased by the use of ideology.

Table 11

Deviant Votes Generated by Party and Ideology:
The Fortas, Haynsworth, Carswell, and Bork Nominations

Nominee	Votes Deviating from Party	Votes Deviating from Ideology	Change in Deviant Votes with Ideology
Fortas	29	9	−20
Haynsworth	36	17	−19
Carswell	30	7	−23
Bork	8	16	+8

The most striking aspect of table 11 is the seeming reversal in the relative strength of party and ideology in explaining Senate voting when the Bork case is compared with the other three cases. While ideology sharply reduced the number of deviant votes in the Fortas, Haynsworth, and Carswell cases relative to party, this does not occur in the case of Bork. Employing party to explain Senate voting in the Fortas case yields twenty-nine deviants compared to nine generated by ideology, a reduction of twenty. On the Haynsworth roll call, party triggers thirty-six inconsistent votes while ideology trims the deviant votes to seventeen, lowering the deviants by nineteen. Likewise, the Carswell roll call reveals thirty inconsistent votes occasioned by employing party but only seven using ideology, a reduction of twenty-three. However, using ideology to explain Senate voting on the Bork nomination produces sixteen deviants while employing party yields eight, an increase of eight.

Additional support for the relative strength of party affiliation as compared to ideology in explaining the Bork roll call vote is provided by table 12. This table indicates that when party affiliation is controlled and Democrat "Liberals" are compared to Democrat "Conservatives" and Republican "Liberals" to GOP "Conservatives," the differences between these ideological groups in supporting Bork are markedly reduced, especially in the case of the Democrats. Table 10 indicated "Liberals" generally supported Bork at an eight percent rate while "Conservatives" compiled a seventy-six percent approval rate. But as table 12 reveals, "Liberals" within the Democrat party provided zero percent (none of forty-one), while their "Conservative" colleagues responded only slightly more favorably at approximately a fifteen percent rate (two of thirteen).

In less evident fashion, the differences between the ideological group-ings in supporting Bork are reduced when party is controlled and the Republican vote is examined. Table 12 shows that while slightly more than forty-four percent (four of nine) of GOP "Liberals" favored Bork, approximately ninety-seven percent (thirty-six of thirty-seven) of Repub-lican "Conservatives" were so inclined. Although the small number of Democrat "Conservatives" and Republican "Liberals" can distort the comparison, the reduction of the percentage differences between these ideological groups in supporting Bork when party is controlled further suggests, at least preliminarily, that party was a more dominant force than ideology in the confirmation roll call.[49]

Table 12
Ideology and the Vote on the Bork Nomination:
Party Affiliation Controlled

	Votes For Confirmation	Votes Against Confirmation	Total	Percent in Favor
Democrats				
Liberals	0	41	41	0%
Conservatives	2	11	13	15%
Total	2	52	54	4%
Republicans				
Liberals	4	5	9	44%
Conservatives	36	1	37	97%
Total	40	6	46	87%

What is one to make of the evidence ostensibly pointing to the dominant role of party affiliation over ideology in the Bork vote? There are several caveats to bear in mind in assessing this evidence. First, it is likely that the impact of party and ideology are so intertwined as to make questionable any explanation as to the dominance of one factor over the other. This is especially the case when the conclusion as to which factor is dominant is reached solely by statistical analysis of the roll call vote and does not take into consideration the nature of the Senate debate on the nomination. In addition, confidence in distinguish-ing the independent pull of party and ideology decreases as the numeri-cal differences between the two factors in generating deviants are reduced. As table 11 indicates, the differences between the numbers of deviants generated by ideology compared to party in the Fortas, Haynsworth, and Carswell cases were respectively twenty, nineteen, and twenty-three, with ideology sharply reducing the inconsistent votes. But the difference between the deviants produced by ideology compared to party in the Bork case is just eight, with party only moderately lowering the inconsistent votes. Given the relatively greater numerical differences in the Fortas, Haynsworth, and Carswell roll calls, these cases likely provided a better opportunity to compare the influence of party and ideology. Furthermore, there is the obvious difficulty of gauging the ideology of senators with different measuring devices at different time periods, a difficulty compounded by the fact that between the 1968-1970 period and the Bork nomination in 1987, the ideological cohesion within each party reportedly increased significantly, making party and ideology even more intertwined.[50]

Despite these caveats, the roll call analysis on the Bork nomination still suggests party was a stronger influence than ideology. But this appears so inconsistent with the ideological tenor of the debate on Bork as well as with the dominant influence of ideology in the relatively recent Fortas, Haynsworth, and Carswell cases as to be highly suspect.[51] Before the argument proceeds, then, the apparent dominance of party in the Bork roll call must be put in proper perspective.

A clearer perspective on the relative strength of the factors of party and ideology in the Bork nomination is provided by examining those senators who were categorized as deviants in the roll call analysis. Of the twelve senators classified as "Conservatives" who voted against Bork's confirmation, ten were from the South and nine of these ten deviant southerners were Democrats.[52]

The consistent opposition to Bork on the part of "Conservative" Democrats from the South helps provide a different perspective on the influence of ideology and party in the Bork vote. This perspective suggests that many, if not all, of these Dixie senators were led to oppose Bork because of considerations involving both ideology and party. Understanding the actions of these senators and the role of ideology and party in their deliberations requires an appreciation of the changing nature of southern politics.

In recent years, two key developments have profoundly altered the political landscape of the South. First, there has been a significant increase in black voting in the years following passage of the 1965 Voting Right Act. In addition, there has been the emergence of a growing Republican party strong enough to break the Democrats' one-party rule throughout the region and to rekindle a competitive two-party system. These developments have had a telling impact on the campaign strategies of those seeking public office in the South. Because many white voters have migrated into the rejuvenated Republican party or are at least willing to support more conservative GOP candidates in the general election, few southern Democratic senators can expect to be supported by a majority of the white voters in their states. Consequently, blacks have achieved significant new clout within the Democratic party throughout the South as their votes have become indispensible to the election victories sought by southern Democrats.[53]

Those southern Democratic senators who had recently won election, many in campaigns in which they had railed against their GOP opponents' endorsement of President Reagan's pledge to appoint more conservative judges, were acutely aware of the growing influence of black voters. For example, Richard C. Shelby (D, Ala.) and John B. Breaux (D, La.) won election to the Senate in 1986, receiving only forty percent of the white vote while gaining approximately ninety percent of the black vote.[54] In addition, both Terry Sanford (D, N.C.) and Howell Heflin (D, Ala.) gained their Senate seats during the Reagan years with less than majority support from white voters but with the overwhelming support of blacks.[55]

As a result of the changing political climate, many Democratic senators in the South confronted a combination of both party and ideological considerations impelling them to oppose Bork. While these senators may not have disapproved of Bork's conservative ideology in most areas, they were particularly concerned about his perceived conservative, if not reactionary, stance on civil rights. These southern senators realized that the key to their electoral success was held by a bloc of constituents who would interpret a vote to confirm Bork as direct evidence of their lack of sincere commitment to civil rights and as grounds for opposing them in future elections.[56]

Accordingly, the combination of these senators' desire to maintain the essential support of a key bloc of their Democratic constituency and Bork's perceived anti-civil rights views, whether depicted accurately or distortedly, led them to vote against confirmation. In effect, a unique blend of the factors of ideology and party explain to some extent the deviation of "Conservative" Democrats from their anticipated pro-Bork course.

Support for this conclusion is directly supplied by a southern senator involved in the Bork deliberations. After noting that his black supporters were making the Bork vote a "litmus test" issue, Senator Breaux assessed how he and his southern Democratic colleagues would approach the Senate roll call on the nomination:[57]

> Those who helped us get elected—the black voters, the working people—
> are united in their opposition to Bork, and don't think for a moment that
> we are going to ignore that.[58]

Under closer examination, it appears that ideology was the dominant factor in the Senate's rejection of the Bork nomination. The initially perceived dominance of party over ideology in the Bork roll call
was traceable to the defection of a number of southern Democratic "Conservatives" from their anticipated support of a conservative nominee.
Because even this defection had ideological overtones, as evinced in
Bork's perceived civil rights stance, it is difficult to maintain, especially
in the face of a Senate debate focused primarily on the nominee's judicial philosophy, that ideology was not the dominant factor.

PRESIDENTIAL MANAGEMENT AND THE BORK NOMINATION

President Reagan's management of the confirmation process played a
pivotal contributory role in the Senate's rejection of Bork. Leading the
list of Reagan's actions contributing to the Senate's negative action is
his critical decision to select Bork as Powell's replacement. In addition,
the White House delayed in actively seeking to round up Senate support
for the nomination, providing opponents the opportunity to build a
strong case against the nominee. Finally, the administration unwisely
elected to present Bork as a moderate despite an extensive record indicating his conservative if not ultraconservative ideology.

Selection and Delay

Because the designation of Bork as the nominee and the deferred
effort in drumming up support in his behalf are intertwined, the discussion of presidential management of the nomination begins with a
focus on both of these aspects.

Ambivalent Strategy. Reagan had received conflicting advice regarding
the merits of nominating Bork to the Supreme Court. There appeared to
be general agreement that the designation of Bork as Powell's replacement would be controversial. Bork's forceful defense of original intent,
as well as his ringing criticisms of liberal Supreme Court decisions, was
a source of that controversy. In addition, in 1973, Bork was Solicitor

General of the United States, the third ranking official in the Justice Department, when President Nixon ordered Attorney General Elliot L. Richardson to fire Archibald Cox, the special prosecutor charged with investigating the Nixon administration's role in the Watergate break-in. Bork carried out the order after Richardson resigned and the second-ranking member of the Justice Department, Deputy Attorney General William D. Ruckelshaus, was fired, after both had refused to follow the presidential directive to discharge Cox. In retrospect, Bork's firing of Cox contributed little to his 1987 rejection by the Senate. Nevertheless, the controversy surrounding that event, coupled with the nominee's outspoken ideological views, signaled difficulties in the event Bork were nominated to succeed Powell.

While Reagan's advisors agreed that Bork would be a controversial nominee, they argued over the merits of nominating him. One group, led by White House Chief of Staff Baker, counseled against nominating Bork. Aware of the GOP's weakened political position given the Democrats' recapture of the Senate majority in 1986; of the time-consuming if not debilitating Iran-Contra affair; of the inopportune time of the vacancy, late in Reagan's last term; and of the already openly expressed hostility of liberal senators to Bork, this group privately advocated caution in selecting the nominee to replace Powell.[59] Accordingly, Baker's group advised a sufficient degree of compromise in order to avoid a bruising and protracted fight over the Powell replacement effort and favored nominating a moderate or at least a conservative less controversial than Bork.

Another circle of advisors, headed by Attorney General Edwin Meese III, pushed for the president to nominate Bork. In this group's view, Bork stood alone in possessing the ideal philosophy and legal acumen to contribute significantly to attaining the Reagan agenda on the Supreme Court. And while the members of Meese's group were aware that a less controversial nominee would more easily gain the Senate's assent, they remained confident Bork would be confirmed.[60]

· Given this conflicting advice, Reagan opted for an ambivalent strategy on the nomination. He eagerly agreed to follow the Meese line regarding the designation of Bork as the nominee. Indeed, the president reportedly had wanted to select Bork almost immediately upon learning of the Powell vacancy, and the advice from Meese's group only bolstered him in that resolve.[61] The Meese group also advocated an immediate, aggressive, hard-sell campaign stressing Bork's right-wing views on abortion, school prayer, and crime, in order to trigger the early support of Reagan's conservative admirers.[62] Evidently influenced, however, by the conciliatory approach recommended by Baker's group, the president rejected, or at least acquiesced in, discarding this type of campaign and opted for the delayed, low keyed, conciliatory one recommended by Baker and his colleagues. As a result, the White House urged conservative groups eager to lobby in Bork's behalf to lay low during the Senate's deliberations and demanded that pro-Bork forces refrain from using the controversial abortion issue in seeking to drum up support for the nominee.[63]

The White House strategy of remaining relatively passive in Bork's defense had a significant impact on the Senate's deliberations as it played directly into the hands of those opposed to the nomination.[64] Before the identity of Powell's replacement was announced, liberal interest groups such as the Leadership Conference on Civil Rights were prepared to mount an immediate, all-out effort to defeat the nomination in the event Bork were the nominee.[65] Consequently, the primed anti-Bork forces went on the offensive immediately after the nomination was announced, while the nominee's supporters remained relatively unresponsive, stripped of the timely opportunity to rebut the charges leveled against the nominee by the White House order for a laid-back approach.

Altering the Debate. The most critical aspect of the anti-Bork forces' unchallenged early assault on the nominee's record can be seen in how these attacks changed the public debate on the nomination. The White House had anticipated that the debate would focus primarily on the issues of crime and abortion, and that Bork's perceived conservative stance on these matters would generate sufficient support in the Senate to gain confirmation. In particular, Bork's conservative law and order position was counted upon to win the votes of key southern senators.[66] But the anti-Bork forces calculatedly employed their early and generally uncontested attacks on the nomination, culminating in the hearings, to refocus the debate on issues more likely to stir Senate opposition.[67]

Instead of specific concentration on the abortion issue, the anti-Bork forces were able to expand the debate to the broader topic of the right to privacy. Consequently, Bork's denouncing of the reasoning in *Roe* v. *Wade* was seen not so much as being in line with the conservative stance on abortion but rather as being outside the mainstream view on the broader topic of the right to privacy. As one report noted, the term "privacy," which was widely understood as a metaphor for abortion, took on an entirely different meaning after the Bork hearings:

It came to stand for the whole theme of fundamental rights, the concept of an expansive Constitution in contrast to Judge Bork's view that the Constitution was limited by its precise language and the intent of 18th Century framers.

The abortion question itself became subsumed into the broader question of a generalized right to privacy, a concept that politicians were suddenly rushing to embrace.[68]

Additionally, the shift in the debate enabled the anti-Bork forces to focus the discussion on civil rights rather than on crime. Consequently, Bork's perceived strong law and order position never materialized as a major issue despite Reagan's belated attempt to make it so.[69] Instead of highlighting the crime issue likely to gain votes for Bork in the South, the Senate debate focused sharply on the nominee's perceived anti-civil-rights record, a move destined to strip him of the essential southern support needed to gain confirmation. As one report explaining the rejection noted:

> Judge Bork's opponents succeeded in focusing the debate on whether he would reverse civil rights gains—a question of critical importance to black voters who provide crucial electoral support to Southern Democrats.[70]

Another account concluded that in the South it was "the civil rights issue that turned the political tide against the nomination."[71]

Outside the Mainstream. In the Fortas, Haynsworth, and Carswell cases, senators seeking to undermine the nominations succeeded because in addition to the ideological considerations underlying their disapproval, they were able to develop non-ideological, non-partisan grounds upon which to base their opposition. But Bork was not credibly vulnerable to either the ethical charges that sapped Fortas's and Haynsworth's support or the incompetence accusations that eroded Carswell's strength. Nevertheless, Bork's opponents realized that for the nomination to be defeated, they would have to expand the opposition beyond the ideological criticisms being voiced by Senate liberals disturbed by the nominee's conservatism.

In this context, the anti-Bork forces' success in shifting the focus of the debate was crucial, because it enabled them to expand the opposition by depicting the nominee not merely as a conservative but as an extremist. For example, the Judiciary Committee report recommending Senate rejection of the nomination noted:

> Judge Bork's approach to liberty and enumerated rights sets him apart from every other Supreme Court Justice. Indeed, not one of the 105 past and present Justices of the Supreme Court has ever taken a view of liberty as narrow as that of Judge Bork . . . .
>
> In particular, Judge Bork's philosophy is outside the mainstream of such great judicial conservatives as Justices Harlan, Frankfurter, and Black, as well as such recent conservatives as Justices Stewart, Powell, O'Connor and Chief Justice Burger.[72]

Notably, Bork's positions on the general right to privacy and civil rights were consistently employed to portray him as an extremist and therein lies the significance of the opponents' success in shifting the focus of the debate to these issues.[73]

Senators sought to increase the opposition against Bork by using the extremist charge in two related but distinct ways. They frequently questioned his support of settled and fundamental elements of law, arguing that while they were willing to support a nominee who disagreed with their ideology, they could not support one who would repudiate principles long cherished in the United States legal tradition. For example, the Judiciary Committee report concluded Bork was a threat to "age-old constitutional commitments."[74]

In addition, senators maintained that since Bork was so rigidly committed to his extremist ideology and approach to constitutional interpretation, he would not address each case with the objectivity and dispassion demanded of a justice. While this attack was a subtle one, moving from a concern about Bork's strong ideological stance to doubts about his judicial temperament, it was nevertheless made by opponents. Witness the comments of Senator David H. Pryor (D, Ark.), who noted he could not support confirmation because "something . . . seems to be absent from the makeup of Robert Bork. And that is 'judicial temperament.' " Pryor added:

> I supported Justices O'Connor and Scalia, as well as Chief Justice Rehnquist. But the question of Robert Bork is not an issue of a person being conservative or liberal, Republican or Democrat. It is a larger question of temperament and understanding.[75]

An indication of the breadth and intensity of the anti-Bork forces' effort to depict the nominee as an extremist outside the mainstream can be glimpsed in the language used by opponents as well as the media to characterize Bork. Opponents pointed out that the nominee was "not conservative" but a "radical."[76] In their view, Bork did not merely possess an ideology, he was an "ideologue," unfavorably implying a more rigid, uncompromising adherence to a point of view.[77] Additionally, Bork was likely to be branded an "ultra-conservative," an "ideological extremist," and "intemperate activist", a "reactionary anti-legal ideologue," an "extremely conservative activist, "a "right-wing ideologue" and even a "right-wing kook."[78]

Impact on the Senate. The effort of the anti-Bork forces to portray the nominee as an extremist had its most significant impact on the pivotal Democratic senators from the South. Because many southern Democrats had endorsed Reagan's nominations of Republican conservatives O'Connor, Rehnquist, and Scalia, the White House counted upon them for the additional votes needed to secure Bork's confirmation in the Democratic-controlled Senate.[79]

As noted above, the anti-confirmation votes of the nine deviant "Conservative" southern Democrats can be explained by the combination of Bork's perceived lack of support for civil rights and the significant increase in black voting throughout the South. But these considerations only present part of the explanation because the anti-Bork forces' depiction of the nominee not as a mainstream conservative but as an extremist was also instrumental in convincing many conservative southern senators, as well as some moderates outside the South, to oppose Bork.

Polling information on the Bork nomination in the South provides evidence supporting this conclusion. An Atlanta *Constitution* poll published shortly after the hearings on the nomination were concluded in October, 1987, showed that in the twelve southern states, fifty-one percent of the voters opposed confirmation, thirty-one percent supported it, and the remainder expressed no opinion.[80] And while one might attribute the anti-Bork majority to the overwhelming disapproval of blacks, the poll revealed whites as well as blacks were against confirmation by a substantial margin. But the most telling testimony that the anti-confirmation forces had made a convincing case that Bork's views put him outside mainstream thought in the South is the poll's finding that even those southerners who described themselves as conservatives were firm in their opposition to confirmation.

The loss of the support of southern voters of both races and across the ideological spectrum confirms that Bork was perceived not as a legitimate conservative but as an extremist. The South's less than favorable view of the nominee's ideology was not unnoticed by southern senators, and it reportedly led them to vote against confirmation. As one observer analyzing the polling data concluded:

With the growth of the Republican party in the South, many southern Democrats had come to depend upon overwhelming support from blacks; leaders in the black community were putting strong pressure on these senators to vote against Bork's confirmation. Had their white constituents favored confirmation, however, southern Democratic senators would have been under intense political cross-pressure. The poll's findings that even their white constituents favored a "No" vote clearly made such a vote the easy choice politically.[81]

Evidence supporting the conclusion that Bork's perceived extremist ideology influenced conservative southern senators and moderates outside the South to oppose confirmation can also be found in analyzing their public statements on the nomination. Many of these senators sounded a common theme, indicating that Bork was not fit to sit on the Supreme Court because his views consistently placed him outside the mainstream. The statements of four Democratic senators, three of them classified as "Conservatives," Heflin of Alabama, J. Bennett Johnston of Louisiana, and Lloyd Bentsen of Texas, and one categorized as a "Liberal" but with a relatively moderate Conservative Coalition Opposition score of sixty-three, DeConcini of Arizona, illustrate the impact of the anti-Bork forces' effort to stigmatize the nominee as an extremist.[82]

Heflin, a former federal judge, has been described as Reagan's most reliable Democratic supporter on the Judiciary Committee. He was the only Democrat on the committee to back Daniel A. Manion, a conservative Republican, for a federal appeals court seat. In addition, the Alabama Democrat split with the majority of his Democratic colleagues in voting to approve Rehnquist's elevation to chief justice and Meese's nomination as attorney general. Heflin's conservative ideological leaning is further reflected in his backing of all but two of over 300 judicial nominations made by Reagan before the Bork nomination.[83] Finally, the Alabama senator's Conservative Coalition Opposition score of six, tying him for the second lowest score of all Democrats, marked him as one of the least liberal members of the party.

Early in the Senate's deliberations on the Bork nomination, Heflin's vote was seen as crucial to the outcome. The White House aggressively sought the Alabama senator's support, viewing his eventual decision on the Bork nomination as a "bellwether" for southern Democrats.[84] Given Heflin's prior service as a federal judge, his position on the Judiciary Committee, and his conservative credentials, his decision on the Bork nomination could indeed influence all senators, especially his southern colleagues.[85]

Before announcing his decision, Heflin suggested that his assess-ment of where Bork's views placed him on the ideological spectrum would determine how he would vote on confirmation.

> If Judge Bork is a true conservative who guards against activism, our now fundamental precepts of a fair and just society, which include peo-ple's rights, will be protected. On the other hand, if he is an extremist, whose concept of the Constitution calls for the reversal of decisions deal-ing with human rights and individual liberties, then people's rights will be threatened.
>
> As the hearings have proceeded, I have endeavored to find an answer. Frankly, I would favor a conservative appointment on the Court. I have supported . . . [President Reagan's appointees] to the federal bench . . . because I felt they would, in most instances, become good conservative and impartial jurists. But, on the other hand, I don't want an extremist on the United States Supreme Court.[86]

Heflin also told a group of Alabama constituents that the key question confronting him was whether Bork was "a conservative in the true sense of the word" or "a de facto right-wing freak."[87]

When Heflin announced his decision, it was clear that the anti-Bork forces' effort to depict the nominee as possessing an ideology out-side the mainstream had been influential in tilting him away from confirmation. Heflin's statement concluded that he would vote against confirmation because Bork "has continued to exhibit—and may still possess—a proclivity for extremism."[88]

Senators Johnston's and Bentsen's public statements opposing Bork focused directly on what they perceived as the nominee's extremist posi-tions on civil rights and the right of privacy. Johnston rebuked the White House for nominating a supposed conservative who in reality was out of touch with prevailing conservative opinion in these two areas.

> Of all the great conservative minds they could have brought forward, there are enough who haven't called public accommodations "unsurpassed ugliness." There's not a civil rights advance in the last 20 years that he hasn't criticized.
>
> Then, on top of that, you have his not recognizing a right to privacy. And that is very big with everyone.[89]

Bentsen's statement expressed apprehension that Bork's promotion to the Supreme Court would "turn back the clock on civil rights."[90] In addition, Jack Martin, Bentsen's 1988 Senate campaign director, defended the senator's announced opposition to Bork by stressing how the nominee's reported rejection of a general right to privacy would be received in the lone star state.

> From a Texas perspective, here's a former Yale professor who wants to deny these people their right to privacy. He might as well be saying he wants to deny their right to bear arms.[91]

Finally, Senator DeConcini indicated that he opposed Bork because the nominee's views placed him too far to the right of Reagan's other conservative but mainstream Supreme Court designees, all of whom the Arizona Democrat supported.

> Judge Bork is different from Justice Sandra Day O'Connor, Chief Justice William Rehnquist and Antonin Scalia. He has spent his career as a legal scholar criticizing in the harshest terms the Court and its decisions. He has used inflammatory terms to criticize the decisions that most people in this country credit with giving some measure of equality and respect to all of us.[92]

DeConcini chastised the president for nominating Bork and attempting to pass him off as a legitimate conservative. He concluded that in choosing Bork, Reagan had

> selected someone that, indeed, is outside the mainstream of conservatism in this country. He selected him, I think, knowing that he was outside the mainstream, and he attempted, through the White House, to sell this person for something he was not.[93]

The Perils of Delay. The evidence presented above leads to the conclusion that Reagan's selection of the controversial Bork and the White House's critical delay in aggressively seeking support for the beleaguered nominee were instrumental in the Senate's rejection of the nomination. This conclusion is widely supported.

Senator Johnston traced the White House defeat directly to the fatal decision to nominate Bork, noting: "It's just real ineptitude to have picked him. He was done before he started."[94] Johnston's view was reportedly shared by at least some White House officials who believed "the key mistake was choosing Judge Bork in the first place."[95]

Extensive criticism of the handling of the Bork affair, voiced by both friends and foes of the White House, focused on the administration's critical delay in attempting to build support for the nominee.[96]

One administration official charged: "We were late getting out of the blocks. We underestimated what the opponents could do." Noted conservative Richard A. Viguerie concluded that because of the delay, the liberals were able to frame the debate and put Bork on the defense. Senator Charles E. Grassley (R, Iowa), a conservative and strong supporter of Bork's, complained that the nomination was lost because the White House was "on vacation during August and asleep at the switch." It was Grassley's view that "while Ron and Nancy were riding horses in August, the opposition was organizing." Southerners Breaux and Shelby shared Grassley's view. Breaux noted, "had I been handling it, I would have put on a much stronger lobbying effort." He also maintained that the White House officials "took some people for granted—Southern Democrats. There was a lack of intensity on their part." In Shelby's view, the Bork nomination was defeated in part because "the President was late in getting into the game."

Additionally, Justice Department officials at odds with Chief of Staff Baker over how to handle the drive toward confirmation openly sniped at the White House's delayed effort on Bork's behalf. According to these officials, the reserved approach by the White House allowed opponents to seize the initiative and dictate the terms of battle.[97] One Justice Department administrator, after complaining that while the liberals were using the critical summer months to gear up for the confirmation fight White House officials took a leisurely approach as the president vacationed in California, concluded "the Bork nomination was lost on the beaches of California. They [White House officials] didn't want to turn the level of heat up. The idea . . . was just drift him in."[98]

Criticism of the administration's tactic of delay even came from within the halls of the White House, adding credibility to the Justice Department's appraisal. A senior White House aide confided that the administration had been too passive in Bork's defense, allowing opponents to run away with the debate. In this official's view, "the agenda we're all discussing now is their (Bork's opponents') agenda, not ours. It's privacy, women's issues . . . not crime and the issues where Bork is strongest."[99]

Finally, Bork himself was critical of the White House effort in his behalf, reportedly having felt "a certain amount of anger and betrayal" at how the nomination was handled. The nominee apparently met with White House aides during the Senate's deliberations and berated them for not doing enough in his behalf.[100] Another report of this meeting indicates that Bork had "sharply criticized the administration effort and asked why President Reagan, Vice President Bush, and Mr. Baker couldn't do more to save the nomination."[101]

Bork as a Moderate?

An additional consideration generating opposition against confirmation was the White House effort to present Bork as a moderate despite his extensive record reflecting his conservative if not extremist ideology. Baker apparently succeeded in convincing Reagan that the balance of power in the Senate was held by the approximately two dozen moderates who were unlikely to agree with Bork's conservative views.[102] Consequently, the president gave the go-ahead to the attempt to portray Bork as a centrist after the Meese group had failed in persuading Reagan to pursue a confirmation campaign emphasizing the nominee's extensive conservative credentials.[103]

There is ample evidence that the effort to present Bork as a moderate was a calculated one coordinated by the White House. A few days after Bork was nominated, setting off a wave of liberal criticism, an administration official confided: "we're citing some of the cases he's been fairly liberal on, such as the First Amendment."[104] Underscoring the urgency in the White House attempt to recast Bork's ideology, one report noted that "almost overnight, the legal darling of the right-wing has been converted to a raging pragmatist."[105] The recasting effort continued with the president's first major address on the nomination, in which he described Bork as a "moderate" and buttressed his case by stressing themes in the nominee's record sharply divergent from the views championed by the administration's more conservative supporters.[106]

Additionally, a briefing book distributed by the White House for the pro-Bork forces to use in rounding up support for the nomination emphasized the moderate aspects of the nominee's record. In deference to the mainstream strategy of the White House, an earlier Justice Department draft of the briefing book, detailing Bork's conservative record, had been toned down. In the revised version, Bork was described as being to the left of both the conservative Scalia and the moderate Powell. In addition, the briefing book disingenuously concluded that Bork was so in line with the moderate views of Powell, his ascension to the Court "will not alter the present balance in any way."[107] Such conclusions led one observer to describe the briefing book as "part of a well-orchestrated effort to mask, if not distort, much of Judge Bork's record—the same record that made him attractive to staunch conservatives."[108]

In concert with the White House mainstream strategy, if not on White House orders, Bork began de-emphasizing his reputation as a conservative. While he had previously proudly accepted the conservative label, faced with mounting pressure to his confirmation before the hearings had even commenced, he told an interviewer: "I don't consider myself a conservative."[109] In his opening testimony at the hearings, Bork must have surprised television viewers and, no doubt, some senators by proclaiming, "my philosophy is neither liberal nor conservative."[110] In later testimony, he asked to be judged not by what he called "speculative" writings as a law professor but rather by his behavior as solicitor general, as a practicing lawyer, and as a federal appellate judge. In these last three roles, Bork told some skeptical members of the committee, "I have not been extreme in any way."[111] In his testimony, Bork frequently disavowed conservative positions he had previously taken on civil rights, freedom of speech and the press, sex discrimination, abortion, and the right of privacy.[112] For example, one report on the hearings concluded:

> One of the most remarkable aspects of Judge Robert H. Bork's five days of testimony . . . was his recantation and qualification of some controversial views he has stated, forcefully and repeatedly, in the past, as long ago as 1971 and as recently as this year.[113]

Reading the "New" Bork. The effort to present Bork as a moderate undermined his chances for confirmation. One report attributed Bork's defeat in part to the effort to repackage the nominee:

> The resulting hybrid, that of a judge of well-documented conservative views trying to portray himself as a moderate, simply did not sell, either to the public or to the Senate. A result was a confused and somewhat slippery image that failed to excite the judge's supporters, while enraging his opponents.[114]

Another report concurred in this conclusion by noting, "it appears in retrospect that it was a mistaken strategy for Bork supporters to try to picture him as a moderate, mainstream jurist . . . . Whatever else he was, Judge Bork was not that, as his academic record and his writings clearly showed." This report went on to conclude:

> Judge Bork might have survived his own record, except for the fact that, on questioning from the Senate Judiciary Committee, he repeatedly denied it. Apparently having agreed to the strategy of being depicted as a moderate, he found himself time and time again forced to say that he no longer believed something he had written in the past, or that he wouldn't vote that way on the Court. This appearance of a "confirmation conversion"—saying anything necessary to win senators' approval—diluted his supporters' arguments that he was a man of strong and independent judgment.[115]

Even conservative observers outside the Senate appeared offended by the White House effort to portray Bork as a moderate and the nominee's seeming complicity in this endeavor. Few liberal critics could match the scorn Bruce Fein, conservative legal scholar and former Justice Department official in the Reagan administration, heaped upon the White House for pursuing the mainstream strategy. In Fein's view, adoption of that strategy merited the White House an A-plus for "ineptitude and cuteness." He had prophetically predicted before the hearings began that the attempt to portray Bork as a moderate would collapse when committee members say to the judge, "the White House says you're just like Powell. Do you agree?" Fein had anticipated that Bork "can't possibly say yes."[116] After observing Bork's attempt to do just that or something close to it before the Judiciary Committee, Fein was brutal in his assessment of the nominee, concluding the hearings had become

> a magnificent triumph for the liberals. The basic message sent by the hearings so far is that courts are about where they should be, that no great changes are needed. Bork is bending his views to improve his confirmation chances and it's a shame.
>
> His ambition perhaps exceeds his intellectual devotion. There are not a lot of Socrates running around saying, "O.K., I'll take the hemlock."[117]

Other conservatives expressed dissatisfaction with the White House by directing their anger at Baker, whom they perceived as the force behind the strategy to portray the nominee as a moderate instead of as a bona fide conservative.[118] One report indicated the strategy had hindered the effort of conservative groups to raise sufficient funds to match the extensive anti-Bork media campaign launched by the nomination's opponents. According to this account, conservatives refrained from making financial contributions to the confirmation effort in part because of "the White House strategy of selling Bork as a moderate." In the view of Curt Anderson, president of the conservative Coalition for America, the administration was taking the effort to portray Bork as a moderate "too far, to the point where anybody can ask, 'why are we getting excited about him?'"[119]

When Bork's conservatism was seemingly contradicted by the White House effort to cast him as a moderate and the nominee's own qualifications of his record, several senators were left uncertain and wary of supporting a Supreme Court designee whose ideology appeared so inconstant and/or incalculable. As one report noted, "repositioning Bork as a moderate . . . gave senators a safe reason to vote against him: his unpredictability."[120] And whether the difficulty in clearly determining the nature of Bork's ideology was used in a genuine or disingenuous way, its availability to opposition senators can be traced to the White House strategy to portray Bork as a moderate.

The impact Bork's ambiguous record had on the confirmation roll call is made evident by focusing upon those moderate-to-conservative senators who noted the nominee's inconsistency or unpredictability in making known their decisions to oppose the nomination. One very important vote lost because of the nominee's unpredictability was that of Senator Specter, a Pennsylvania Republican. Specter had earlier expressed distress regarding the lack of consistency in Bork's record by noting during the hearings: "The concern I have is: where's the predictability in Judge Bork? What are the assurances that this committee and the Senate has?"[121] When Specter later announced his opposition to confirmation he reiterated his concern about Bork's inconsistent record, specifically linking it to the nominee's professed support for equal protection of the law.

> For the first time, at his confirmation hearings, Judge Bork said he would apply equal protection broadly in accordance with the Court's settled doctrine . . . . I have substantial doubt about Judge Bork's application of this fundamental legal principle where he has over the years disagreed with the scope of coverage and has a settled philosophy that constitutional rights do not exist unless specified or are within original intent.[122]

Because Specter was considered one of the most insightful and thoughtful members of the Judiciary Committee, and the administration counted heavily on his support to influence a number of undecided moderate Republicans, his decision to vote against confirmation reportedly dealt a serious blow to Bork's chances for confirmation.[123]

Several other conservative-to-moderate senators, particularly from the South, made reference to Bork's unpredictability and inconsistency in arriving at their decisions to oppose confirmation. Senator Sanford, of North Carolina, concluded:

> In the course of his public life Robert Bork has been a socialist, a libertarian, a conservative and now, most recently, a moderate. There is no way to predict what he will be as a member of the Supreme Court.[124]

Pryor, of Arkansas, traced his opposition to Bork's ideological inconsistencies.

Having gone from extreme positions in his youth to unexplainable positions in later life, Robert Bork continues to wrestle with what he believes. Today, he remains an unknown man with unknown beliefs.

There is something sad about the whole issue of Judge Bork's nomination. Here is a brilliant scholar, going through the agony of public hearings and public scrutiny. And yet we don't know him any better than we did months ago. I would even submit the respectful opinion . . . that he does not know himself.[125]

Johnston, of Louisiana, confided that he had expected to vote in favor of confirmation until Bork's testimony before the Judiciary Committee revealed that he "had blazed such a trail of erratic decisions."[126]

Alabama's Heflin's concern about Bork's unpredictability can be glimpsed in a statement he made to the nominee early in the Judiciary Committee hearings:

You're gone through a lot of changing ideas. I wish I was a psychiatrist rather than a lawyer and member of this committee to try and figure out what you would do if you get on the Supreme Court.[127]

A short time later, when asked by reporters which of the many ideological faces presented by the nominee was the "real Bork," Heflin replied, "maybe all of them."[128] Heflin's uncertainty about Bork's ideology clearly formed part of the basis upon which he later rested his opposition to the nomination. Unable to determine whether Bork was a true conservative or a right-wing extremist, Heflin elected, as he put it in announcing his opposition, to follow the old saying of "when in doubt, don't."[129]

Arizona's DeConcini, a moderate Democrat and member of the Judiciary Committee, also appears to have been influenced by Bork's unpredictability in arriving at his determination to oppose confirmation.[130] Upon listening to the nominee's testimony, DeConcini noted that he had serious concerns about Bork's significant shifts in ideology during the course of his academic and judicial career.

The judge has made some very strong, what I consider radical views known over the years of being a judge and particularly before being a judge. And now he has changed.[131]

Finally, liberal Democrat and Judiciary Committee member Leahy of Vermont noted that Bork's apparent backing away from his conservative stance when testifying at the hearings raised serious doubts in the minds of many senators whether the nominee could be believed. According to Leahy, Bork's backing away created a "credibility issue": "The question is whether he [Bork] was really running for office for 20 years and is now having to eat his campaign promises."[132]

EXPLAINING THE SENATE'S ACTIONS

Having examined the roles of ideology and presidential management, it is now possible to present an explanation of the Senate's rejection of the Bork nomination. Insights gleaned from this explanation will in turn be used to account for the Senate's refusal to confirm Ginsburg and its eventual assent to Kennedy as Powell's successor.

Explaining the Bork Rejection

Understanding Bork's rejection begins with the realization that the vacancy occasioned by Powell's resignation took place under less than ideal circumstances. The Bork nomination was forwarded to a Senate in which the Republicans were in the minority, signaling greater potential ideological opposition to Bork than that faced by Reagan's three previous successful Supreme Court nominees, all of whom were nominated when the president's party controlled the upper house. Analysis of the Senate debate and the roll call on the Bork nomination confirms both the activation and significance of this ideological opposition. In addition, the GOP's minority status meant that the Democrats commanded the machinery of the Senate, and that the liberal Joseph Biden (D, Del.) had replaced the conservative Strom Thurmond (R, S. C.) as chair of the Judiciary Committee with the resultant power to determine when the hearings would begin and which witnesses would be heard.[133] Control of this machinery was reportedly instrumental in the anti-Bork forces' critical and successful effort to focus the public debate on issues detrimental to confirmation.[134]

The Bork nomination was not forwarded to the Senate during Reagan's last full year in office. However, in being sent to the Senate no more than six months before the start of Reagan's last year in office, the Bork nomination did suffer from some of the unfavorable effects of a so-called "lame-duck" nomination. For example, one report noted that Senate Democrats were emboldened to oppose Bork on ideological grounds because they believed "a lame-duck President should not be able to use his appointment power to further a social agenda that he cannot get through Congress."[135] Another account traced Bork's rejection in part to Reagan's power having waned because he "had now entered the 'lame duck' period, the last two years in office."[136]

The presence of one of the warning signs of potential confirmation opposition, the Democrats' control of the Senate, should have alerted Reagan his selection of Powell's replacement could encounter trouble. Even more, the appearance of a second caution signal, a Supreme Court vacancy's occurring late in his last term, should have convinced Reagan that extraordinary care was essential if Senate rejection were to be avoided. The president should have realized that the relative ease with which his three previous Supreme Court nominations gained confirmation stemmed in part from the hospitable GOP ratio in the Senates considering them as well as the favorable early-in-the-term time at which they were made.[137]

Additionally, Reagan should have been more appreciative of the difficulties inherent in seeking to replace Powell, a centrist and the swing vote on the Court, with a decided conservative. In this regard, Reagan may have been lulled into a sense of complacency by his earlier successes in appointing individuals to the Court. But he should have recognized that these successes were due in part to the general perception that the Senate's confirmation of his nominees would not greatly alter the Supreme Court's ideological composition. For example, the moderate-to-conservative Potter Stewart was replaced by O'Connor, who had similar ideological inclinations and the conservatives Chief Justice Warren Burger and Associate Justice Rehnquist were respectively succeeded by the equally conservative Rehnquist and Scalia.[138] Now, however, especially after having acquiesced to three Reagan nominees, liberal senators, and perhaps some moderates as well, might feel differently about a departing president's attempting to reshape the Court by replacing a pivotal centrist justice with a pronounced conservative.[139]

Despite these warning signals, Reagan approached the finding of a replacement for Powell as if the Senate setting remained favorable, even though it now demanded astute presidential management. At a time demanding a careful and conciliatory course, the president elected to challenge potential opponents in the Senate by nominating a controversial individual they could portray and attack as an extremist. Indeed, the selection of Bork was immediately seen by liberals and eventually viewed by moderates and southern Democrats not as a conciliatory move by the departing president but rather as a confrontational one.[140] For example, Senator DeConcini saw the selection of Bork as Reagan's way of throwing down "a gauntlet" that Senate liberals had to pick up.[141]

The critical mistake, and the one almost inevitably leading to other tactical moves working against confirmation, was the selection of Bork. Surely there were other nominees possessing a conservative ideology approaching Bork's but lacking his perceived contentiousness who would have easily gained the Senate's approval.[142]

Only after the nomination was made, and the die cast, did White House officials become concerned that the unfavorable setting in the Senate was not conducive to confirmation of a nominee as controversial as Bork. In an attempt to offset the extensive early and unanticipated opposition to Bork, an effort was undertaken by the pro-confirmation forces to make the nomination appear less contentious. The White House sought to cool the heated debate surrounding the nomination by delaying its own effort in Bork's behalf, instructing right-wing groups to lay low in expressing support for him, and eventually attempting to reposition the nominee as a moderate. Indeed, Bork's apparent backing away from his conservative views in testifying before the Judiciary Committee was seen as part of this repositioning effort.[143] And as the analysis of presidential management above indicated, the White House effort was not only unsuccessful in offsetting the early opposition to Bork, it was instrumental in generating additional votes against confirmation.

It must be emphasized that Reagan's primary error in failing to gain Senate confirmation of Powell's replacement in this instance was his unreflective selection of Bork.[144] While the subsequent counterproductive tactical moves of delaying the White House effort in Bork's behalf, quieting the vocal support of right-wing groups, and attempting to recast the nominee as a moderate undermined confirmation, they can at least be seen as reasonable endeavors to salvage a nomination that was in serious trouble from the beginning because of the selection of a controversial nominee.[145] In retrospect, the selection of Bork immediately painted the White House into a corner from which it could extricate itself only by some risky tactical moves. Not surprisingly, these moves had a double edge, holding out the hope of snaring victory from defeat but also the peril of increasing Senate opposition and erasing any chance for confirmation. And while it is difficult to determine whether the risky tactical moves gained any votes for Bork, the evidence presented in previous pages clearly indicate they directly influenced some senators to oppose confirmation.

When the rejection of the Bork nomination is compared to the refusals to confirm Fortas, Haynsworth, and Carswell, continuity rather than change in the factors accounting for the Senate's negative action is evident. For while the Bork rejection was marked by a greater willingness of senators to attribute their negative votes to ideological concerns, and by the presence of a massive effort on the part of pressure groups having more in common with an election campaign than the appointment of a justice, the basic factors providing an explanation of the Senate's negative actions in all four instances are more similar than dissimilar.

The presence of the adverse structural considerations of a Senate controlled by the Democrats and a vacancy occurring late in Reagan's term signaled the potential for extensive ideological opposition to a conservative nominee. The selection of the outspokenly conservative Bork activated the opposition of liberal Democrats, increasing the likelihood of negative Senate action."[146] But the disapproval of liberal Democrats would not have been sufficient to defeat the nomination, for, as in the Fortas, Haynsworth, and Carswell cases, the anti-confirmation forces had to expand the opposition, and this could only occur with the development of an additional factor (or factors) leading other senators to oppose the nomination. And while Johnson and Nixon had obliged opponents by selecting candidates vulnerable to the non-ideological, non-partisan criticism of ethical insensitivity or incompetence, these criticisms could not convincingly be leveled at Bork. Nevertheless, Reagan obliged by nominating an individual whose ideological views had been so passionately and contentiously expressed that opponents could convincingly depict the nominee as being outside the ideological mainstream.

Reagan further played into the hands of opposition senators by delaying the White House effort to defend Bork's record, leaving the anti-Bork forces free to more easily portray the nominee's ideological views as outside the mainstream. When the White House finally entered the fray and sought to increase support for confirmation by attempting to posture the nominee as a moderate, Reagan further accommodated Bork's opponents. This effort, including Bork's own moderation of his views, served to increase the opposition because now senators could also ground their disapproval on Bork's inconsistency, his unpredictability, or even his alleged duplicity.

As in the Fortas, Haynsworth, and Carswell cases, anti-Bork senators had an array of negative considerations, which some employed sincerely to oppose confirmation, and which others used to conceal the ideological or partisan basis for their opposition. Bork could be opposed not only on the forthright but politically dangerous grounds that he was a mainline conservative but also on the safer grounds that he was a right-wing extremist outside the mainstream, and was unpredictable if not outright deceitful. The choice of a conservative less controversial than Bork, and more careful management of the post-nomination process, would have limited the credible opposition to the nominee's perceived ideology and increased the chances for favorable Senate action. To the extent President Reagan failed to promote this favorable setting, he contributed to the Senate rejection of Bork.

A Note on Ginsburg

After the Bork rejection, the political setting confronting Reagan remained unchanged. The Democrats' control of the Senate, and the unfavorable timing of the Powell vacancy, necessitated careful presidential management to ensure confirmation of the next nominee. Because the president could not expect smooth sailing were he to nominate a decided conservative in the Bork mold, he might have established a more favorable atmosphere in the Senate by nominating a moderate like Justice Powell. Eschewing this approach, he might have sought to build a solid base of support by selecting a conservative whose judicial or scholarly record was so outstanding as almost to ensure confirmation by the Democratic-controlled Senate, no matter how reluctantly. In nominating Ginsburg, the president was perceived as following neither of these prudent steps.

The mood established by the choice of Ginsburg was one of confrontation. Ginsburg was identified as the choice of Attorney General Meese and other hard-line conservatives in the administration, and the president did little to discourage this view.[147] Before announcing the nomination, Reagan had promised to select a nominee who would upset liberals "just as much" as Bork.[148] In announcing the Ginsburg selection, the president opted to emphasize conflict rather than conciliation by blasting senators for having done a "disservice to the Court and to the nation" by opposing Bork.[149] And despite Ginsburg's slender and relatively undeveloped judicial record in the criminal justice area, after having served on the District of Columbia Court of Appeals for only fourteen months, Reagan elected to highlight in confrontational fashion the nominee's supposed strong law and order stance. In an implied but obvious slap at liberals for being unduly concerned about providing criminal defendants with basic constitutional protections, the president praised Ginsburg for understanding that "no one has rights when criminals are allowed to prey on society."[150]

Reagan's rhetoric, whether justified or not, helped lead some liberal senators to perceive the nominee as being as far to the right as Bork.

For example, Senator Kennedy described Ginsburg as "an ideological clone of Judge Bork—a Judge Bork without a paper trail."[151] Kennedy's assessment was soon voiced by other liberal critics of the nomination, increasing the likelihood of their opposition to confirmation if for no other reason than that Ginsburg appeared to share Bork's ideology.

Reagan's perceived disinclination to compromise on ideology, however, did not alone doom the Ginsburg nomination as even the solid opposition of liberal Democrats would not have been sufficient to defeat confirmation. It was in failing to oversee an effective screening of Ginsburg's background that the president ensured that his nominee would go down to defeat. For in relying heavily on Meese's rushed assessment of Ginsburg's suitability to replace Powell, Reagan was denied vital information about his eventual choice. A thorough screening of Ginsburg would likely have indicated to the White House, in more timely fashion, the damaging aspect of Ginsburg's involvement, while a Justice Department official, in a possible conflict of interest situation, handling a cable broadcast case at the same time he held a $140,000 stock interest in a cable television company.[152] More importantly, Ginsburg's smoking of marijuana, which occurred while he was a Cornell student and while he was a Harvard law professor, as recently as 1978, would likely have been brought to the president's attention. Pre-nomination discovery of the alleged conflict of interest and especially of the marijuana incidents would have fully alerted Reagan to the dangers inherent in the selection of Ginsburg, and provided the opportunity for the White House to make a more confirmable choice.

As it was, the discovery of this information after the Ginsburg nomination was announced fatally wounded the nominee. The marijuana reports in particular represented the non-ideological, nonpartisan criticism guaranteed to increase the opposition to Ginsburg's confirmation, because liberals now had safer non-ideological grounds on which to base their disapproval. Additionally, the conservatives and moderates who were expected to rally behind Ginsburg began to withhold their support, aware that their call for strong law and order justices would appear hypocritical, if not ridiculous, were they to support a nominee who admitted to breaking the law by smoking marijuana. Accordingly, Ginsburg, denied a firm basis of support, was left with the unenviable choice of confronting Senate rejection or requesting the president to withdraw his nomination. He eventually chose the latter course, ending his short but bitter ordeal.

In summary, the Democrats' control of the Senate created a situation in which an expected core of liberal senators would likely be dissatisfied with Reagan's choice of a replacement for Powell. The president could have reduced the anticipated opposition of Senate liberals by adopting a conciliatory approach and by conveying at least the appearance, if not the reality, of compromising on ideology. Rather than pursuing this course, however, he adopted a combative approach by selecting Ginsburg and even before by proclaiming that his nominee would be as objectionable to liberals as was Bork. The president further solidified the opposition of liberals, and triggered the lethal disapproval of moderates and conservatives, by not carefully overseeing the pre-nomination screening of the nominee. Not unlike Fortas, Haynsworth, Carswell, and Bork, Ginsburg was refused confirmation because of ideological concerns and a failure in presidential management.

A Note on Kennedy

Appearing to have learned from the Bork and Ginsburg refusals, Reagan handled the Kennedy nomination with a belated but nevertheless effective display of presidential management. The president took several critical steps in ensuring that the Senate would approve his third effort to find a replacement for Justice Powell.

Reagan clearly adopted a conciliatory approach toward the Senate in announcing the Kennedy nomination. Unlike the Ginsburg announcement, which was used to castigate Bork's opponents, the president now confided that the Senate's deliberations regarding his two unsuccessful nominees had "made us all a bit wiser." He also expressed the hope Kennedy would be confirmed "in the spirit of cooperation and bipartisanship." And rather than emphasizing the nominee's generally conservative ideology, the president noted that Kennedy "seems to be popular with many senators of varying political persuasions."[153]

In selecting Kennedy, the president also conveyed a willingness to compromise in regard to ideology. This became even more apparent when the nominee appeared before the Judiciary Committee and his views, while conservative, were perceived to contrast starkly with those expressed by Bork.[154] Indeed, and whether rightly or not, Kennedy's ideology was almost universally viewed as differing from Bork's alleged extremism. For example, conservative legal scholar Fein suggested that Kennedy's views placed him "probably between Bork and Powell."[155] Liberal Harvard law professor Tribe concluded that the nomination of Kennedy "replaces the dogmatism of Robert Bork with a sense of decency and moderation."[156] The liberal Senator Metzenbaum described Kennedy's ideology as "well within the constitutional mainstream."[157] Conservative Democrat Heflin, in an oblique but obvious reference to Bork's perceived ideological rigidity, concluded that Kennedy's "conservatism, while pronounced, is not so severe as to prevent him from listening."[158] Additionally, Reagan's newly discovered pragmatism regarding the ideology of his Supreme Court nominee was not missed by reporters, as one concluded,

> Reagan has finally yielded to the imperative of winning in the Senate. After the fiasco of Judge Douglas H. Ginsburg, he had to abandon his preference for a tamper-proof ideologue in the Robert H. Bork image. He pointedly introduced Judge Kennedy as something the critics said Judge Bork was not: "a true conservative."[159]

Another noted,

> In turning this time to a consensus nominee, President Reagan was yielding to a political reality that includes Democratic control of the Senate and his own weakened powers as he enters his last year in office.[160]

An additional step Reagan took in ensuring success in his third attempt to fill the Powell vacancy involved the screening of Kennedy's record. After the rushed and shallow review of Ginsburg, both Democrats and Republicans had urged administration officials "to take their time and make sure there are no surprises this time."[161] The White House evidently followed this bipartisan urging as one senior administration official confided that Kennedy's background check was so exhaustive "we know when he stopped sucking his thumb."[162] The thorough screening of Kennedy enabled the White House to avoid the embarrassing post-nomination discovery of incidents in the nominee's past detracting from his outstanding and extensive judicial record. Indeed, the nominee was even prepared to finesse a minor flap over his membership in private clubs excluding women or blacks by maintaining he had worked to change the discriminatory policies and resigned when he was unsuccessful.[163]

Had the steps of taking a conciliatory approach, compromising on ideology, and guarding against embarrassing post-nomination disclosures been taken earlier, the White House would have been spared the anguish of the Senate's refusals to confirm the Bork and Ginsburg nominations. Effective presidential management of the Kennedy nomination held in check the potential liberal opposition and paved the way for confirmation. And when an exhausted Senate approved the nomination by a 97-0 count on February 3, 1988, the search for Powell's successor had ended.

FINAL NOTE

In the future, a Supreme Court nominee is going to be refused confirmation by the Senate. It is not possible to determine when that will occur, but the pattern of previous unsuccessful nominations can suggest the setting and factors likely to be present when the Senate withholds its consent. The president's party is likely to be in the minority in the Senate, or the vacancy on the Court will have occurred late in his/her term. Of course, the presence of both of these conditions would increase the expectation the nomination will not be confirmed. The dominant factor leading senators to vote against confirmation will be the nominee's perceived ideology. And even though the Bork case appears to have made the Senate's examination of a nominee's ideology more acceptable and legitimate, senators will remain reluctant to base their opposition to confirmation publicly on ideological grounds. Accordingly, the generation of the additional non-ideological, non-partisan opposition essential to undermining the nomination will most likely involve a cover and/or legitimate issue traceable to the factor of presidential management. In essence, the Senate's action in refusing to confirm some future Supreme Court nominee will be, as it always has been, supremely political.

Appendix 1

THE FOLLOWING TABLE provides information pertinent to all Supreme Court nominations made between 1789 and 1988. The abbreviations employed in the table are as follows:

Fd = Federalist
DR = Democratic-Republican
NR = National Republican
D = Democrat
R = Republican
W = Whig
F = Favorable, i.e., the president's party was in control of the Senate or the vacancy occurred other than in the president's last full year in office or in the interregnum period.
H = Hostile, i.e., the president's party was not in control of the Senate
U = Unfavorable, i.e., the vacancy occurred during the president's last full year in office or during the interregnum period
C = Confirmed
* = Chief Justice nomination.

Supreme Court Nominations 1789-1988

Nominee	Nominating President	Approximate Date of Nomination	Senate	Time	Outcome
John Jay (Fd)*	Washington (Fd)	Sept. 24, 1789	F	F	C
William Cushing (Fd)	Washington (Fd)	"	F	F	C
John Rutledge (Fd)*	Washington (Fd)	"	F	F	C
James Wilson (Fd)	Washington (Fd)	"	F	F	C

Supreme Court Nominations, 1789-1988 (continued)

Nominee	Nominating President	Approximate Date of Nomination	Senate	Time	Outcome
Robert Harrison (Fd)	Washington (Fd)	"	F	F	C
John Blair (Fd)	Washington (Fd)	"	F	F	C
James Iredell (Fd)	Washington (Fd)	Feb. 9, 1790	F	F	C
Thomas Johnson (Fd)	Washington (Fd)	Nov. 1, 1790	F	F	C
William Paterson (Fd)	Washington (Fd)	Mar. 4, 1793	F	F	C
John Rutledge (Fd)	Washington (Fd)	Nov. 5, 1795	F	F	Rejected
William Cushing (Fd)	Washington (Fd)	Jan. 26, 1796	F	F	C (declined)
Samuel Chase (Fd)	Washington (Fd)	Jan. 26, 1796	F	U	C
Oliver Ellsworth (Fd)*	Washington (Fd)	Mar. 3, 1796	F	U	C
Bushrod Washington (Fd)	Adams (Fd)	Dec. 19, 1798	F	F	C
Alfred Moore (Fd)	Adams (Fd)	Dec. 6, 1799	F	F	C
John Jay (Fd)	Adams (Fd)	Dec. 18, 1800	F	U	C
John Marshall (Fd)*	Adams (Fd)	Jan. 20, 1801	F	U	C
William Johnson (DR)	Jefferson (DR)	Mar. 22, 1804	F	U	C
Henry B. Livingston (DR)	Jefferson (DR)	Dec. 15, 1806	F	F	C
Thomas Todd (DR)	Jefferson (DR)	Feb. 28, 1807	F	F	C
Levi Lincoln (DR)	Madison (DR)	Jan. 2, 1811	F	F	C
Alexander Wolcott (DR)	Madison (DR)	Feb. 4, 1811	F	F	Rejected
John Quincy Adams (DR)	Madison (DR)	Feb. 21, 1811	F	F	C (declined)
Joseph Story (DR)	Madison (DR)	Nov. 15, 1811	F	F	C
Gabriel Duval (DR)	Madison (DR)	Nov. 15, 1811	F	F	C
Smith Thompson (DR)	Monroe (DR)	Dec. 8, 1823	F	F	C
Robert Trimble (NR)	John Q. Adams (DR)	Apr. 11, 1826	F	F	C
John Crittenden (W)	John Q. Adams (DR)	Dec. 18, 1828	H	U	Postponed
John McLean (D)	Jackson (D)	Mar. 6, 1829	F	F	C
Henry Baldwin (D)	Jackson (D)	Jan. 5, 1830	F	F	C
James Wayne (D)	Jackson (D)	Jan. 7, 1835	F	F	C
Roger Taney (D)	Jackson (D)	Jan. 15, 1835	H	F	Postponed
Roger Taney (D)*	Jackson (D)	Dec. 28, 1835	F	F	C
Philip Barbour (D)	Jackson (D)	Dec. 28, 1835	F	F	C
William Smith (D)	Jackson/Van Buren	Mar. 3, 1837	F	F	C (declined)
John Catron (D)	Jackson/Van Buren	Mar. 3, 1837	F	F	C
John McKinley (D)	Van Buren (D)	Sep. 18, 1837	F	F	C
Peter Daniel (D)	Van Buren (D)	Feb. 27, 1841	F	U	C
John Spencer (W)	Tyler (D)	Jan. 9, 1844	H	U	Rejected

Supreme Court Nominations, 1789-1988 (continued)

Nominee	Nominating President	Approximate Date of Nomination	Senate	Time	Outcome
Reuben Walworth (D)	Tyler (D)	Mar. 3, 1844	H	U	Postponed Withdrawn
Edward King (D)	Tyler (D)	June 5, 1844	H	U	Postponed Withdrawn
Samuel Nelson (D)	Tyler (D)	Feb. 6, 1845	H	U	C
John Read (D)	Tyler (D)	Feb. 7, 1845	H	U	No action
George Woodward (D)	Polk (D)	Dec. 23, 1845	F	F	Rejected
Levi Woodbury (D)	Polk (D)	Dec. 23, 1845	F	F	C
Robert Grier (D)	Polk (D)	Aug. 3, 1846	F	F	C
Benjamin Curtis (W)	Fillmore (W)	Dec. 11, 1851	H	F	C
Edward Bradford (W)	Fillmore (W)	Aug. 16, 1852	H	U	No action
George Badger (W)	Fillmore (W)	Jan. 10, 1853	H	U	Postponed
William Micou (W)	Fillmore (W)	Feb. 24, 1853	H	U	No action
John Campbell (D)	Pierce (D)	Mar. 21, 1853	F	F	C
Nathan Clifford (D)	Buchanan (D)	Dec. 9, 1857	F	F	C
Jeremiah Black (D)	Buchanan (D)	Feb. 6, 1861	H	U	Postponed
Noah Swayne (R)	Lincoln (R)	Jan. 22, 1862	F	F	C
Samuel Miller (R)	Lincoln (R)	July 16, 1862	F	F	C
David Davis (R)	Lincoln (R)	Dec. 1, 1862	F	F	C
Stephen Field (D)	Lincoln (R)	Mar. 7, 1863	F	F	C
Salmon Chase (R)*	Lincoln (R)	Dec. 6, 1864	F	F	C
Henry Stanbery (R)	Johnson (D)	Apr. 16, 1866	H	F	No action
Ebenezer Hoar (R)	Grant (R)	Dec. 15, 1869	F	F	Rejected
Edwin Stanton (R)	Grant (R)	Dec. 20, 1869	F	F	C
William Strong (R)	Grant (R)	Feb. 8, 1870	F	F	C
Joseph Bradley (R)	Grant (R)	Feb. 8, 1870	F	F	C
Ward Hunt (R)	Grant (R)	Dec. 6, 1872	F	F	C
George Williams (R)	Grant (R)	Dec. 2, 1873	F	F	Withdrawn
Caleb Cushing (R)	Grant (R)	Jan. 9, 1874	F	F	Withdrawn
Morrison Waite (R)*	Grant (R)	Jan. 19, 1874	F	F	C
John M. Harlan (R)	Hayes (R)	Oct. 17, 1877	F	F	C
William Woods (R)	Hayes (R)	Dec. 15, 1880	H	U	C
Stanley Matthews (R)	Hayes (R)	Jan. 26, 1881	H	U	No action
Stanley Matthews (R)	Garfield (R)	Mar. 18, 1881	H	F	C
Horace Gray (R)	Arthur (R)	Dec. 19, 1881	H	F	C

Supreme Court Nominations, 1789-1988 (continued)

Nominee	Nominating President	Approximate Date of Nomination	Senate	Time	Outcome
Roscoe Conkling (R)	Arthur (R)	Feb. 24, 1882	H	F	C
Samuel Blatchford (R)	Arthur (R)	Mar. 13, 1883	F	F	C
Lucius Lamar (D)	Cleveland (D)	Dec. 12, 1887	H	F	C
Melville Fuller (D)*	Cleveland (D)	May 2, 1888	H	U	C
David Brewer (R)	Harrison (R)	Dec. 4, 1889	F	F	C
Henry Brown (R)	Harrison (R)	Dec. 23, 1890	F	F	C
George Shiras, Jr. (R)	Harrison (R)	July 19, 1892	F	U	C
Howell Jackson (D)	Harrison (R)	Feb. 2, 1893	F	U	C
William Hornblower (D)	Cleveland (D)	Sept. 19, 1893	F	F	Rejected
Wheeler Peckham (D)	Cleveland (D)	Jan. 22, 1894	F	F	Rejected
Edward White (D)	Cleveland (D)	Feb. 19, 1894	F	F	C
Rufus Peckham (D)	Cleveland (D)	Dec. 3, 1895	H	F	C
Joseph McKenna (R)	McKinley (R)	Dec. 16, 1897	H	F	C
Oliver Holmes (R)	Roosevelt (R)	Dec. 2, 1902	F	F	C
William Day (R)	Roosevelt (R)	Feb. 19, 1903	F	F	C
William Moody (R)	Roosevelt (R)	Dec. 3, 1906	F	F	C
Horace Lurton (D)	Taft (R)	Dec. 13, 1909	F	F	C
Edward White (D)*	Taft (R)	Dec. 12, 1910	F	F	C
Charles Hughes (R)	Taft (R)	Apr. 25, 1910	F	F	C
Willis VanDevanter (R)	Taft (R)	Dec. 12, 1910	F	F	C
Joseph Lamar (D)	Taft (R)	Dec. 12, 1910	F	F	C
Mahlon Pitney (R)	Taft (R)	Feb. 19, 1912	F	U	C
James McReynolds (D)	Wilson (D)	Aug. 19, 1914	F	F	C
Louis Brandeis (D)	Wilson (D)	Jan. 28, 1916	F	U	C
John Clarke (D)	Wilson (D)	July 14, 1916	F	U	C
William Taft (R)*	Harding (R)	June 30, 1921	F	F	C
George Sutherland (R)	Harding (R)	Sept. 5, 1922	F	F	C
Pierce Butler (D)	Harding (R)	Nov. 23, 1922	F	F	C
Edward Sanford (R)	Harding (R)	Jan. 24, 1923	F	F	C
Harlan Stone (R)	Coolidge (R)	Jan. 5, 1925	F	F	C
Charles Hughes (R)*	Hoover (R)	Feb. 3, 1930	F	F	C
John Parker (R)	Hoover (R)	Mar. 21, 1930	F	F	Rejected
Owen Roberts (R)	Hoover (R)	May 9, 1930	F	F	C
Benjamin Cardozo (D)	Hoover (R)	Feb. 15, 1932	F	U	C
Hugo Black (D)	Roosevelt (D)	Aug. 12, 1937	F	F	C

Supreme Court Nominations, 1789-1988 (continued)

Nominee	Nominating President	Approximate Date of Nomination	Senate	Time	Outcome
Stanley Reed (D)	Roosevelt (D)	Jan. 15, 1938	F	F	C
Felix Frankfurter (D)	Roosevelt (D)	Jan. 5, 1939	F	F	C
William Douglas (D)	Roosevelt (D)	Mar. 20, 1939	F	F	C
Frank Murphy (D)	Roosevelt (D)	Jan. 4, 1940	F	U	C
Harlan Stone (R)	Roosevelt (D)	June 12, 1941	F	F	C
James Byrnes (D)	Roosevelt (D)	June 12, 1941	F	F	C
Robert Jackson (D)	Roosevelt (D)	June 12, 1941	F	F	C
Wiley Rutledge (D)	Roosevelt (D)	Jan. 11, 1943	F	F	C
Harold Burton (R)	Truman (D)	Sept. 19, 1945	F	F	C
Fred Vinson (D)*	Truman (D)	June 6, 1946	F	F	C
Tom Clark (D)	Truman (D)	Aug. 2, 1949	F	F	C
Sherman Minton (D)	Truman (D)	Sept. 15, 1949	F	F	C
Earl Warren (R)*	Eisenhower (R)	Sept. 30 1953	F	F	C
John M. Harlan (R)	Eisenhower (R)	Jan. 10, 1955	H	F	C
William Brennan (D)	Eisenhower (R)	Oct. 16, 1956	H	U	C
Charles Whittaker (R)	Eisenhower (R)	Mar. 2, 1957	H	F	C
Potter Steward (R)	Eisenhower (R)	Jan. 17, 1959	H	F	C
Byron White (D)	Kennedy (D)	Apr. 3, 1962	F	F	C
Arthur Goldberg (D)	Kennedy (D)	Aug. 31, 1962	F	F	C
Abe Fortas (D)	Johnson (D)	July 28, 1965	F	F	C
Thrugood Marshall (D)	Johnson (D)	June 13, 1967	F	F	C
Abe Fortas (D)*	Johnson (D)	June 26, 1968	F	U	Withdrawn
Warren Burger (R)*	Nixon (R)	May 21, 1969	H	F	C
Clement Haynsworth (R)	Nixon (R)	Aug. 18, 1969	H	F	Rejected
G. Harrold Carswell (R)	Nixon (R)	Jan. 19, 1970	H	F	Rejected
Harry Blackmun (R)	Nixon (R)	Apr. 14, 1970	H	F	C
Lewis F. Powell (D)	Nixon (R)	Oct. 21, 1970	H	F	C
William H. Rehnquist (R)	Nixon (R)	Oct. 21, 1970	H	F	C
John Paul Stevens (R)	Ford (R)	Dec. 1, 1975	H	F	C
Sandra Day O'Connor (R)	Reagan (R)	Aug. 19, 1981	F	F	C
William H. Rehnquist*	Reagan (R)	June 17, 1986	F	F	C
Antonin Scalia	Reagan (R)	June 17, 1986	F	F	C
Robert H. Bork	Reagan (R)	July 2, 1987	H	F	Rejected
Douglas H. Ginsburg	Reagan (R)	Oct. 20, 1987	H	F	Withdrawn
Anthony M. Kennedy	Reagan (R)	Nov. 12, 1987	H	F	C

APPENDIX 2

THE IDEOLOGY INDEX AND SENATE
VOTING ON THE FORTAS, HAYNSWORTH,
AND CARSWELL NOMINATIONS

The roll call data employed to construct the ideology index are drawn from the *Congressional Quarterly Almanac*. The *Almanac* for 1968 provides the data employed to construct the index for those senators taking part in the cloture vote on the Fortas nomination. Data employed to construct the index for those senators voting on the Haynsworth and Carswell nominations are drawn from the *Almanac* for 1969. For the Fortas case, the index represents the percentage of time each senator voted in behalf of the interests of lower or less privileged economic and social groups in the United States on fifteen selected roll calls occurring in 1968. For the Haynsworth and Carswell cases, the index is based upon twelve roll calls in the Senate during 1969 which involved the interests of lower or less privileged groups. In constructing the index for both 1968 and 1969, live pairs, announcements for or against, and responses to the *Congressional Quarterly* poll have been counted along with the recorded votes on each roll call. A failure to vote or otherwise be recorded on the roll call lowers an individual senator's score.

Congressional Quarterly assigns each roll call appearing in the *Almanac* a specific identifying number. Knowing the roll call number and consulting the *Almanac* will enable the reader to ascertain the specific nature of the roll calls used.

For 1968, fifteen selected roll calls were used. Those for which a "yea" vote was designated the liberal response were: 8 (motion to invoke cloture on an open housing provision), 32 (appropriation for the Head Start program), 67 (amendment to exempt spending for the war on poverty, and other related programs from spending cuts), 105, 106, 107, 117 (all amendments deleting conservative provisions from the Omnibus Crime Bill) and 135 (amendment to delete language from an agriculture bill that would reduce funds available for food distribution programs). Those for which a "nay" vote was designated the liberal response were: 9 and 12 (amendments to exempt all privately owned single-family housing from various open housing provisions), 20 (amendment to provide penalties of fine and imprisonment for those assisting others in using firearms in civil disorders), 76 (adoption of a conference report reducing funding for youth manpower training programs and for Head Start), 171 (amendment to delete authorization for the Federal Trade Commission to seek temporary restraining orders to prevent fraudulent or deceptive practices affecting the consumer), 174 (amendment to transfer the Head Start program to the Office of Education from the Office of Economic Opportunity), and 183 (amendment to reduce appropriations for model city grants and urban renewal projects).

For 1969, twelve roll calls were used. Those for which a "yea" vote was designated the liberal response were: 29 (amendment exempting certain educational assistance programs from the fiscal 1970 spending ceiling), 30 (amendment exempting health activities of HEW from the spending ceiling), 84 (authorization of free food stamps for needy families), 126 (amendment increasing funds for urban renewal), 142 (amendment reducing the depletion allowance on oil and gas), 150 (amendment allowing tax-exempt foundations to finance nonpartisan voter registration drives in more than one state), 156 (amendment increasing social security payments and funding), 218 (amendment increasing appropriations for the Office of Economic Opportunity), 220 (amendment adding "except as required by the Constitution" to school desegregation provisions), and 222 (amendment deleting from the Labor/HEW appropriation bill the provision dealing with campus disorders). Those for which a "nay" vote was designated the liberal response were: 102 (amendment giving Governors veto power over legal services projects) and 104 (amendment cutting funding for the Office of Economic Opportunity)

While the designation whether a "yea" or "nay" vote represented the liberal response was made by the writer, this interpretation was cross-checked by ascertaining the positions of the Americans for Democratic Action (ADA), a liberal interest group, and the Americans for Constitutional Action (ACA), a conservative interest group, on each of the roll calls used. For every roll call employed the response designated as "liberal" was in accordance with the ADA's stated position and/or in disagreement with the ACA's stance. All data regarding the ADA's and

ACA's positions on the roll calls for 1968 can be found in the *Congressional Quarterly Almanac* for 1968, pp. 868-878. For the positions on the 1969 roll calls, see *Congressional Quarterly Weekly Report*, February 20, 1970, pp. 567-574.

The following tables provide information on the Fortas cloture roll call in 1968 and the Haynsworth and Carswell roll calls in 1969 and 1970 respectively. The ideology index for each senator is recorded as well as his/her vote on the roll call pertinent to the Fortas, Haynsworth, or Carswell nominations. Abbreviations employed in the tables are as follows:

Y = Voted in favor of cloture (Fortas) or confirmation (Haynsworth and Carswell)

N = Voted against cloture or confirmation

? = Absent and unrecorded

— = Announced against cloture or confirmation or responded to *Congressional Quarterly* poll as against

PY = Paired in favor of cloture or confirmation

PN = Paired against cloture or confirmation

X = No index compiled

Ideology Indexes and Senate Voting on the Fortas Cloture Roll Call: 1968

Senator	Index	Vote on Cloture
Democrats		
Anderson (N.M.)	33	Y
Bartlett (Alaska)	80	?
Bayh (Ind.)	60	Y
Bible (Nev.)	13	—
Brewster (Md.)	60	Y
Burdick (N.D.)	87	Y
Byrd, Jr., (Va.)	0	N
Byrd (W.Va.)	20	N
Cannon (Nev.)	40	N
Church (Idaho)	53	PY
Clark (Pa.)	93	Y
Dodd (Conn.)	60	N
Eastland (Miss.)	0	N
Ellender (La.)	13	—
Ervin (N.C.)	0	N

Ideology Indexes and Senate Voting on the Fortas Cloture Roll Call: 1968 (continued)

Senator	Index	Vote on Cloture
Fulbright (Ark.)	13	N
Gore (Tenn.)	27	Y
Gruening (Alaska)	87	PN
Harris (Okla.)	73	Y
Hart (Mich.)	93	Y
Hartke (Ind.)	67	Y
Hayden (Ariz.)	7	Y
Hill (Ala.)	7	N
Holland (Fla.)	7	N
Hollings (S.C.)	13	N
Inouye (Hawaii)	93	Y
Jackson (Wash.)	73	Y
Jordan (N.C.)	0	N
Kennedy (Mass.)	73	Y
Lausche (Ohio)	20	N
Long (La.)	13	N
Long (Mo.)	53	?
McCarthy (Minn.)	87	Y
McClellan (Ark.)	0	N
McGee (Wyo.)	53	Y
McGovern (S.D.)	40	?
McIntyre (N.H.)	73	Y
Magnuson (Wash.)	67	Y
Mansfield (Mont.)	40	Y
Metcalf (Mont.)	100	Y
Mondale (Minn.)	73	Y
Monroney (Okla.)	47	Y
Montoya (N.M.)	47	Y
Morse (Ore.)	93	PY
Moss (Utah)	80	Y
Muskie (Maine)	93	Y
Nelson (Wis.)	67	Y
Pastore (R.I.)	83	Y
Pell (R.I.)	87	Y
Proxmire (Wis.)	67	Y
Randolph (W.Va.)	67	Y
Ribicoff (Conn.)	73	Y

Ideology Indexes and Senate Voting on the Fortas Cloture Roll Call: 1968
(continued)

Senator	Index	Vote on Cloture
Russell (Ga.)	7	N
Smathers (Fla.)	7	?
Sparkman (Ala.)	13	N
Spong (Va.)	33	N
Stennis (Miss.)	7	N
Symington (Mo.)	67	Y
Talmadge (Ga.)	7	N
Tydings (Md.)	93	Y
Williams (N.J.)	93	Y
Yarborough (Tex.)	80	Y
Young (Ohio)	93	Y
Republicans		
Aiken (Vt.)	53	—
Allott (Colo.)	13	N
Baker (Tenn.)	33	N
Bennett (Utah)	0	N
Boggs (Del.)	53	N
Brooke (Mass.)	87	Y
Carlson (Kan.)	7	N
Case (N.J.)	100	Y
Cooper (Ky.)	73	Y
Cotton (N.H.)	33	N
Curtis (Neb.)	7	N
Dirksen (Ill.)	13	N
Dominick (Colo.)	33	Y
Fannin (Ariz.)	7	N
Fong (Hawaii)	60	N
Goodell (N.Y.)	X	Y
Griffin (Mich.)	53	N
Hansen (Wyo.)	7	N
Hatfield (Ore.)	87	Y
Hickenlooper (Idaho)	0	N
Hruska (Neb.)	7	N
Javits (N.Y.)	93	Y
Jordan (Idaho)	20	N
Kuchel (Calif.)	53	Y

Ideology Indexes and Senate Voting on the Fortas Cloture Roll Call: 1968 (continued)

Senator	Index	Vote on Cloture
Miller (Iowa)	13	N
Morton (Ky.)	47	?
Mundt (S.D.)	0	N
Murphy (Calif.)	20	N
Pearson (Kan.)	27	N
Percy (Ill.)	80	Y
Prouty (Vt.)	40	N
Scott (Pa.)	60	Y
Smith (Maine)	20	—
Thurmond (S.C.)	0	N
Tower (Tex.)	0	N
Williams (Del.)	0	N
Young (N.D.)	7	N

Ideology Indexes and Senate Voting on the Haynsworth and Carswell Roll Calls: 1969-1970

Senator	Index	Haynsworth Nomination	Carswell Nomination
Democrats			
Allen (Ala.)	8	Y	Y
Anderson (N.M.)	25	N	?
Bayh (Ind.)	100	N	N
Bible (Nev.)	42	N	Y
Burdick (N.D.)	83	N	N
Byrd, Jr. (Va.)	0	Y	Y
Byrd (W.Va.)	42	Y	Y
Cannon (Nev.)	50	N	N
Church (Idaho)	75	N	N
Cranston (Calif.)	75	N	N
Dodd (Conn.)	83	N	N
Eagleton (Mo.)	100	N	N
Eastland (Miss.)	0	Y	Y
Ellender (La.)	0	Y	Y
Ervin (N.C.)	0	Y	Y

Ideology Indexes and Senate Voting on the Haynsworth and Carswell Roll Calls: 1969-1970
(continued)

Senator	Index	Haynsworth Nomination	Carswell Nomination
Fulbright (Ark.)	67	Y	N
Gore (Tenn.)	75	N	N
Gravel (Alaska)	92	Y	N
Harris (Okla.)	83	N	N
Hart (Mich.)	100	N	N
Hartke (Ind.)	100	N	N
Holland (Fla.)	0	Y	Y
Hollings (S.C.)	50	Y	Y
Hughes (Iowa)	100	N	N
Inouye (Hawaii)	92	N	N
Jackson (Wash.)	100	N	N
Jordan (N.C.)	0	Y	Y
Kennedy (Mass.)	100	N	N
Long (La.)	0	Y	Y
McCarthy (Minn.)	100	N	N
McClellan (Ark.)	8	Y	Y
McGee (Wyo.)	67	N	N
McGovern (S.D.)	100	N	N
McIntyre (N.H.)	83	N	N
Magnuson (Wash.)	75	N	N
Mansfield (Mont.)	58	N	N
Metcalf (Mont.)	100	N	N
Mondale (Minn.)	92	N	N
Montoya (N.M.)	83	N	N
Moss (Utah)	92	N	N
Muskie (Maine)	83	N	N
Nelson (Wis.)	100	N	N
Pastore (R.I.)	92	N	N
Pell (R.I.)	100	N	PN
Proxmire (Wis.)	67	N	N
Randolph (W.Va.)	75	Y	Y
Ribicoff (Conn.)	92	N	N
Russell (Ga.)	17	Y	Y
Sparkman (Ala.)	0	Y	Y
Spong (Va.)	67	Y	N

Ideology Indexes and Senate Voting on the Haynsworth and Carswell Roll Calls: 1969-1970
(continued)

Senator	Index	Haynsworth Nomination	Carswell Nomination
Stennis (Miss.)	0	Y	Y
Symington (Mo.)	75	N	N
Talmadge (Ga.)	0	Y	Y
Tydings (Md.)	100	N	N
Williams (N.J.)	100	N	N
Yarborough (Tex.)	92	N	N
Young (Ohio)	100	N	N
Republicans			
Aiken (Vt.)	58	Y	Y
Allott (Colo.)	0	Y	Y
Baker (Tenn.)	25	Y	Y
Bellmon (Okla.)	17	Y	Y
Bennett (Utah)	0	Y	PY
Boggs (Del.)	33	Y	Y
Brooke (Mass.)	92	N	N
Case (N.J.)	92	N	N
Cook (Ky.)	58	Y	N
Cooper (Ky.)	17	N	Y
Cotton (N.H.)	17	Y	Y
Curtis (Neb.)	0	Y	Y
Dole (Kan.)	25	Y	Y
Dominick (Colo.)	33	Y	Y
Fannin (Ariz.)	0	Y	Y
Fong (Hawaii)	42	Y	N
Goldwater (Ariz.)	0	Y	Y
Goodell (N.Y.)	83	N	N
Griffin (Mich.)	42	N	Y
Gurney (Fla.)	0	Y	Y
Hansen (Wyo.)	0	Y	Y
Hatfield (Ore.)	83	N	N
Hruska (Neb.)	0	Y	Y
Javits (N.Y.)	92	N	N
Jordan (Idaho)	17	N	Y

Ideology Indexes and Senate Voting on the Haynsworth and Carswell Roll Calls: 1969-1970
(continued)

Senator	Index	Haynsworth Nomination	Carswell Nomination
Mathias (Md.)	83	N	N
Miller (Iowa)	8	N	Y
Mundt (S.D.)	0	Y	—
Murphy (Calif.)	25	Y	Y
Packwood (Ore.)	50	N	N
Pearson (Kan.)	33	Y	Y
Percy (Ill.)	75	N	N
Prouty (Vt.)	67	Y	N
Saxbe (Ohio)	50	N	Y
Schweiker (Pa.)	83	N	N
Scott (Pa.)	67	N	Y
Smith (Ill.)	30	Y	Y
Smith (Maine)	17	N	N
Stevens (Ark.)	50	Y	Y
Thurmond (S.C.)	0	Y	Y
Tower (Tex.)	0	Y	Y
Williams (Del.)	8	N	Y
Young (N.D.)	0	Y	Y

APPENDIX III

THE FOLLOWING TABLE indicates Senate voting on the Bork nomination as well as the Conservative Coalition Opposition scores of each senator. Abbreviations employed are:

Y = voted in favor of confirmation
N = voted against confirmation.

Coalition Scores and Senate Voting on the Bork Roll Call

Senator	Coalition Score	Vote on Bork
Democrats		
Adams (Wash.)	93	N
Baucus (Mont.)	56	N
Bentsen (Tex.)	31	N
Biden (Del.)	90	N
Bingaman (N.M.)	41	N
Boren (Okla.)	3	Y
Bradley (N.J.)	60	N
Breaux (La.)	19	N
Bumpers (Ark.)	61	N
Burdick (N.D.)	75	N
Byrd (W.Va.)	56	N
Chiles (Fla.)	16	N
Conrad (N.D.)	53	N
Cranston (Calif.)	90	N
Daschle (S.D.)	55	N
DeConcini (Ariz.)	63	N
Dixon (Ill.)	16	N

Coalition Scores and Senate Voting on the Bork Roll Call
(continued)

Senator	Coalition Score	Vote on Bork
Dodd (Conn.)	68	N
Exon (Neb.)	28	N
Ford (Ky.)	34	N
Fowler (Ga.)	47	N
Glenn (Ohio)	70	N
Gore (Tenn.)	73	N
Graham (Fla.)	44	N
Harkin (Iowa)	84	N
Heflin (Ala.)	6	N
Hollings (S.C.)	12	Y
Inouye (Hawaii)	57	N
Johnston (La.)	12	N
Kennedy (Mass.)	93	N
Kerry (Mass.)	90	N
Lautenberg (N.J.)	79	N
Leahy (Vt.)	90	N
Levin (Mich.)	71	N
Matsunaga (Hawaii)	75	N
Melcher (Mont.)	56	N
Metzenbaum (Ohio)	97	N
Mikulski (Md.)	87	N
Mitchell (Maine)	69	N
Moynihan (N.Y.)	81	N
Nunn (Ga.)	6	N
Pell (R.I.)	81	N
Proxmire (Wis.)	69	N
Pryor (Ark.)	46	N
Reid (Nev.)	56	N
Riegle (Mich.)	81	N
Rockefeller (W.Va.)	72	N
Sanford (N.C.)	55	N
Sarbanes (Md.)	94	N
Sasser (Tenn.)	62	N
Shelby (Ala.)	17	N
Simon (Ill.)	78	N

Coalition Scores and Senate Voting on the Bork Roll Call
(continued)

Senator	Coalition Score	Vote on Bork
Stennis (Miss.)	15	N
Wirth (Colo.)	56	N
Republicans		
Armstrong (Wash.)	6	Y
Bond (Mo.)	0	Y
Boschwitz (Minn.)	16	Y
Chafee (R.I.)	69	N
Cochran (Miss.)	3	Y
Cohen (Maine)	37	Y
D'Amato (N.Y.)	29	Y
Danford (Mo.)	20	Y
Dole (Kan.)	7	Y
Domenici (N.M.)	12	Y
Durenberger (Minn.)	52	Y
Evans (Wash.)	37	Y
Garn (Utah)	3	Y
Gramm (Tex.)	13	Y
Grassley (Iowa)	31	Y
Hatch (Utah)	6	Y
Hatfield (Ore.)	58	Y
Hecht (Nev.)	16	Y
Heinz (Pa.)	43	Y
Helms (N.C.)	3	Y
Humphrey (N.H.)	16	Y
Karnes (Neb.)	3	Y
Kassebaum (Kan.)	23	Y
Kasten (Wis.)	9	Y
Lugar (Ind.)	14	Y
McCain (Ariz.)	27	Y
McClure (Idaho)	0	Y
McConnell (Ky.)	6	Y
Murkowski (Alaska)	7	Y
Nickels (Okla.)	9	Y
Packwood (Ore.)	57	N
Pressler (S.D.)	13	Y

Coalition Scores and Senate Voting on the Bork Roll Call
(continued)

Senator	Coalition Score	Vote on Bork
Quayle (Ind.)	10	Y
Roth (Del.)	12	Y
Rudman (N.H.)	7	Y
Simpson (Wyo.)	14	Y
Specter (Pa.)	59	N
Stafford (Vt.)	66	N
Stevens (Alaska)	19	Y
Symms (Idaho)	0	Y
Thurmond (S.C.)	16	Y
Trible (Va.)	9	Y
Wallop (Wyo.)	3	Y
Warner (Va.)	10	N
Weicker (Conn.)	67	N
Wilson (Calif.)	22	Y

NOTES

IN THE FOLLOWING notes, four abbreviations have been employed: "LBJL" for the Lyndon Baines Johnson Library, Austin, Texas; "NPMP" for the Nixon Presidential Materials Project, Washington, D.C.; "RBRML" for the Richard B. Russell Memorial Library, Athens, Georgia; and "WHCF" for White House Central Files. Additionally, references to "Files Pertaining to Fortas and Thornberry" have been shortened to "Fortas/Thornberry Files."

INTRODUCTION

1. U. S., Constitution, Art. 2, sec. 2, cl. 2 states that the president "shall nominate, and by and with the advice and consent of the Senate, shall appoint . . . Judges of the Supreme Court."

2. There has been some confusion in the literature regarding how many Supreme Court nominations have been made as well as how many have been refused confirmation by the Senate. This confusion stems in part from how one counts resubmitted nominations of the same individual for the same vacancy as well as what one considers a "refusal to confirm" by the Senate. In the text, "refusal to confirm" refers to occasions when the Senate rejects a nominee outright, postpones action on the nomination causing the president to withdraw it, postpones action on the nomination and fails to act further, or fails to take any action whatsoever on the nomination. Individuals nominated more than once for the same vacancy by the same president and subsequently refused confirmation are counted as one refusal to confirm. Individuals nominated more than once for the same vacancy and subsequently confirmed are not counted as a refusal to confirm. However, Stanley Matthews, refused confirmation and subsequently nominated for the same vacancy by a *different* president and confirmed, is counted as one refusal to confirm. Not counting the nomination of Homer Thornberry, contingent upon Fortas's confirmation as chief justice, and George Washington's withdrawal of the nomination of William

Patterson because of a constitutional disqualification, there have been twenty-six refusals to confirm as of 1988.

3. Samuel Krislov, *The Supreme Court in the Political Process* (New York: The Macmillan Company, 1965), p. 13. With the single exception of the rejection of John Parker in 1930, the Senate, up to 1965, had not refused to confirm a Supreme Court nominee since it rejected Wheeler Peckham in 1894.

4. The literature on Supreme Court nominations is extensive but the following sources deal directly with the factors associated with unsuccessful nominations: John P. Frank, "The Appointment of Supreme Court Justices: Prestige, Principles and Politics," *Wisconsin Law Review*, 1941 (July, 1941); Daniel S. McHargue, "Appointments to the Supreme Court of the United States: The Factors That Have Affected Appointments (1789-1932)" (unpublished Ph.D. dissertation, University of California, Los Angeles, 1949); William F. Swindler, "The Politics of 'Advice and Consent,'" *American Bar Association Journal*, 56 (June, 1970); Henry J. Abraham and Edward M. Goldberg, "A Note on the Appointment of Justices of Supreme Court of the United States," *American Bar Association Journal*, 46 (February, 1960); Kenneth C. Cole, "The Role of the Senate in the Confirmation of Judicial Nominations," *American Political Science Review*, 28 (1934); Cortez A. M. Ewing, *The Judges of the Supreme Court: A Study of Their Qualifications* (Minneapolis: The University of Minnesota Press, 1938); George H. Haynes, *The Senate of the United States: Its History and Practice* (Boston: Houghton Mifflin Company, 1938); Joseph P. Harris, *The Advice and Consent of the Senate: A Study of the Confirmation of Appointments by the United States Senate* (Berkley: University of California Press, 1953); Richard K. Burke, "The Path to the Court: A Study of Federal Judicial Appointments" (unpublished Ph.D. dissertation, Vanderbilt University, 1958); Glendon A. Schubert, *Constitutional Politics: The Political Behavior of Supreme Court Justices and the Constitutional Policies That They Make* (New York: Holt, Rinehart & Winston, Inc., 1960); John R. Schmidhauser, *The Supreme Court: Its Politics, Personalities, and Procedures* (New York: Holt, Rinehart & Winston, 1960); David J. Danelski, *A Supreme Court Justice is Appointed* (New York: Random House, 1964); Samuel Krislov, *The Supreme Court in the Political Process* (New York: The Macmillan Co., 1965); Joel B. Grossman and Stephen Wasby, "Haynsworth and Parker: History Does Live Again," *South Carolina Law Review*, 23, no. 3 (1971); Robert Scigliano, *The Supreme Court and the Presidency* (New York: The Free Press, 1971); John R. Schmidhauser and Larry L. Berg, *The Supreme Court and Congress* (New York: The Free Press, 1972); Henry J. Abraham, *Justices and Presidents: A Political History of Appointments to the Supreme Court* (2d edition; New York: Oxford University Press, 1985); and Jeffrey A. Segal and Harold J. Spaeth, "If a Supreme Court Vacancy Occurs, Will the Senate Confirm a Reagan Nominee?" *Judicature*, 69, no. 4 (December-January 1986), 186-190.

5. On the Fortas nomination, see Robert Shogan, *A Question of Judgment: The Fortas Case and the Struggle for the Supreme Court* (Indianapolis: The

Bobbs-Merrill Company, 1972) and Bruce Allen Murphy, *Fortas: The Rise and Ruin of a Supreme Court Justice* (New York: William Morrow and Company, Inc., 1988). For an analysis of the factors involved in Haynsworth's rejection, see Joel B. Grossman and Stephen L. Wasby, "The Senate and Supreme Court Nominations: Some Reflections," *Duke Law Journal*, 72 (August, 1972). On the Carswell nomination, see Richard Harris, *Decision* (New York: E. P. Dutton and Co., 1971).

6. Jerome Corsi, *Judicial Politics: An Introduction* (Englewood Cliffs, New Jersey: Prentice-Hall, Inc., 1984), p. 149.

7. John P. Frank, *Marble Palace: The Supreme Court in American Life* (New York: Alfred A. Knopf, 1958), pp. 8-9.

8. Schmidhauser, p. 6; see also Laurence H. Tribe, *God Save This Honorable Court: How the Choice of Supreme Court Justices Shapes Our History* (New York: New American Library, 1986).

9. Henry J. Abraham, *The Judicial Process: An Introductory Analysis of the Courts of the United States, England and France* (2d ed. rev.; New York: Oxford University Press, 1968), p. 86. I am aware in later editions Abraham reconsiders his conclusion regarding the lack of opposition to Supreme Court nominees on the basis of their qualifications.

10. See Harris, *The Advice and Consent of the Senate*, p. 9.

CHAPTER 1

1. Abe Fortas graduated from the Yale Law School in 1933. In 1946, after extensive experience as an administrator in several New Deal agencies and as a member of the Yale faculty, Fortas and his partners, Thurman Arnold and Paul Porter, began to build Arnold, Fortas and Porter into one of Washington D.C.'s most prestigious law firms. President Lyndon B. Johnson appointed Fortas an associate justice of the Supreme Court in 1965. At the time of his appointment to the Court, Fortas, a Democrat, had earned a reputation as one of the nation's finest and most powerful attorneys. This renown was enhanced by his generally recognized role as an intimate friend and advisor to Lyndon Johnson.

2. Haynsworth, from Greenville, South Carolina, received his degree from Harvard Law School in 1936. In 1957, Republican President Dwight D. Eisenhower appointed him to the United States Court of Appeals for the Fourth Circuit. Although Haynsworth was a Democrat at the time of his appointment to the Court of Appeals, he switched to the GOP in 1964. That same year, he was designated Chief Judge of the Fourth Circuit.

3. Carswell graduated from Mercer University Law School, Macon, Georgia, in 1948. After an unsuccessful bid for a seat in the Georgia state legislature,

he moved to Tallahassee, Florida, in 1949 and began private practice. Carswell had been a Democrat until 1952 when he switched to the GOP and supported Dwight D. Eisenhower for the presidency. In 1953, President Eisenhower appointed him United States Attorney for the Northern District of Florida. Five years later, the thirty-eight-year-old Carswell was named a federal district judge in Florida's Northern District. In May, 1969, President Richard M. Nixon named Carswell to the United States Court of Appeals for the Fifth Circuit.

4. "Ideology" and "philosophy" will be utilized interchangeably to mean an organized, systematic set of beliefs enabling an individual to respond to particular stimuli. As its roots run deep, an individual's ideology is less susceptible to change than other considerations which can influence Senate voting on Supreme Court nominations. See Robert E. Lane, *Political Ideology* (New York: The Free Press of Glencoe, 1962), pp. 13-16.

5. U. S., Congress, Senate, Committee on the Judiciary, *Hearings on the Nomination of Abe Fortas, of Tennessee, to be Chief Justice of the United States and the Nomination of Homer Thornberry, of Texas, to be Associate Justice of the Supreme Court of the United States*, 90th Cong., 2d Sess., 1968, p. 275. Hereafter cited as *Hearings on the Nomination of Fortas.*

6. For an interesting discussion of this point, see Joel B. Grossman and Stephen L. Wasby, "Haynsworth and Parker: History Does Live Again," *South Carolina Law Review*, 23, no. 3 (1971), 345-359.

7. For a complete discussion of each nominee's judicial record, see U. S., Senate, Committee on the Judiciary, *Hearings* relevant to each nomination.

8. 384 U. S. 436 (1966).

9. 389 U. S. 258 (1967).

10. Memorandum from Warren Christopher, Deputy Attorney General, to Larry Temple, Special Counsel to the President, December 20, 1968, Fortas/Thornberry Files, Box 3, LBJL; see also memorandum from Fred Drogula, Staff, Justice Department, to Warren Christopher, July 24, 1968, Christopher Papers, Box 17, LBJL.

11. 323 F. 2d 959 (4th Cir. 1963), *cert. denied*, 376 U. S. 938 (1964).

12. 372 F. 2d 338 (4th Cir. 1967), *rev'd*, 391 U. S. 430 (1968).

13. U. S., Congress, Senate, Committee on the Judiciary, *Hearings on the Nomination of Clement F. Haynsworth, Jr., of South Carolina, to be Associate Justice of the Supreme Court of the United States*, 91st Cong., 1st Sess., 1969, p. 443. Hereafter cited as *Hearings on the Nomination of Haynsworth.*

14. 386 F. 2d 562 (4th Cir. 1967).

15. *Hearings on the Nomination of Haynsworth*, pp. 363-364.

16. 325 F. 2d 682 (4th Cir. 1963), *rev'd*, 380 U. S. 263 (1965).

17. *Hearings on the Nomination of Haynsworth*, p. 364.

18. Unreported decision (N. D. Fla., 1965), *rev'd*, 371 F. 2d 395 (5th Cir. 1967).

19. U. S., Senate, Committee on the Judiciary, *Hearings on the Nomination of G. Harrold Carswell, of Florida, to be Associate Justice of the Supreme Court of the United States*, 91st Cong., 2nd Sess., 1970, pp. 223-224. Hereafter cited as *Hearings on the Nomination of Carswell*.

20. Unreported decision (N. D. Fla., 1964), *rev'd*, 356 F. 2d 771 (5th Cir. 1966).

21. *Hearings on the Nomination of Carswell*, p. 286.

22. See *Black's Law Dictionary*, 4th ed. rev. All subsequent references to specific canons can be found in this source.

23. *Hearings on the Nomination of Fortas*, pp. 1299-1306.

24. Letter from Senator Richard B. Russell to President Johnson, September 26, 1968, Fortas/Thornberry Files, Box 3, LBJL.

25. While opponents of the nomination cited at least five cases, the major case discussed was *Darlington Manufacturing Co. and Deering Milliken v. NLRB*, 325 F. 2d 682 (4th Circ. 1963).

26. U. S., Congress, Senate, Committee on the Judiciary, *Report Together with Individual Views to Accompany the Nomination of Clement F. Haynsworth, Jr.*, Executive Report No. 12, 91st Cong., 1st Sess., November 12, 1969, pp. 24, 40-43. Hereafter cited as *Report on the Nomination of Haynsworth*.

27. The major case cited by opponents was *Brunswick v. Long*, 392 F. 2d 337 (4th Cir. 1968). See *Report on the Nomination of Haynsworth*, pp. 46-47.

28. U. S., *Congressional Record*, 91st Cong., 1st Sess., 1969, p. 29235.

29. *Hearings on the Nomination of Carswell*, 1970, p. 242.

30. U. S., *Congressional Record*, 91st Cong., 2d Sess., 1970, pp. 9607-9610.

31. Carswell's white supremacy speech is reprinted in part in *The New York Times*, January 22, 1970, p. A22.

32. For a more thorough presentation of the charges and rebuttals presented during the Senate's consideration of the nominations, see the following: U. S. Senate, Committee on the Judiciary, *Report Together with Individual Views to*

Accompany the Nomination of Abe Fortas, Executive Report no. 8, 90th Cong., 2d Sess., 1968; *Report on the Nomination of Haynsworth; Report Together with Individual Views to Accompany the Nomination of G. Harrold Carswell*, Executive Report no. 14, 91st Cong., 2d Sess., February 27, 1970. Hereafter these sources will be cited in the shortened form, e. g., *Report on the Nomination of Fortas*, etc.

33. A. Mitchell McConnell, Jr., "Haynsworth and Carswell: A New Senate Standard of Excellence," *Kentucky Law Journal*, 59, no. 1 (Fall, 1970), 13. For similar views, see U. S., *Congressional Record*, 90th Cong., 2d Sess., 1968, p. 28756, and 91st Cong., 1st Sess., 1969, pp. 30661, 33570, 33662; see also President Richard M. Nixon's comment that a nominee's "philosophy" is not a proper basis for Senate rejection of a Supreme Court nomination in *The New York Times*, October 21, 1969, p. A34. For a dissenting view, see Charles L. Black, Jr., "A Note on Senatorial Consideration of Supreme Court Nominees," *The Yale Law Journal*, 79, no. 4 (March, 1970), 663-64.

34. *The New Republic*, November 1, 1969, p. 14. See also *Commonweal*, 91, no. 1 (October 3, 1969), 4.

35. Kenneth M. Dolbeare and Patricia Dolbeare, *American Ideologies: The Competing Political Beliefs of the 1970s*, (Chicago: Markham Publishing Co., 1971), pp. 17ff.

36. Milton C. Cummings, Jr., and Robert L. Peabody, "The Decision to Enlarge the Committee on Rules: An Analysis of the 1961 Vote," *New Perspectives on the House of Representatives*, ed. Robert L. Peabody and Nelson w. Polsby (2d ed., Chicago: Rand McNally and Co., 1969), pp. 257-58; Lawrence K. Pettit, "Constitutional Ambiguity and Legislative Decision Making: The Establishment Clause and Aid to Higher Education," *The Legislative Process in the U. S. Senate*, ed. Lawrence K. Pettit and Edward Keynes (Chicago: Rand McNally and Co., 1969), pp. 266-269.

37. The following discussion of the index of likeness is drawn from Lee F. Anderson, Meredith W. Watts, Jr., and Allen R. Wilcox, *Legislative Roll-Call Analysis* (Northwestern University Press, 1966), pp. 43-45.

38. It should be noted that in controlling for party and comparing "Liberals" and "Conservatives" in each party to each other i.e., Democratic "Liberals" to Democratic "Conservatives" and Republican "Liberals" to Republican "Conservatives," the indexes of likeness for the ideological groups remain substantially lower than the indexes produced when the Senate is divided along party lines.

39. Memorandum from Mike N. Manatos, Administrative Assistant to the President, June 25, 1968, Fortas/Thornberry Files, Box 1, LBJL.

40. Ibid.

41. U. S., *Congressional Record*, 90th Cong., 2d Sess., 1968, p. 23785.

42. Memorandum from Harry C. McPherson, Special Counsel to the President, to Manatos, July 2, 1968, Fortas/Thornberry Files, Box 4, LBJL.

43. *The New York Times*, July 14, 1968, p. 28.

44. U. S., *Congressional Record*, 90th Cong., 2d Sess., 1968, p. 28748.

45. *Report on the Nomination of Fortas*, p. 18.

46. Ibid., p. 20.

47. Memorandum from Manatos to President Johnson, June 25, 1968, Fortas/Thornberry Files, Box 1, LBJL.

48. U. S., *Congressional Record*, 90th Cong., 2d Sess., 1968, p. 28159.

49. Letter from Senator Richard B. Russell to Doctor William T. Bedenhamer, August 19, 1968, Political Patronage Series, Presidential Appointments Subseries, RBRML.

50. U. S., *Congressional Record*, 90th Congress, 2d Sess., 1968, p. 28273.

51. Memorandum from Harold Barefoot Sanders, Jr., Legislative Counsel to the President, to Postmaster General Marvin Watson, July 8, 1968, Fortas/Thornberry Files, Box 2, LBJL.

52. Letter from Senator Spessard L. Holland to Louis J. Hector, July 17, 1968, Fortas/Thornberry Files, Box 2, LBJL.

53. *Report on the Nomination of Fortas*, p. 39.

54. Memorandum from Larry Temple, Special Counsel to the President, to President Johnson, July 2, 1968, Fortas/Thornberry Files, Box 2, LBJL.

55. Letter from Senator Norris Cotton to Eugene F. Bogan (with enclosures), August 20, 1968, Papers of Paul Porter 1968, Box 5, LBJL.

56. Oral history of Senator Everett Dirksen (R, Ill.), March 21, 1969, tape #1, p. 12, LBJL.

57. *Report on the Nomination of Fortas*, p. 42.

58. Memorandum from Drogula to Christopher, July 24, 1968, Christopher Papers, Box 17, LBJL.

59. Memorandum from McPherson to Manatos, September 10, 1968, Fortas/Thornberry Files, Box 3, LBJL and memorandum from Manatos to President Johnson, September 16, 1968, LBJL.

60. Memorandum from Postmaster General Watson to Temple, September 20, 1968, Fortas/Thornberry Files, Box 3, LBJL.

61. Memorandum from Christopher to Temple, December 20, 1968, p. 8, Fortas/Thornberry Files, Box 3, LBJL.

62. Memorandum from Manatos to President Johnson, September 16, 1968, Fortas/Thornberry Files, Box 3, LBJL.

63. U. S., *Congressional Record*, 91st Cong., 1st Sess., 1969, p. 35377.

64. Ibid., p. 28353.

65. Ibid., p. 35376.

66. Ibid., p. 35131.

67. Memorandum from Bryce N. Harlow, Assistant to the President, for the Staff Secretary, November 11, 1969, President's Office Files, Folder "Beginning Nov. 9, 1969," NPMP.

68. Letter from Senator Edward R. Brooke to President Nixon, October 1, 1969, WHCF—FG-51 (Supreme Court), Box 3, NPMP.

69. Memorandum from Jack A. Gleason, Assistant to the Secretary of Commerce, for Harry S. Dent, Special Counsel to the President, November 5, 1969, White House Special Files of Harry S. Dent, Box 6, NPMP.

70. Letter from Senator Strom Thurmond to President Nixon, May 21, 1969, WHCF—FG-51 (Supreme Court), Box 1, NPMP.

71. U. S., *Congressional Record*, 91st Cong., 1st Sess., 1969, p. 35369.

72. Ibid., pp. 28211-12.

73. Ibid., p. 34275.

74. Letter from Peter M. Flanigan, Assistant to the President, to Barry T. Leithead, December 30, 1969, WHCF—FG-51 (Supreme Court), Box 2, NPMP.

75. Letter from John D. Ehrlichman, Counselor to the President, to Warren Parker, November 26, 1969, WHCF—FG-31, Box 4, NPMP.

76. U. S., *Congressional Record*, 91st Cong., 2d Sess., 1970, p. 9780.

77. Ibid., p. 4874.

78. Ibid., p. 8064.

79. Ibid., p. 4962.

80. Ibid., p. 4273.

81. Ibid., p. 2526.

82. Memorandum from William E. Timmons, Assistant to the President for Congressional Relations, to President Nixon, March 20, 1970, President's Office Files, Box 6, NPMP.

83. Memorandum from William H. Rehnquist, Assistant Attorney General, to Attorney General John N. Mitchell, October 12, 1971, White House Special Files of John Dean, Box 70, NPMP.

84. The term "lame-duck" may be offensive to those who correctly maintain the president has the constitutional power to nominate individuals to the Court at any time during his term. Nevertheless, the term was generally employed by several senators who opposed the nomination. See, for example, *The New York Times*, June 22, 1968, p. A1.

85. See *Congressional Quarterly Almanac*, 1968, p. 532 for the identities of the Republican senators who signed the statement.

86. Letter from Senator Howard H. Baker, Jr., to Edwin M. Marks, August 12, 1968, Porter Papers, Box 6, LBJL.

87. Memorandum from Manatos to President Johnson, July 9, 1968, WHCF, Subject File FG-535A, Box 360, LBJL.

88. Robert Shogan, *A Question of Judgment: The Fortas Case and the Struggle for the Supreme Court* (Indianapolis: The Bobbs-Merrill Company, 1972), p. 159. As indicated in the following chapter, Russell had other reasons to oppose the Fortas nomination.

89. John Massaro, " 'Lame-Duck' Presidents, Great Justices?" *Presidential Studies Quarterly*, 8 no. 3 (Summer, 1978).

90. Memorandum from Finley to Christopher, July 3, 1968, Fortas/Thornberry Files, Box 2, LBJL.

91. Memorandum from Sanders to Temple, September 24, 1968, Fortas/Thornberry Files, Box 3, LBJL.

92. *The Courier Journal* (Louisville, Kentucky), October 2, 1968, p. A5.

93. Memoranda from Manatos to President Johnson, September 18, 1968, and September 25, 1968, Fortas/Thornberry Files, Box 3, and Executive and General FG-535A, Box 358, LBJL.

94. Memorandum from Manatos to President Johnson, June 26, 1968, Fortas/Thornberry Files, Box 1, LBJL.

95. Memorandum from Joseph Califano, Special Assistant to the President, to President Johnson, August 13, 1968, Fortas/Thornberry Files, Box 2, LBJL.

96. Memorandum from Sanders to Temple, September 24, 1968, Fortas/Thornberry Files, Box 3, LBJL.

97. Letter from Senator George S. McGovern to John Massaro, December 12, 1973.

98. Memorandum from Manatos to President Johnson, September 16, 1968, Fortas/Thornberry Files, Box 3, LBJL.

99. Memorandum from Manatos to President Johnson, September 25, 1968, Executive and General FG-535A, Box 358, LBJL.

100. Memorandum from Sanders to Temple, September 24, 1968, Fortas/Thornberry Files, Box 3, LBJL.

101. Memorandum from Irv Sprague to Sanders, September 24, 1968, Sanders Papers, Box 19, LBJL.

102. Memorandum from Jim Jones [James R. Jones], Special Assistant to the President, August 22, 1968, Fortas/Thornberry Files, Box 2, LBJL.

103. Memorandum from George Reedy, Special Consultant to the President, to President Johnson, July 2, 1968, Fortas/ Thornberry Files, Box 4, LBJL.

104. Letter from Paul A. Porter to Fred Lazarus, Jr., August 1, 1968, Porter Papers, Box 5, LBJL; see, also, the oral history of Porter, tape #1, pp. 27-28, LBJL.

105. Ibid.

106. Ibid.

107. *The New York Times*, September 15, 1968, p. 76.

108. Oral history of Temple, tape #6, p. 2, LBJL.

109. Oral history of Manatos, tape #1, p. 24, LBJL.

110. Letter from Porter to Thomas R. Mulroy, August 16, 1968, Porter Papers, Box 5, LBJL.

111. Oral history of Homer Thornberry, tape #1, p. 39, LBJL.

112. Oral history of Abe Fortas, p. 33, LBJL.

113. Oral history of Manatos, tape #1, p. 23, LBJL.

114. Memorandum from Irv Sprague to Sanders, September 24, 1968, Sanders Papers, Box 19, LBJL.

115. Letter from Porter to Troy V. Post, October 15, 1968, Porter Papers, Box 3, LBJL.

116. Oral history of Senator Robert Griffin, tape #1, p. 8, LBJL.

CHAPTER 2

1. See also Robert Scigliano, *The Supreme Court and the Presidency* (New York: The Free Press, 1971), p. 96, updated through November, 1987.

2. Prior to the Twentieth Amendment, which went into effect in 1936, the interregnum period extended until March 4 of the year following a presidential election. Under the amendment, the interregnum period now extends only until January 20 of the year following a presidential election.

3. On the key role of ideology and timing in previous unsuccessful Supreme Court nominations, see John R. Schmidhauser and Larry L. Berg, *The Supreme Court and Congress* (New York: The Free Press, 1972), pp. 100-28; Robert Scigliano, *The Supreme Court and the Presidency* (New York: The Free Press, 1971), and Jeffrey A. Segal and Harold J. Spaeth, "If a Supreme Court Vacancy Occurs, Will the Senate Confirm a Reagan Nominee?" *Judicature*, 69, no. 4 (December-January 1986), 186-190.

4. On the long-standing relationship which has existed between party affiliation and ideology, see the following: John R. Schmidhauser, *The Supreme Court: Its Politics, Personalities and Procedures* (New York: Holt, Rinehart and Winston, Inc., 1960), pp. 48 and 61, n. 32; Scigliano, pp. 120-121; and Fred I. Greenstein, *The American Party System and the American People*, 2d ed. (Englewood Cliffs, New Jersey: Prentice-Hall, Inc., 1970), pp. 86-90.

5. In 1866, Democrat President Andrew Johnson's nomination of Henry Stanbery was refused confirmation by the Republican-controlled Senate even though it was made at a favorable time. In 1835, Democrat President Andrew Jackson's controversial nomination of Roger B. Taney to be associate justice was indefinitely postponed by a Senate not controlled by the Democrats.

6. Some of the material on the Fortas nomination presented in this chapter appears in Bruce Allen Murphy, *Fortas: The Rise and Ruin of a Supreme Court Justice* (New York: William Morrow and Company, Inc., 1988). Murphy has kindly acknowledged his reliance on my previous work on the Fortas nomination as well as on the study undertaken by Hugh Jones. For my work, see John L. Massaro, "Advice and Dissent: Factors in the Senate's Refusal to Confirm Supreme

Court Nominees, with Special Emphasis on the Cases of Abe Fortas, Clement F. Haynsworth, Jr., and G. Harrold Carswell," (unpublished Ph.D. dissertation, Southern Illinois University, 1972), and "LBJ and the Fortas Nomination for Chief Justice," *Political Science Quarterly*, 97, no. 4 (Winter 1982-83), 603-21. For the Jones study, see Hugh Jones, "The Defeat of the Nomination of Abe Fortas as Chief Justice of the United States," (unpublished Ph.D. dissertation, Johns Hopkins University, 1976). In drawing upon Murphy's book in adding to and clarifying my analysis of the Fortas case, I gratefully acknowledge my debt to him and Professor Jones.

7. Oral history of Ramsey Clark, interview June 3, 1969, tape #1, p. 19, LBJL.

8. Ibid.

9. Memorandum from Harold Barefoot Sanders, Jr., Legislative Counsel to the President, to Temple, September 24, 1968, Fortas/Thornberry Files, Box 3, LBJL.

10. Memorandum from William T. Finley, Jr., Assistant Deputy Attorney General, to Christopher, July 3, 1968, Fortas/Thornberry Files, Box 2, LBJL.

11. Memorandum from Harry C. McPherson, Jr., Special Counsel to the President, to Mike N. Manatos, Administrative Assistant to the President, September 20, 1968, Fortas/Thornberry Files, Box 3, LBJL.

12. U. S., *Congressional Record*, 90th Cong., 2d Sess., 1968, pp. 28928-29.

13. Daily Diary (of President Johnson), Box 14, March 31, 1968, LBJL.

14. *The New York Times*, April 1, 1968, p. A1.

15. Ibid., June 27, 1968, p. A.30.

16. U. S., *Congressional Record*, 90th Cong., 2d Sess., 1968, p. 10452.

17. Memorandum from Manatos to President Johnson, July 2, 1968, Fortas/Thornberry Files, Box 2, LBJL.

18. Robert Shogan, *A Question of Judgment: The Fortas Case and the Struggle for the Supreme Court* (Indianapolis: The Bobbs-Merrill Company, 1972), p. 162.

19. Oral history of Senator Robert Griffin, tape #1, p. 7, LBJL.

20. See Chief Justice Earl Warren's letter to John Massaro, December 10, 1973, and memorandum from Attorney General Clark to President Johnson, June 24, 1968, Christopher Papers, Box 19, LBJL.

21. Letter from Warren to Massaro, December 10, 1973.

22. Memorandum for the record from James R. Jones, Special Assistant to the President, June 13, 1968, Earl Warren Name File, LBJL.

23. Letter from Warren to President Johnson, June 13, 1968, reprinted in *The New York Times*, June 27, 1968, p. A30. On this point, see Murphy, p. 272.

24. Memorandum from McPherson to President Johnson, June 28, 1968, Office Files of McPherson, LBJL.

25. Letter from President Johnson to Warren, June 26, 1968, reprinted in *The New York Times*, June 27, 1968, p. A.30.

26. Shogan, p. 146.

27. Claudia Anderson, Archivist at The Lyndon Baines Johnson Library has confirmed that the initials "AF" on White House communications during this period signify Abe Fortas.

28. Draft letter from President Johnson to Warren, June 24, 1968, Executive and General FG-535A, Box 358, LBJL.

29. Memorandum from "Jim J" (James R. Jones), June 27, 1968, Fortas/Thornberry Files, Box 4, LBJL. For additional material on this point, see Murphy, pp. 309-310.

30. Murphy, pp. 270-273.

31. Memorandum from Christopher to Temple, December 20, 1968, p. 1, Fortas/Thornberry Files, Box 3, LBJL.

32. Letter from Senator Albert Gore to President Johnson, July 11, 1968, Fortas/Thornberry Files, Box 4, LBJL.

33. *The New Republic*, September 28, 1968, p. 22.

34. Letter from Senator Roman L. Hruska to Louis E. Lipp, July 19, 1968, Papers of Paul Porter, Box 6, LBJL.

35. U.S., Senate, Committee on the Judiciary, *Report Together With Individual Views to Accompany the Nomination of Abe Fortas*, Executive Report No. 8, 90th Cong., 2d Sess., p. 20. Hereafter cited as *Report on the Nomination of Fortas*.

36. Shogan, p. 182.

37. Ibid., p. 149.

38. For example, see Senator Allott's views in memorandum from Manatos to President Johnson, July 2, 1968, Fortas/Thornberry Files, Box 2, LBJL.

39. Shogan, p. 159.

40. Memorandum from McPherson to Manatos, July 2, 1968, Fortas/Thornberry Files, Box 4, LBJL.

41. Memorandum from Sanders to Jones, July 10, 1968, Daily Diary Backup, Box 105, LBJL.

42. *Hearings on the Nomination of Fortas*, p. 46.

43. Houston, Texas, *Tribune*, July 11, 1968, p. 1, included in Porter Papers, Box 6, LBJL.

44. Memorandum from George Reedy, Special Consultant to the President, to President Johnson, July 2, 1968, Fortas/Thornberry Files, Box 4, LBJL.

45. Memorandum from James Gaither, Staff Assistant to Joseph A. Califano, to Joseph A. Califano, Special Assistant to the President, July 2, 1968, Fortas/Thornberry Files, Box 2, LBJL.

46. "Report to Constituents from Senator Norris Cotton," July 25, 1968, included in letter from Cotton to Eugene F. Bogan, August 20, 1968, Porter Papers, 1968, Box 5, LBJL.

47. Memorandum from Sanders to President Johnson, July 2, 1968, Sanders Papers, Box 19, LBJL.

48. Letter from Porter to Fred Lazarus, Jr., August 1, 1968, Porter Papers, Box 5, LBJL.

49. Memorandum from Finley to Christopher, June 28, 1968, Clark Papers, Box 47, LBJL.

50. Oral history of Manatos, tape #1, pp. 39-40, LBJL.

51. Lyndon Baines Johnson, *The Vantage Point: Perspectives of the Presidency 1963-1969* (New York: Holt, Rinehart, and Winston, 1971), p. 545.

52. Memorandum from McPherson to President Johnson, June 24, 1968, FG-535, Box 357, LBJL.

53. Oral history of Temple, tape #6, p. 6., LBJL.

54. Ibid.

55. Memorandum from Manatos to President Johnson, June 25, 1968, Fortas/Thornberry Files, Box 1, LBJL.

56. Shogan, p. 182.

57. Oral history of Manatos, tape #1, p. 40, LBJL.

58. Memorandum from Temple to Manatos, July 10, 1968, Fortas/Thornberry Files, Box 5, LBJL.

59. Oral history of McPherson, tape #4, p. 38, LBJL. One source notes that the individual expressing this view was Senator Eastland; see also Murphy, p. 361.

60. Letter from Porter to Troy V. Post, October 15, 1968, Porter Papers, Box 3, LBJL.

61. Note from Associate Justice Abe Fortas to Porter, August 19, 1968, Porter Papers, Box 6, LBJL.

62. Oral history of Senator Everett M. Dirksen, tape #1, p. 10, LBJL.

63. Shogan, p. 156. See also memorandum from E. Ernest Goldstein, Special Assistant to the President, to President Johnson, undated, Fortas/Thornberry Files, Box 3, LBJL and Murphy, p. 362. For Javits's comments, see U.S., *Congressional Record*, 90th Cong., 2d Sess., 1968, p. 28299.

64. Oral history of Temple, tape #6, p. 1, LBJL. See also Goldstein's comments in his memo to President Johnson, undated, Fortas/Thornberry Files, Box 3, LBJL.

65. Shogan, p. 151.

66. Memorandum, untitled, June 28, 1968, Fortas/Thornberry Files, Box 1, LBJL. The comment in the memorandum is attributed to Eugene Wyman, Democrat National Committeeman from California. For evidence of Fortas's alleged involvement in raising the anti-Semitism issue, see Murphy, pp. 321-22; 469.

67. Shogan, pp. 155-156. See also Murphy, p. 481.

68. Memorandum from McPherson, to President Johnson, July 11, 1968, McPherson Office Files, LBJL; see also Temple's comment that the anti-Semitism charges could be "beneficial" to Fortas's chances for confirmation in his memorandum to Manatos, July 10, 1968, Fortas/Thornberry Files, Box 5, LBJL.

69. Letter from Porter to Senator Thruston B. Morton, September 4, 1968, Porter Papers, Box 5, LBJL. For additional details on the use of the anti-Semitism issue to gain Nixon's support of Fortas, see Murphy, pp. 464-76.

70. Shogan, p. 157.

71. Ibid.

72. St. Louis, Missouri, *Post-Dispatch*, August 3, 1968, included in Christopher Papers, Box 18, LBJL. See also Murphy, pp. 306-308.

73. Oral history of Temple, tape #5, p. 42, LBJL.

74. Memorandum from McPherson, to President Johnson, June 28, 1968, McPherson Office Files, LBJL.

75. For Eastland's comments see, *The New York Times*, June 28, 1968, p. A1. For Ervin's view, see memorandum from Temple to President Johnson, July 2, 1968, Fortas/Thornberry Files, Box 2, LBJL.

76. Shogan, pp. 16ff.

77. Ibid., p. 177.

78. *The New York Times*, September 5, 1968, p. A24, and U.S., *Congressional Record*, 90th Cong., 2d Sess., 1968, p. 26142.

79. Johnson, *The Vantage Point*, p. 547.

80. Memorandum from Sanders to President Johnson, December 9, 1968, FG-535, Box 357, LBJL.

81. Shogan, p. 177.

82. Johnson, *The Vantage Point*, p. 547.

83. See the oral history of Clark, interview June 3, 1969, tape #1, p. 19, LBJL, and Shogan, p. 178.

84. Shogan, p. 182.

85. Oral history of Temple, tape #6, pp. 1-2, LBJL.

86. Shogan, p. 182.

87. Oral history of Sanders, tape #2, p. 29, LBJL.

88. Shogan, p. 178.

89. Murphy, pp. 503-504.

90. Memorandum from Manatos to President Johnson, September 16, 1968, Fortas/Thornberry Files, Box 3, LBJL.

91. U.S., *Congressional Record*, 90th Cong., 2d Sess., 1968, p. 28114.

92. Memorandum from Christopher to Temple, December 20, 1968, p. 14, Fortas/Thornberry Files, Box 3, LBJL.

93. Murphy, pp. 504-05.

94. Memorandum from Goldstein to President Johnson, undated, Fortas/Thornberry Files, Box 3, LBJL.

95. Memorandum from McPherson, to President Johnson, July 10, 1968, Fortas/Thornberry Files, Box 5, LBJL, and memorandum from Califano to President Johnson, July 15, 1968, Fortas/Thornberry Files, Box 5, LBJL.

96. Memorandum from Sanders to Temple, September 24, 1968, Fortas/Thornberry Files, Box 3, LBJL.

97. Memorandum from Manatos to President Johnson, August 13, 1968, Fortas Name File, LBJL.

98. Untitled White House memorandum, June 28, 1968, Fortas/Thornberry Files, Box 1, LBJL.

99. Letter from Senator Richard B. Russell to President Lyndon B. Johnson, September 26, 1968, Series VII: Political Patronage, Subseries B.1: Presidential Appointments, Box 5, RBRML, The University of Georgia, Athens, Georgia.

100. Oral history of Temple, tape #5, p. 23, LBJL; see also Shogan, pp. 150-155. For a contrary view of Eastland's reaction to the Fortas nomination, see Murphy, p. 301.

101. Ibid.

102. Ibid., tape #6, pp. 8-9.

103. Memorandum from Manatos to President Johnson, June 26, 1968, Fortas/Thornberry Files, Box 1, LBJL.

104. Memorandum from Gaither to Califano, July 2, 1968, Fortas/Thornberry Files, Box 2, LBJL.

105. Memorandum from Fred Drogula, Staff, Office of the Deputy Attorney General, to Christopher, July 24, 1968, Christopher Papers, Box 17, LBJL. See also, Murphy, p. 447.

106. Memorandum from "Jim" (most likely James R. Jones) for the record, June 27, 1968, Fortas/Thornberry Files, Box 4, LBJL.

107. Memorandum from Gaither to Califano, July 2, 1968, Fortas/Thornberry Files, Box 2, LBJL.

108. Memorandum from Manatos to President Johnson, June 25, 1968, Fortas/Thornberry Files, Box 1, LBJL. See also Johnson, *The Vantage Point*, p. 547.

109. Memorandum from Christopher to Temple, December 20, 1968, p. 2, Fortas/Thornberry Files, Box 3, LBJL.

110. Ibid.

111. Ibid.

112. James C. Millstone, "Fortas's Chances Dimming," St. Louis, Missouri, *Post-Dispatch*, August 4, 1968, p. 1B.

113. Portland, Maine, *Press-Herald*, October 5, 1968, editorial page.

114. Letter from Porter to Troy V. Post, October 15, 1968, Porter Papers, 1968, Box 3, LBJL.

115. As cited in Millstone, St. Louis, Missouri *Post-Dispatch*, August 4, 1968, p. 1B.

116. Oral history of Manatos, tape #1, p. 47. LBJL.

117. Johnson, *The Vantage Point*, p. 158.

118. Shogan, p. 150.

119. Oral history of Temple, tape #5, p. 42, LBJL.

120. Memorandum from Manatos to President Johnson, July 2, 1968, Fortas/Thornberry Files, Box 2, LBJL.

121. Memorandum from Manatos to President Johnson, July 9, 1968, WHCF, Subject File FG-535A, Box 360, LBJL; see also Senator's Notebook, July 17, 1968, "Court Must Not Be Delayed," Papers, Remarks and Releases, 1930-69, The Everett McKinley Dirksen Congressional Leadership Research Center, Pekin, Illinois.

122. Memorandum from Manatos to the President Johnson, July 29, 1968, Fortas/Thornberry Files, Box 2, LBJL.

123. Memorandum from Sanders to President Johnson, September 12, 1968, Fortas/Thornberry Files, Box 3, LBJL.

124. *Chicago Tribune*, September 28, 1968, p. 1.

125. Ibid. pp. 1-2.

126. Decatur, Illinois, *Herald-Review*, October 1, 1968, p. 6.

127. October 2, 1968, p. 6.

128. *The Washington Post*, October 1, 1968, p. A8.

129. *The New York Times*, September 28, 1968, p. A1.

130. Oral history of Temple, tape #5, p. 32, LBJL.

131. Memorandum from Goldstein to President Johnson, September 30, 1968, WHCF Subject File FG-535A, LBJL.

132. Claudia Alto "Lady Bird" Johnson, *A White House Diary* (New York: Holt, Rinehart, and Winston, 1970), p. 713.

133. *The New York Times*, September 28, 1968, p. A30.

134. Oral history of Dirksen, tape #2, p. 14, LBJL.

135. 391 U.S. 510 (1968).

136. U.S., *Congressional Record*, 90th Cong., 2d Sess., 1968, pp. 28932-28933.

137. Oral history of Dirksen, tape #2, p. 11, LBJL, (italics added).

138. Ibid., p. 14.

139. Letter from Harold E. Rainville, Special Assistant to Senator Everett McKinley Dirksen, to Charles A. Hayer, September 20, 1968, Chicago Office File, Folder #2166, The Dirksen Research Center.

140. Memorandum from McPherson to Manatos, September 20, 1968, Fortas/Thornberry Files, Box 3, LBJL.

141. Memorandum from Manatos to unspecified recipient, July 2, 1968, Fortas/Thornberry Files, Box 2, LBJL, (italics added).

142. Decatur, Illinois, *Herald-Review*, October 1, 1968, p. 6.

143. Boise, Idaho, *Statesman*, October 5, 1968, p. 4.

144. Neil MacNeil, *Dirksen: Portrait of a Public Man* (New York: The World Publishing Co., 1970), p. 336.

145. *The New York Times*, September 29, 1968, sec. 4, p. 7. See also MacNeil, *Dirksen*, p. 336.

146. Shogan, p. 155.

147. Winston-Salem, North Carolina, *Journal*, October 1, 1968, p. 10.

148. Letter from Senator Richard B. Russell to Alexander Lawrence, February 13, 1968, Series I, Sub-series D. 1., RBRML.

149. Memorandum from Clark to President Johnson, May 13, 1968, WHCF—FG-530, Box 355, LBJL.

150. Ibid.

151. Oral history of Temple, tape #5, pp. 19-20, LBJL.

152. Letter from Russell to President Johnson, May 20, 1968, Series I, Sub-series D. 1., RBRML. All references to the language and substance of the letter are taken from this source.

153. Ibid.

154. Memorandum from W. Thomas Johnson to Temple, July 2, 1968, WHCF—FG-530, Box 355, LBJL.

155. Letter from Russell to Clark, June 14, 1968, Series I, Sub-series D. 1., RBRML.

156. Oral history of Temple, tape #5, p. 20, LBJL.

157. Letter from Alexander A. Lawrence to Mills B. Lane, Jr., June 19, 1968, WHCF—FG-530, Box 355, LBJL.

158. Note from Jones to President Johnson, June 24, 1968, WHCF—FG-530, Box 355, LBJL.

159. Oral History of Temple, tape #5, p. 21, LBJL.

160. Letter from Griffin B. Bell to Russell, May 30, 1968, Series VII, Subseries E.1, Box 19, RBRML.

161. Oral history of Temple, tape #5, p. 22, LBJL. According to Murphy, pp. 344-45, Johnson knew at this time that he would eventually make the Lawrence nomination. Accordingly, the president ordered the Jenner investigation in the hope that a highly positive report from Jenner might convince Attorney General Clark to withdraw his objections to Lawrence.

162. Ibid., p. 22.

163. Letter from Russell to H.H. Perry, Jr., June 5, 1968, Series VII, Subseries E.1., Box 19, RBRML.

164. Letter from Russell to F.M. Scarlett, June 24, 1968, Series VII, Subseries E.1., Box 19, RBRML.

165. Memorandum from W. Thomas Johnson to President Johnson, May 28, 1968, Name File (Richard B. Russell), LBJL.

166. Oral history of Temple, tape #5, p. 24, LBJL.

167. Ibid., p. 23.

168. Ibid.

169. Ibid.

170. Oral history of Homer Thornberry, tape #1, p. 39, LBJL. See also Murphy, p. 348.

171. Oral history of Temple, tape #5, p. 24, LBJL.

172. Ibid., p. 29.

173. Ibid., p. 25.

174. Ibid., pp. 25, 29-30.

175. Memorandum from Temple to President Johnson, July 1, 1968, Fortas/Thornberry Files, Box 2, LBJL.

176. Letter from Russell to President Johnson, Series I, Sub-series D.1, RBRML.

177. Ibid.

178. Ibid.

179. Letter from Russell to Griffin B. Bell, July 2, 1968, Series I, Sub-series D.1., RBRML.

180. Ibid.

181. Oral history of Temple, tape #5, pp. 32-33, LBJL.

182. Ibid., pp. 32-35.

183. Oral history of Temple, tape #5, pp. 37-38, LBJL.

184. Ibid.

185. Oral history of Temple, tape #5, p. 37, and memorandum from Manatos to President Johnson, July 9, 1968, WHCF, Subject File FG-535A, Box 360, both in LBJL.

186. Murphy, p. 356.

187. See letter from Christopher to Senator Wayne Morse, July 27, 1968, with enclosures, Fortas/Thornberry Files, Box 2, LBJL.

188. See letter from Russell to President Johnson, September 26, 1968, Series VII, Sub-series B.1., Box 5, RBRML.

189. Oral history of Temple, tape #5, p. 34, LBJL.

190. Shogan, p. 159.

191. Oral history of William H. Darden, tape #1, p. 21, LBJL.

192. Oral history of Temple, tape #5, pp. 24-25, LBJL.

193. Ibid., p. 36. For more on the nature of the Johnson-Clark relationship, see Murphy, pp. 295-298, 341.

194. Letter from Russell to Frank M. Scarlett, April 2, 1968, Series I, Sub-series D.1., RBRML.

195. Letter from Russell to Griffin B. Bell, June 7, 1968, Series I, Sub-series D.1., RBRML; see also Murphy, pp. 342, 350.

196. Johnson, *The Vantage Point*, p. 158. See also Murphy, pp. 332-336.

197. For a contrary view, expressed by Fortas, that liberals would understand the necessity of appointing Lawrence to placate the powerful Russell and not be upset by it, see Murphy, p. 344.

198. Letter from Joseph L. Rauh, Jr., to Porter, September 20, 1968, Porter Papers, 1968, Box 3, LBJL.

199. Oral history of Griffin, I, p. 9., LBJL. See also Shogan, pp. 158-159.

200. Murphy, p. 356.

201. Ibid.

CHAPTER 3

1. See Bruce Allen Murphy, *Fortas: The Rise and Ruin of a Supreme Court Justice* (New York: William Morrow and Co., Inc., 1988), pp. 545-577 for details on the events leading to Fortas's resignation.

2. Memorandum from Patrick J. Buchanan, Special Assistant to the President, to President Nixon, May 6, 1969, WHCF—FG (Supreme Court), Box 1, NPMP.

3. Letter from Judge Warren E. Burger, United States Court of Appeals, to President Nixon, May 8, 1969, WHCF—FG (Supreme Court), Box 1, NPMP (italics in original).

4. Memorandum from Alexander P. Butterfield, Deputy Assistant to the President, to Attorney General John N. Mitchell, May 14, 1969, WHCF—FG (Supreme Court), Box 1, NPMP.

5. Written notes of Buchanan, undated, White House Special Files of Buchanan, Box 13, NPMP.

6. For the comments of the following senators see U.S., *Congressional Record*, 91st Cong., 1st Sess., 1969: Eagleton (p. 25626); Inouye (pp. 28601-02); McGee (p. 35135); Symington (pp. 33997-8); Cooper (pp. 35165-66); Hatfield (p. 35398); Mathias (p. 35147); Miller (p. 33414); and Smith (pp. 29040-29041). For the respective comments of Bayh, Tydings, and Griffin, see U.S. Senate, Committee on the Judiciary, *Report on the Nomination of Haynsworth*, pp. 25-26; 50-52; 47. For Scott's comments, see *The New York Times*, November 22, 1969, p. A20.

7. *Report on the Nomination of Haynsworth*, p. 50.

8. U.S., *Congressional Record*, 91st Cong., 1st Sess., 1969, p. 35135.

9. Ibid., p. 25626.

10. Ibid., p. 35398.

11. Ibid., p. 35147.

12. Memorandum from Thomas L. Lias, Deputy Special Assistant to the President, to Kevin Phillips, Special Assistant to the Attorney General, October 16, 1969, White House Special Files of Harry S. Dent, Special Counsel to the President, Box 6, NPMP.

13. Memorandum from Bryce N. Harlow, Counselor to the President, and Kenneth E. Belieu, Deputy Assistant to the President for Senate Relations, to President Nixon, October 20, 1969, WHCF—FG (Supreme Court), Box 3, NPMP.

14. U.S., *Congressional Record*, 91st Cong., 1st Sess., 1969, pp. 29040-41.

15. Letter from Senator Margaret Chase Smith to President Nixon, September 30, 1969, in the files of the Margaret Chase Smith Library Center, Skowhegan, Maine.

16. U.S., *Congressional Record*, 91st Cong., 1st Sess., 1969, pp. 29040-29041.

17. Richard Harris, *Decision* (New York: E.P. Dutton and Co., 1971), p. 159, and *The New York Times*, October 2, 1969, pp. A1, A22.

18. *The New York Times*, October 9, 1969, p. A44.

19. Ibid., p. A1.

20. *The New York Times*, November 22, 1969, p. A20.

21. Memorandum from Harlow and Belieu to President Nixon, October 20, 1969, WHCF—FG (Supreme Court), Box 3, NPMP.

22. Ibid.

23. Notes of John D. Ehrlichman, Assistant to the President for Domestic Affairs, of meeting with President Nixon, November 13, 1969, White House Special Files of Ehrlichman, Box 3, NPMP.

24. Memorandum from President Nixon to Harlow, October 21, 1969, WHCF—FG (Supreme Court), Box 3, NPMP.

25. Memorandum from Harlow for the Staff Secretary, October 23, 1969, WHCF—FG (Supreme Court), Box 3, NPMP.

26. Memorandum from Nyle M. Jackson, Assistant Postmaster General's Office, for Dent, October 24, 1969, White House Special Files of Dent, Box 6, NPMP.

27. Memorandum from Clark Mollenhoff, Special Counsel to the President, to President Nixon, October 13, 1969, WHCF—FG (Supreme Court), Box 3, NPMP.

28. Notes of Ehrlichman of meeting with President Nixon, October 1, 1969, White House Special Files of Ehrlichman, Box 3, NPMP.

29. Rowland Evans, Jr., and Robert D. Novak, *Nixon in the White House: The Frustration of Power* (New York: Random House, 1971), p. 164.

30. *Newsweek*, October 6, 1969, pp. 76, 81.

31. U.S., *Congressional Record*, 91st Cong., 1st Sess., 1969, p. 34848.

32. See chapter 1.

33. *Commonweal*, December 5, 1969, p. 294.

34. Joel B. Grossman and Stephen L. Wasby, "Haynsworth and Parker: History Does Live Again," *South Carolina Law Review*, 23, no. 3 (1971), 353.

35. Notes of President Nixon on Supreme Court, for conversation with newsmen, May 22, 1969, President's Personal Files, Box 19, NPMP.

36. Memorandum from Murray M. Chotiner, General Counsel for Trade Negotiations, to President Nixon, May 18, 1970, Papers of H. R. Haldeman, Assistant to the President, Folder: "HRH—Staff Memos April, May, June, 1970," NPMP.

37. Letter from Peter M. Flanigan, Assistant to the President, to Barry T. Leithead, December 30, 1969, WHCF—FG-51 (Supreme Court), Box 2, NPMP, (italics added).

38. Memorandum from William H. Rehnquist, Assistant Attorney General, to Mitchell, October 12, 1971, White House Special Files of John Dean, Assistant Deputy Attorney General for Legislation, Box 70, NPMP.

39. Letter from William Loeb to Senator Winston L. Prouty, October 21, 1969, WHCF—FG-51 (Supreme Court), Box 2, NPMP.

40. U.S., *Congressional Record*, 91st Cong., 1st Sess., 1969, pp. 34825-34828.

41. Harris, p. 135.

42. Memorandum from Jack A. Gleason, Assistant to the Secretary of Commerce, to Dent, November 5, 1969, White House Special Files of Dent, Box 6, NPMP.

43. U.S., *Congressional Record*, 91st Cong., 1st Sess., 1969, pp. 34287-88.

44. Ibid., p. 33414.

45. Letter from Margaret Chase Smith to John Massaro, September 8, 1983.

46. Letter from Margaret Chase Smith to Mrs. William H. Erskine, November 25, 1969, in the files of the Margaret Chase Smith Library Center.

47. Letter from Margaret Chase Smith to Bachman S. Smith, November 19, 1969, in the files of the Margaret Chase Smith Library Center.

48. *The New York Times*, November 7, 1969, p. A20.

49. Ibid., November 22, 1969, p. A20.

50. Notes of Ehrlichman of meeting with President Nixon, October 1, 1969, White House Special Files of Ehrlichman, Box 3, NPMP.

51. Memorandum from Harlow and Belieu to President Nixon, October 20, 1969, WHCF—FG (Supreme Court), Box 3, NPMP. (emphasis in original).

52. Memorandum from Harlow, recipient unspecified, October 17, 1969, WHCF—FG (Supreme Court), Box 3, NPMP.

53. Ibid.

54. Ibid.

55. Memorandum from Harlow to President Nixon, October 28, 1969, WHCF—FG (Supreme Court), Box 3, NPMP.

56. Clark R. Mollenhoff, *Game Plan for Disaster: An Ombudsman's Report on the Nixon Years* (New York: W.W. Norton and Company, Inc., 1976), p. 63.

57. *The New York Times*, November 22, 1969, p. A20.

58. Memorandum from Harlow to President Nixon, October 14, 1969, WHCF—FG (Supreme Court), Box 3, NPMP.

59. Notes of Buchanan, undated (but approximately October 11, 1969), White House Special Files of Buchanan, Box 13, NPMP.

60. Notes of Ehrlichman of meeting with President Nixon, October 5, 1969, White House Special Files of Ehrlichman, Box 3, NPMP.

61. Mollenhoff, p. 50.

62. Ibid.

63. As quoted ibid., p. 52.

64. Ibid., pp. 52-53.

65. As quoted ibid., p. 53.

66. *The New York Times*, October 11, 1969, p. A15.

67. Mollenhoff, p. 60.

68. Memorandum from Mollenhoff to President Nixon, October 29, 1969, WHCF—FG (Supreme Court), Box 3, NPMP.

69. Ibid., p. 59.

70. Ibid.; see also Mollenhoff, p. 60.

71. Ibid., p. 51.

72. Ibid., pp. 64-65.

73. Notes of Haldeman, October 3, 1969, Haldeman Papers, Box 40, NPMP.

74. See the following: *The New York Times*, November 21, 1969, p. A1; *Time*, October 17, 1969, p. 24; *Newsweek*, October 20, 1969, p. 36; and U.S., *Congressional Record*, 91st Cong., 1st Sess., 1969, p. 30956.

75. Letter from Senator Edward W. Brooke to President Nixon, October 1, 1969, WHCF—FG (Supreme Court), Box 3, NPMP.

76. Memorandum from Buchanan to President Nixon, October 14, 1969, containing notes of the Legislative Leadership Meeting on October 14, 1969, President's Office Files, NPMP.

77. Memorandum from President Nixon to Dent, October 21, 1969, WHCF—FG (Supreme Court), Box 3, NPMP.

78. Notes of Ehrlichman of meeting with President Nixon, October 8, 1969, White House Special Files of Ehrlichman, Box 3, NPMP.

79. Notes of Haldeman, October 21, 1969, Haldeman Papers, Box 40, NPMP.

80. Memorandum from Dent to Belieu, October 17, 1969, White House Special Files of Dent, Box 6, NPMP and memorandum from Dent to Mitchell and Harlow, October 27, 1969, White House Special Files of Ehrlichman, Box 34, NPMP.

81. Memorandum from Dent to Mitchell and Harlow, October 27, 1969, White House Special Files of Ehrlichman, Box 34, NPMP.

82. *The New York Times*, September 28, 1969, sec. 4, p. 11.

83. Memorandum from Kenneth R. Cole, Jr., Deputy Assistant to the President for Domestic Affairs, to Herbert G. Klein, Director of Communications, October 15, 1969, containing a portion of the president's news summary of Ted Lewis's October 10 column in the New York *Daily News*, White House Special Files of Dent, Box 6, NPMP. See also *The New York Times*, September 28, 1969, sec. 4, p. 11, and ibid., October 5, 1969, sec. 4, p. 1.

84. *Newsweek*, December 1, 1969, pp. 22-24.

85. Memorandum from Harlow to Staff Secretary, November 24, 1969, WHCF—FG (Supreme Court), Box 3, NPMP.

86. *Newsweek*, December 1, 1969, p. 4.

87. Memorandum from Dent to Mitchell, October 23, 1969, White House Special Files of Dent, Box 6, NPMP.

88. Memorandum from Dent to President Nixon, November 24, 1969, containing newspaper clipping from *The State* (Columbia, South Carolina), November 23, 1969, WHCF—FG (Supreme Court), Box 3, NPMP.

89. *Newsweek*, December 1, 1969, p. 24.

90. Memorandum from Lias to Dent, October 21, 1969, White House Special Files of Dent, Box 6, NPMP.

91. *Newsweek*, October 20, 1969, p. 36.

92. Memorandum from Harlow to President Nixon, October 17, 1969, WHCF—FG (Supreme Court), Box 3, NPMP.

93. Ibid.

94. Memorandum from Gleason to Dent, November 5, 1969, p. 2, White House Special Files of Dent, Box 6, NPMP.

95. Memorandum from Dent to Mitchell and Harlow, October 27, 1969, p. 8, White House Special Files of Ehrlichman, Box 34, NPMP.

96. Memorandum from Gleason to Dent, November 5, 1969, p. 2, White House Special Files of Dent, Box 6, NPMP.

97. Undated press review contained in memorandum from Harlow, December, 1969, Haldeman Papers, Box 55, NPMP.

98. U.S., *Congressional Record*, 91st Cong., 1st Sess., 1969, p. 34288.

99. Mollenhoff, p. 59.

100. Memorandum from Donald E. Johnson, Administrator of Veteran Affairs, to Harlow, October 20, 1969, White House Special Files of Dent, Box 6, NPMP.

101. Harris, p. 99. The reference would indicate Miller because he alone appears to fit the description of a mid-western, conservative Republican who voted against the nomination.

102. Memorandum from Dent to Belieu, October 17, 1969, White House Special Files of Dent, Box 6, NPMP.

103. Memorandum from Gleason to Dent, October 14, 1969, White House Special Files of Dent, Box 6, NPMP.

104. Memorandum from Gleason to Phillips, October 15, 1969, White House Special Files of Dent, Box 6, NPMP.

105. Memorandum from Gleason to Phillips, October 17, 1969, White House Special Files of Dent, Box 6, NPMP.

106. Ibid.

107. Memorandum from Dent to Mitchell and Harlow, October 27, 1969, White House Special Files of Ehrlichman, Box 34, NPMP.

108. Memorandum from Gordon S. Brownell to Dent, October 16, 1969, White House Special Files of Dent, Box 6, NPMP.

109. Memorandum from Gleason to Phillips, October 17, 1969, White House Special Files of Dent, Box 6, NPMP.

110. Memorandum from Gleason to Dent, November 4, 1969, White House Special Files of Dent, Box 6, NPMP.

111. *The New York Times*, November 21, 1969, p. A20.

112. As quoted in *Newsweek*, November 24, 1969, p. 36; see also *Time*, November 28, 1969, p. 15.

113. Ibid.

114. Undated press review contained in memorandum from Harlow, December, 1969, Haldeman Papers, Box 55, NPMP.

115. Mollenhoff, p. 59.

116. *The New York Times*, November 1, 1969, p. A16.

117. Memorandum from Gleason to Phillips, October 22, 1969, White House Special Files of Dent, Box 6, NPMP; see also ibid., October 17, 1969, p. 2.

118. Memorandum from Cole to Klein, October 15, 1969, containing portion of the president's news summary for October 10, 1969 of Ted Lewis's column in *New York Daily News*, October 10, 1969, White House Special Files of Dent, Box 6, NPMP.

CHAPTER 4

1. *Newsweek*, February 2, 1970, p. 19.

2. Jeb Stuart Magruder, *An American Life: One Man's Road to Watergate* (New York: Antheneum, 1974), p. 110.

3. William Safire, *Before the Fall: An Inside View of the Pre-Watergate White House* (Garden City, New York: Doubleday & Company, Inc., 1975), p. 267.

4. *The New York Times*, January 31, 1969, p. A14; February 13, 1970, p. A18; and February 21, 1970, p. A50.

5. John Osborne, "The Nixon Watch: A Look at John Mitchell," *The New Republic*, February 7, 1970, p. 13.

6. Ibid.

7. Ibid.

8. Rowland Evans, Jr. and Robert D. Novak, *Nixon in the White House: The Frustration of Power* (New York: Random House, 1971), p. 165.

9. News summary (undated), President's Office Files, Box 31, Folder: "News Summaries, February, 1970," NPMP.

10. Memorandum from William E. Timmons, Deputy Assistant to the President, to President Nixon, March 19, 1970, WHCF—FG (Supreme Court), Box 4, NPMP.

11. News summary (undated), President's Office Files, Box 31, Folder: "News Summaries, March, 1970," NPMP.

12. Joel B. Grossman and Stephen L. Wasby, "The Senate and Supreme Court Nominations: Some Reflections," *Duke Law Journal*, August, 1972, p. 579.

13. *The New York Times*, April 12, 1970, sec. 4, p. 13.

14. See chapter 1.

15. *The Washington Post*, April 12, 1970, p. A2.

16. Memorandum from William H. Rehnquist, Assistant Attorney General, to John W. Dean, Assistant Deputy Attorney General for Legislation, October 12, 1971, White House Special Files of John W. Dean, Box 70, NPMP.

17. *The New York Times*, March 17, 1970, p. A21.

18. These senators, with appropriate citations from the *Congressional Record*, were: Harold E. Hughes (D, Iowa), p. 7856; Mike Gravel (D, Alaska), p. 8064; Abraham A. Ribicoff (D, Conn.), pp. 8715-17; Stuart Symington (D, Mo.), p. 8652; Frank Church (D, Idaho), p. 8704; Claiborne Pell (D, R.I.), p. 8911; Thomas F. Eagleton (D, Mo.), p. 8805; Henry M. Jackson (D, Wash.), p. 9263. Vance Hartke's remarks are reported in *The New York Times*, March 21, 1979, p. A11.

19. Senators J. William Fulbright (D, Ark.), Quentin N. Burdick (D, N.D.), and Richard S. Schweiker (R, Pa.); see *The New York Times*, March 20, 1970, p. A11.

20. Senators Winston L. Prouty (R, Vt.), Marlow W. Cook (R, Ky.), George D. Aiken (R, Vt.), and Hiram L. Fong (R, Hawaii); see *The New York Times,* March 21, 1970, p. A11.

21. *The Washington Post,* April 12, 1970, p. A2.

22. The designations of "Liberals" and "Conservatives" refer to the categories of "Liberals" and "Conservatives" established by use of the ideology index presented in chapter 1.

23. Richard Harris, *Decision* (New York: E. P. Dutton and Co., 1971), p. 187.

24. U.S., Senate, Committee on the Judiciary, *Report on the Nomination of Carswell,* pp. 7-9. Cook had given his assent to the report's conclusion that Carswell was a "constitutional conservative" deserving of confirmation.

25. *Newsweek,* April 6, 1970, p. 26.

26. Memorandum from Timmons to President Nixon, March 20, 1970, President's Office Files, Box 6, NPMP.

27. Memorandum for President Nixon, April 6, 1970 (writer unspecified), WHCF—FG (Supreme Court), Box 4, NPMP.

28. Evans and Novak, pp. 167-168.

29. *The Washington Post,* April 9, 1970, p. A12.

30. Memorandum from Timmons to President Nixon, March 20, 1970, President's Office File, Box 6, NPMP.

31. Notes of H. R. Haldeman, Assistant to the President, of meeting with President Nixon, March 23, 1970, papers of H. R. Haldeman, Box 41, NPMP.

32. Memorandum for President Nixon, April 6, 1970, (writer unspecified), WHCF—FG (Supreme Court), Box 4, NPMP.

33. Memorandum from Bryce N. Harlow, Counselor to the President, to Staff Secretary, April 7, 1970, President's Office Files, Box 80, NPMP.

34. Memorandum from Timmons to President Nixon, March 20, 1970, President's Office Files, Box 6, NPNP.

35. Ibid.

36. Harris, pp. 190-191.

37. As discussed below, an ill-conceived White House effort to gain her support also contributed to Smith's defection.

38. Letter from Margaret Chase Smith to Mrs. Verna S. Phelan, April 20, 1970, in the files of the Margaret Chase Smith Library Center, Skowhegan, Maine.

39. Harris, p. 58.

40. Ibid.

41. It should be noted that at least twenty-two Democrats had indexes above ninety.

42. U.S., *Congressional Record*, 91st Cong., 2d Sess., 1970, p. 10431.

43. Harris, p. 185.

44. *Newsweek*, April 20, 1970, p. 35; see also *New Yorker*, April 18, 1970, p. 138; *Time*, April 6, 1970, p. 10.

45. *The New York Times*, March 17, 1970, p. A21.

46. Ibid., April 10, 1970, p. A15.

47. Evans and Novak, p. 164.

48. Ibid.

49. Herbert G. Klein, *Making It Perfectly Clear* (Garden City, New York: Doubleday & Company, Inc., 1980), p. 339.

50. Notes of John D. Ehrlichman, Assistant to the President, of meetings with President Nixon, January, 1970, Folder: "Carswell [G. Harrold]," and March 25, 1970, Folder: "JDE Notes of Meetings with the President 1-1-70 to 6-30-70 (3 of 5)," White House Special Files of John D. Ehrlichman, Box 3, NPMP.

51. *The New York Times*, January 28, 1970, p. A23.

52. *The Washington Post*, March 25, 1970. p. A1.

53. Harris, pp. 123-124. The contents of the memorandum were generally known to most senators before March 25 but the publication of the memo intensified the impact of the lack of candor issue.

54. Magruder, pp. 110-111.

55. Ibid.

56. Memorandum from Harlow and Timmons to President Nixon, March 21, 1970, WHCF-FG (Supreme Court), Box 4, NPMP.

57. Ibid.

58. *The New York Times*, April 2, 1970, p. A28, contains the complete text of the president's letter to Saxbe.

59. Ibid., April 3, 1970, p. A1.

60. Harris, p. 158.

61. Ibid., p. 156.

62. *The New York Times*, April 9, 1970, p. A72; see also Harris, p. 158.

63. Letter from Margaret Chase Smith to Ruth M. Gonchar, April 21, 1970, in the files of the Margaret Chase Smith Library Center, Skowhegan, Maine.

64. Harris, p. 158.

65. Ibid., p. 159.

66. Magruder, p. 111.

67. Evans and Novak, p. 166.

68. *The New York Times*, April 12, 1970, sec. 4, p. 13.

69. Grossman and Wasby, p. 558 n. 4.

70. James David Barber, *The Presidential Character: Predicting Performance in the White House* (1st ed; Englewood Cliffs, New Jersey: Prentice-Hall, Inc., 1972), p. 428.

71. *The New York Times*, March 24, 1970, p. A20, and March 26, 1970, p. A51.

72. Harris, p. 177.

73. *Time*, April 20, 1970, p. 12.

74. Harris, p. 177.

75. *The New York Times*, April 9, 1970, p. A32.

76. Ibid., April 1, 1970, pp. A1, A24; see also notes of Haldeman of White House Meeting, April 8, 1970, Haldeman Papers, Box 41, NPMP.

77. Evans and Novak, p. 168.

78. Notes of Haldeman of White House Meeting, March 26, 1970, Haldeman Papers, Box 41, NPMP.

79. Harris, p. 164.

80. U.S., *Congressional Record*, 91st Cong., 2d Sess., p. 10600.

81. Harris, pp. 174-175.

82. *The New York Times*, April 12, 1970, sec. 4, p. 13.

83. Harris, p. 174.

84. Grossman and Wasby, p. 579 n. 95.

85. See Senator John O. Pastore's (D, R.I.) comments in U.S., *Congressional Record*, 91st Cong., 2d Sess., p. 10359.

86. As quoted in Harris, p. 62.

87. Memorandum from Harlow to President Nixon, December 3, 1969, WHCF—FG-31-1, NPMP.

88. Harris, pp. 11-12.

89. Notes of Haldeman of White House Meeting, February 14, 1979, Haldeman Papers, Box 41, NPMP.

90. Ibid., February 21, 1970.

91. President's News Summary, March 26, 1970, President's Office Files, Box 31, NPMP.

92. Ibid., undated, but summary contains news clipping from *Indianapolis News*, March 25, 1970; see also memorandum from Jeb S. Magruder, Deputy to Haldeman, to President Nixon, April 8, 1970, White House Special Files of Herbert G. Klein, Director of Communications, Box 5, NPMP.

93. Ibid.

94. Evans and Novak, p. 167.

95. Notes of Ehrlichman of meeting with President Nixon, March 26, 1970, White House Special Files of Ehrlichman, Box 3, NPMP.

96. Ibid.

97. Notes of Haldeman, March 23, 1970, Haldeman Papers, Box 41, NPMP.

98. Ibid., April 8, 1970.

99. Notes of Ehrlichman of meeting with President Nixon, April 25, 1970, Box 8, Folder: "Miscellaneous Notes 1969-1973 (2 of 7)," NPMP.

100. *The New Yorker*, April 18, 1970, p. 144.

101. Harris, pp. 99-100.

102. Ibid.

103. Ibid.

104. *The New York Times*, April 7, 1970, p. A17.

105. Not voting were Wallace F. Bennett (R, Utah), Karl E. Mundt (R, S.D.), Clinton P. Anderson (D, N.M.), and Claiborne Pell (D, R.I.)

106. Memorandum from Harlow to Staff Secretary, April 2, 1970, President's Office File, Box 80, NPMP.

107. Ibid.

108. Memorandum to President Nixon, April 6, 1970, WHCF—FG (Supreme Court), Box 4, NPMP.

109. *Time*, April 20, 1970, p. 12; see also *The New York Times*, April 9, 1970, p. A32, and Harris, p. 197.

110. Ibid.

111. *The New York Times*, April 14, 1970, p. A27; see also *Newsweek*, April 20, 1970, p. 39, and *Time*, April 20, 1970, p. 12.

112. U.S., *Congressional Record*, 91st Cong., 2d Sess., pp. 11472-73, and *The New York Times*, April 14, 1970, p. A27.

113. Interview with Senator Margaret Chase Smith, Skowhegan, Maine, March 10, 1983.

114. *The New York Times*, April 9, 1970, p. A32; see also Harris, p. 197; and *Time*, April 20, 1970, p. A12.

115. On Senator Dodd, see memoranda from Timmons to President Nixon, March 20, 1970, President's Office File, Box 6, and from Patrick J. Buchanan, Special Assistant to the President, to President Nixon, March 30, 1970, WHCF— FG (Supreme Court), Box 4, NPMP.

116. Unless otherwise noted, the following account is based upon Harris, pp. 197-200, and Evans and Novak, p. 168.

117. Interview with Senator Margaret Chase Smith, Skowhegan, Maine, March 10, 1983.

118. *The New York Times*, April 9, 1979, p. A32; Harris, pp. 197-200; and *Time*, April 20, 1970, p. 12.

119. Notes of Haldeman of White House meeting, March 20, 1970, Haldeman Papers, Box 41, NPMP.

120. Memorandum from Harlow to Staff Secretary, April 7, 1970, President's Office File, Box 80, NPMP. A live pair involves two members, one present for the vote, the other absent. The present member casts a vote, withdraws it, and then votes "present." This member then announces a live pair with the absent colleague, identifying how each would have voted on the question. A live pair

consequently subtracts the vote of the present member from the final vote tabulation.

121. Notes of Ehrlichman of meeting with President Nixon, March 26, 1970, White House Special Files of Ehrlichman, Box 3, NPMP.

122. Memorandum from Harlow and Timmons to President Nixon, March 31, 1970, WHCF—FG (Supreme Court), Box 4, NPMP.

123. Harris, p. 142.

124. Memorandum from Lyn Nofziger, Presidential Advisor, for President Nixon's file, October 24, 1969, President's Office Files, NPMP.

125. Harris, p. 142.

126. *The New York Times*, April 10, 1970, p. A14.

127. Memorandum from Dean to Frederic V. Malek, Deputy Under Secretary, Department of Health, Education, and Welfare, April 5, 1971, White House Special Files of Malek, Box 3; memorandum from Egil Krogh Jr., White House Aide, to Ehrlichman, September 24, 1971, White House Special Files of David R. Young, Staff, National Security Council, Box 17, and memorandum from Ehrlichman to President Nixon, October 8, 1971, ibid, NPMP.

CHAPTER 5

1. All statistical data in this chapter relating to unsuccessful nominations are drawn from appendix 1 unless otherwise noted.

2. The nominations of Roger Taney, in 1835, and Henry Stanbery, in 1866, were rejected by Senates in which the president's party was in the minority.

3. John Massaro, "The Forgotten Factor: Presidential Management and Unsuccessful Supreme Court Nominations" (paper delivered at the Northeastern Political Science Association Meeting, November 1987), pp. 18-20. For extensive case studies of the unsuccessful nominations, see: Daniel S. McHargue, "Appointments to the Supreme Court of the United States: The Factors That Have Affected Appointments (1789-1932)" (Ph.D. dissertation, University of California, Los Angeles, 1949), and John Massaro, "Advice and Dissent: Factors in the Senate's Refusal to Confirm Supreme Court Nominees, With Special Emphasis on the Cases of Abe Fortas, Clement F. Haynsworth, Jr., and G. Harrold Carswell" (Ph.D. dissertation, Southern Illinois University at Carbondale, 1972).

4. Stephen Carter, "The Confirmation Mess," *Harvard Law Review*, 101 no. 6, (April 1988), pp. 1189-1191. I am aware that Carter's article questions

whether there exists a genuine concern about a nominee's judicial ideology on the part of senators and their constituents, pp. 1191-1192.

5. Henry J. Abraham, *The Judicial Process* (5th ed.; New York: Oxford University Press, 1986), p. 68. See also David M. O'Brien, *Storm Center: The Supreme Court in American Politics* (New York: W.W. Norton & Co., 1986), p. 57.

6. Bruce A. Ackerman, "Transformative Appointments," *Harvard Law Review*, 101, no. 6 (April 1988), 1175.

7. For discussion of the legitimacy of senators' considering a nominee's ideology, see A. Mitchell McConnell, Jr., "Haynsworth and Carswell: A New Senate Standard of Excellence," *Kentucky Law Journal*, 59, no. 1 (Fall 1970), 13; Charles L. Black, Jr., "A Note on Senatorial Consideration of Supreme Court Nominees," *The Yale Law Journal*, 79, no. 4 (March 1970), 663-64; Paul Simon, "The Senate's Role in Judicial Appointments, *Judicature*, 70 (June-July 1986), 55-60; and Herbert F. Weisberg and John D. Felice, "An Ideological Model of Senate Voting on Supreme Court Nominations, 1955-1988" (paper delivered at the Midwest Political Science Association Annual Meeting in Chicago, Illinois, April 14-16, 1988), pp. 1, 15.

8. Laurence H. Tribe, *God Save This Honorable Court* (New York: Random House, 1985), p. 111; Donald R. Songer, "The Relevance of Policy Values in Senate Consideration of Supreme Court Nominations," *Law and Society Review*, 13, 946; Stephen L. Wasby, *The Supreme Court in the Federal Judicial System* (3d ed.; Chicago: Nelson-Hall Publishers, 1988), pp. 127-128.

9. Wasby, p. 127.

10. These results are based upon a chart "Supreme Court Nominees on Which There Was A Recorded Vote For Confirmation By The Senate" prepared by the Legislative Reference Service, The Library of Congress, and included in White House Special Files of John Dean, Box 70, NPMP. Data of the chart have been updated through June, 1988.

11. James David Barber, *The Presidential Character: Predicting Performance in the White House* (2d ed.; Englewood Cliffs, New Jersey, 1977), p. 12.

12. Ibid.

13. Ibid., pp. 56, 418.

14. Ibid., pp. 426-27.

15. Ibid., pp. 427-28.

16. Henry J. Abraham, *Justices and Presidents: A Political History of Appointments to the Supreme Court* (2d ed.; New York: Oxford University Press), p. 46. For a different view of the likelihood of a senator's winning confirmation, see Jeffrey Segal, "Senate Confirmation of Supreme Court Justices: Partisan and

Institutional Politics," *The Journal of Politics*, 49 (November 1987), 1008.

17. John Massaro, " 'Lame Duck' Presidents, Great Justices?" *Presidential Studies Quarterly*, 8, no. 3, (Summer 1978), 301-302.

18. Joel B. Grossman and Stephen L. Wasby, "The Senate and Supreme Court Nominations: Some Reflections," *Duke Law Journal*, 72 (August 1972), p. 589.

19. The following discussion regarding the two views of the nature of law is drawn from Charles L. Black, Jr., *Capital Punishment: The Inevitability of Caprice and Mistake* (New York: W. W. Norton and Co., Inc., 1974), pp. 75ff.

20. Ibid.

21. Charles A. Johnson and Bradley C. Canon, *Judicial Policies: Implementation and Impact* (Washington, D. C.: Congressional Quarterly, Inc., 1984), p. 231.

22. Bernard Schwartz, *A Basic History of the Supreme Court* (Princeton, New Jersey: D. Van Nostrand Company, Inc., 1968), p. 82.

23. Richard Funston, "The Supreme Court and Critical Elections," *American Political Science Review*, 69, no. 3 (September 1975), 810; see also Robert Dahl, "Decision-Making in a Democracy: The Supreme Court as a National Policy-Maker," *Journal of Public Law*, 6 (Fall 1957), 279-295.

24. Memorandum from President Richard Nixon to H. R. Haldeman, Assistant to the President, April 13, 1970, Papers of H. R. Haldeman, Box 138, NPMP.

25. The following descriptions of the successful nominations of Lewis F. Powell, Jr., William H. Rehnquist, John Paul Stevens, and Sandra Day O'Connor draw heavily from Abraham, *Justices and Presidents*, pp. 19-23, 321-324, 329-339.

26. Ibid. pp. 22-23. It is unclear whether Nixon ever seriously considered selecting a nominee from the list of six or whether he employed the list as a foil for his designation of Powell and Rehnquist. Abraham, *Justices and Presidents*, p. 21, maintains there is little doubt Nixon wanted to appoint Lilley and Friday. For an inside but noncommittal Nixon White House report on the announcements of the Powell and Rehnquist nominations, see "Special Report on the Nominations to the Supreme Court, October 24, 1971," White House Special Files of David R. Young, Staff, National Security Council, Box 17, NPMP.

27. Wasby, p. 129. See also Abraham, *Justices and Presidents*, p. 324.

28. Massaro, " 'Lame Duck' Presidents, Great Justices?" pp. 301-302.

29. There has been some interesting speculation that President Reagan, knowing it would be difficult to achieve confirmation of a new chief justice late in his second term and concerned the Democrats might gain control of the Senate in 1986, attempted successfully to bring about Chief Justice Burger's retirement one year earlier than his expected September, 1987 date for leaving the Court; see Wasby, pp. 129-130.

CHAPTER 6

1. Bork was born on March 1, 1927, in Pittsburgh, Pennsylvania. He attended the University of Pittsburgh and then enlisted in the United States Marine Corps in 1945, serving until 1946. Following military service, he attended the University of Chicago, where he received a Bachelor of Arts degree. During his first year at the University of Chicago Law School, he enlisted in the Marine Corps Reserves and was called back to active duty in 1950, serving until 1952. After receiving his law degree from the University of Chicago in 1953, he became a research associate with the law school's Law and Economic Project. From 1954 to 1962, he engaged in the private practice of law in New York and Chicago. In 1962, he joined the faculty of the Yale Law School, serving as an associate professor from 1962 to 1965 and a full professor from 1965 to 1973. From 1973 to 1977, he was Solicitor General of the United States. During this time, he briefly served as Acting Attorney General from 1973 to 1974. In 1977, he returned to the faculty of the Yale Law School. His book, *The Antitrust Paradox: A Policy At War With Itself*, was published in 1978. At the time he was nominated to the Supreme Court, in 1987, he was serving as a judge on the United States Court of Appeals for the District of Columbia, having been appointed to that post by President Reagan in 1982.

2. Ginsburg was born on May 25, 1946, in Chicago, Illinois. He received an undergraduate degree from Cornell University in 1970 and a law degree from the University of Chicago in 1973. He served as a law clerk for Judge Carl McGowan of the United States Court of Appeals, District of Columbia, from 1973 to 1974, and for Associate Justice Thurgood Marshall from 1974 to 1975. From 1975 to 1983, he taught at the Harvard Law School. In 1983, he was Deputy Assistant Attorney General for Regulatory Affairs, Antitrust Division, United States Department of Justice, and a year later served as Administrator for Information and Regulatory Affairs, Office of Management and Budget. From 1985 to 1986, he was Assistant Attorney General in the Antitrust Division of the Justice Department. When nominated to the Supreme Court, he was serving as a judge on the United States Court of Appeals for the District of Columbia, having been appointed to that position in 1986 by President Reagan.

3. Kennedy was born on July 23, 1936, in Sacramento, California. His undergraduate degree was from Stanford University in 1958 and his law degree from Harvard University in 1961. From 1961 to 1967, he practiced law in San Francisco and later on in Sacramento. From 1967 to 1975, he was a partner in the Sacramento law firm of Evans, Jackson, and Kennedy. When nominated to the Supreme Court in 1987, he was serving as a judge on the United States Court of Appeals for the Ninth Circuit in Sacramento, having been named to that position in 1975 by President Gerald Ford. From 1965 to his nomination to the Supreme Court he also taught constitutional law at McGeorge School of Law, University of the Pacific.

4. For more complete treatment of these issues see U. S., Congress, Senate, Committee on the Judiciary, *Hearings on the Nomination of Robert H. Bork to be an Associate Justice of the United States Supreme Court*, 100th Cong., 1st Sess., 1987; and U. S., Congress, Senate, Committee on the Judiciary, *Report of the Committee on the Judiciary United States Senate together with Additional, Minority, and Supplemental Views on the Nomination of Robert H. Bork to be an Associate Justice of the Supreme Court*, 100th Cong., 1st Sess., 1987. Hereafter cited as *Report* with specific reference to majority views unless otherwise noted.

5. Robert H. Bork, "The Struggle Over the Role of the Court," *National Review*, September 17, 1982, pp. 1127-38.

6. *Report*, p. 9.

U. S., Congress, Senate, Committee on the Judiciary, Hearings on the Confirmation of Federal Judges, 97th Cong., 2d Sess., part 3, January 27, 1982, p. 5.

8. Everett Carll Ladd, *The Ladd Report #7: The Political Battle for the Federal Courts*, (New York: W. W. Norton & Company, Inc., 1988), p. 13.

9. Ibid.

10. William J. Brennan, Jr., "The Constitution of the United States: Contemporary Ratification," Presentation at Text and Teaching Symposium, Georgetown University, Washington, D. C., October 10, 1985.

11. *Report*, p. 11.

12. Ibid., p. 13.

13. *The New York Times*, July 3, 1987, p. A27.

14. *Griswold* v. *Connecticut*, 381 U. S. 484 (1965).

15. *The New York Times*, July 5, 1987, sec. 4, p. 1.

16. *Report*, p. 33.

17. Robert H. Bork, "Civil Rights—A Challenge," *The New Republic*, August 31, 1963, p. 22.

18. *Chicago Tribune*, March 1, 1964, p. 1.

19. *Report*, p. 37.

20. 383 U. S. 666 (1964).

21. *Report*, p. 39.

22. Ibid., p. 40

23. Ibid., pp. 38-43.

24. Ibid., p. 44.

25. Robert H. Bork, "Neutral Principles and Some First Amendment Problems," *Indiana Law Journal*, 47 (Fall 1971), pp. 11, 17.

26. *Report*, p. 46. It should be noted that Bork also expressed changes in his positions on the extent of the First Amendment's protection of dissident political speech, artistic expression, and other forms of speech.

27. Testimony of Laurence H. Tribe before the Senate Judiciary Committee, September 22, 1987, p. 5 of the transcript of Tribe's prepared remarks, as quoted in Ladd, p. 11.

28. *Report*, Minority Views, p. 215.

29. As cited in Ladd, p. 11.

30. *Report*, Minority Views, p. 215.

31. Ibid., p. 310.

32. Ibid., pp. 25, 28-29.

33. U. S., *Congressional Record*, Daily Edition, v. 133, July 1, 1987, p. S9188.

34. *Report*, p. 35.

35. Ibid., p. 34.

36. *The New York Times*, September 22, 1987, p. A1.

37. Ibid., p. B6.

38. *Report*, p. 36.

39. Ibid., pp. 44-45.

40. *The New York Times*, September 30, 1987, p. A25.

41. Ibid., October 1, 1987, p. B9; see also issue of July 9, 1987, p. A24.

42. Ibid., July 5, 1987, sec. 4, p. 1.

43. Ibid., July 9, 1987, p. A24.

44. Ibid., August 13, 1987, p. A31.

45. *The Washington Post*, September 13, 1987, p. D7.

46. These scores represent the percentage of thirty-two recorded votes in 1987 in which a participating senator voted in disagreement with the position of the Conservative Coalition. *Congressional Quarterly* describes the Conservative Coalition as "a voting alliance of Republicans and Southern Democrats

against Northern Democrats" and defines a Conservative Coalition vote as one in which a majority of voting Southern Democrats and a majority of voting Republicans are opposed to the stand taken by a majority of voting Northern Democrats. In the version of the Conservative Coalition Opposition study used here, absences are not counted; therefore failures to vote do not affect scores. For a complete discussion of the Conservative Coalition Opposition scores, see *Congressional Quarterly Weekly Report*, January 16, 1988, pp. 110-115.

47. See *Congressional Quarterly Weekly Report*, January 16, 1988, p. 114, and Herbert F. Weisberg and John D. Felice, "An Ideological Model of Senate Voting on Supreme Court Nominations, 1955-1988" (paper prepared for the Midwest Political Science Association Annual Meeting, in Chicago, Illinois, April 14-16, 1988), pp. 6-9, 19, n. 2.

48. It should be noted that Senators Cohen and Evans tied for the fiftieth "Liberal" position with scores of thirty-seven. The last "Liberal" slot was assigned to Evans on the basis of his more liberal voting on other dimensions of the Conservative Coalition ratings.

49. For a similar conclusion see, Weisberg and Felice, p. 8.

50. Frank J. Sorauf and Paul Allen Beck, *Party Politics in America* (6th ed.; Glenview, Illinois: Scott, Foresman and Company, 1988), pp. 460-461; see also *Congressional Quarterly Weekly Report*, January 16, 1986, pp. 110, 114.

51. Weisberg and Felice, p. 9.

52. The ten southerners were Democrats Lloyd Bentsen (Tex.) John B. Breaux (La.), Lawton Chiles (Fla.), Wendell H. Ford (Ky.), Howell Heflin (Ala.), J. Bennett Johnston (La.), Sam Nunn (Ga.), Richard C. Shelby (Ala.), and John C. Stennis (Miss.) and Republican John W. Warner (Va.). The two non-southerners were Democrats Alan J. Dixon (Ill.) and J. James Exon (Neb.).

53. Tom Wicker, "Bork and Blacks," *The New York Times*, October 5, 1987, p. A23.

54. *The New York Times*, September 27, 1987, p. 26; see also *The Washington Post*, October 4, 1987, p. A12.

55. *The New York Times*, October 8, 1987, p. A34.

56. Ibid., July 9, 1987, p. A24.

57. Ibid., September 26, 1987, p. A32.

58. Ibid., September 27, 1987, p. 26 and October 5, 1987, p. A23.

59. Ibid., October 8, 1987, p. A34.

60. Ibid.

61. *The Washington Post*, October 24, 1987, p. A16.

62. Ibid.; see also *The Wall Street Journal*, October 7, 1987, p. 24.

63. *The Washington Post*, October 24, 1987, p. A16; see also *The Los Angeles Times*, October 4, 1987, part 5 (Opinion), p. 2, and *The New York Times*, October 9, 1987, p. A22.

64. *The Wall Street Journal*, October 9, 1987, pp. 1, 24; see also *The New York Times*, October 8, 1987, p. A34, and October 1, 1987, p. A1.

65. *The New York Times*, July 9, 1987, p. A24; see also *The Los Angeles Times*, October 4, 1987, part 5 (Opinion), p. 2.

66. *The Washington Post*, October 24, 1987, p. A16.

67. Ibid., October 4, 1987, pp. A1, A10.

68. *The New York Times*, October 7, 1987, p. B10, and October 28, 1987, p. B8.

69. Ibid., October 1, 1987, p. A1.

70. *The Wall Street Journal*, October 7, 1987, p. 1.

71. *The Washington Post*, October 4, 1987, p. A10.

72. *Report*, p. 13.

73. In this regard, a poll at this time indicated that a nominee whose ideology is viewed as extreme will face stiffer opposition than one whose philosophy is perceived as being in the mainstream; see *The Washington Post*, August 11, 1987, p. A4 and September 25, 1987, pp. A1, A16.

74. *Report*, p. 98.

75. U. S., *Congressional Record*, 100th Cong., 1st Sess., 1987, 133, S13268.

76. The New York Times, September 1, 1987, p. A10.

77. *The Washington Post*, September 10, 1987, p. A20.

78. Ibid.; see also, *Time*, September 21, 1987, pp. 12, 13, and *The New York Times*, July 30, 1987, p. A16.

79. *The Washington Post*, October 4, 1987, p. A12.

80. Ibid.; see also Ladd, p. 20.

81. Ladd, p. 20.

82. DeConcini's Conservative Coalition Opposition score of sixty-three was below the average "Liberal" rating of 67.6, indicating his relatively moderate leanings when contrasted with other "Liberals."

83. *The New York Times*, October 7, 1987, p. B10.

84. Ibid., October 2, 1987, p. A1.

85. Ibid., September 27, 1987, p. 26.

86. *Report*, Individual Views of Senator Heflin, p. 210.

87. *The New York Times*, October 6, 1987, p. B6.

88. *Report*, Individual Views of Senator Heflin, p. 212. It should be noted that in making this statement at the close of the Judiciary Committee hearings, Heflin reserved the right to change his opinion on confirmation during the ensuing Senate debate, an option he never exercised.

89. *The Washington Post*, October 24, 1987, p. A16.

90. *The New York Times*, September 27, 1987, p. 26.

91. *The Washington Post*, October 4, 1987, p. A12.

92. *The New York Times*, October 6, 1987, p. B6.

93. Ibid., p. B10.

94. *The Washington Post*, October 24, 1987, p. A16.

95. *The New York Times*, October 9, 1987, p. A22.

96. Ibid., October 8, 1987, p. A34, for all quotations in this paragraph.

97. *The Washington Post*, October 24, 1987, p. A16.

98. Ibid.

99. *The New York Times*, October 1, 1987, p. A1.

100. Ibid., October 8, 1987, p. A34.

101. *The Wall Street Journal*, October 7, 1987, p. 24.

102. *The New York Times*, July 9, 1987, p. A24.

103. Ibid.; see also issue of October 9, 1987; *The Los Angeles Times*, October 4, 1987, p. 1; and *The Wall Street Journal*, October 7, 1987, pp. 1, 24.

104. *The New York Times*, July 9, 1987, p. A24.

105. Ibid.

106. Ibid., July 30, 1987, p. A16.

107. *The Washington Post*, August 11, 1987, p. A4; see also Ronald K. L.

Collins and David M. O'Brien, "Just Where Does Judge Bork Stand?" *The National Law Journal*, September 7, 1987, pp. 13, 29.

108. Collins and O'Brien, p. 13.

109. Ibid.

110. *The New York Times*, September 16, 1987, p. A1.

111. Ibid., September 17, 1987, p. A1.

112. Ibid., pp. B10-B11 and September 21, 1987, p. B14.

113. Ibid., September 21, 1987, p. B14.

114. Ibid., October 9, 1987, p. A22.

115. Ibid., October 5, 1987, p. A23.

116. *Time*, September 21, 1987, p. 14.

117. As quoted in Anthony Lewis, "The Bork Surprise," *The New York Times*, September 24, 1987, p. A27.

118. *The New York Times*, October 8, 1987, p. A34.

119. Ronald Brownstein, "The Inside-Outside Battle About Seating Judge Bork," *The Los Angeles Times*, October 4, 1987, part 5, p. 2.

120. Ibid.

121. *The New York Times*, September 18, 1987, p. A22.

122. Ibid., October 2, 1987, p. A17.

123. Ibid., October 2, 1987, p. A1.

124. Ibid.

125. Ibid.

126. Ibid.

127. Ibid., September 17, 1987, p. A1.

128. Ibid., September 19, 1987, p. A10.

129. *Report*, Individual Views of Heflin, p. 212.

130. *The New York Times*, September 18, 1987, p. A22.

131. Ibid., September 21, 1987, p. B14.

132. Ibid., September 19, 1987, p. A10.

133. Ibid., October 9, 1987, p. A22.

134. *The Washington Post*, October 4, 1987, p. A1; see also George Watson and John Stookey, "Supreme Court Confirmation Hearings: A View From The Senate," *Judicature*, 71, no. 4 (December-January 1988), pp. 194-195.

135. *The New York Times*, September 28, 1987, p. B7.

136. Watson and Stookey, p. 195.

137. O'Connor was nominated on July 7, 1981; Rehnquist, as Chief Justice, and Scalia, on June 17, 1986.

138. Watson and Stookey, pp. 195-196; see also *The Washington Post*, August 11, 1987, p. A4.

139. Ibid.; see also Bruce A. Ackerman, "Tranformative Appointments," *Harvard Law Review*, 101, no. 6 (April 1988), 1170.

140. Ibid., pp. 195-196.

141. *The New York Times*, October 4, 1987, p. 39.

142. The ease with which the conservative Kennedy would later win Senate confirmation supports this point.

143. Henry J. Reske, "Did Bork Say Too Much?" *ABA Journal*, December 1, 1987, p. 76.

144. *The New York Times*, October 8, 1987, p. A34.

145. Indeed, the effort to portray Bork as a moderate may have provided the only means of increasing support for confirmation; for, according to Senator Biden, had the nominee not moderated his ardent conservative views he would have been rejected by a significantly greater margin. See Reske, p. 76 and *The Los Angeles Times*, October 4, 1987, part 5, p. 1.

146. Ackerman, pp. 1170, 1175.

147. *The New York Times*, October 30, 1987, pp. A34 and D23.

148. Ibid., October 14, 1987, p. A1.

149. Ibid., October 30, 1987, p. A1.

150. Ibid., p. D23.

151. Ibid.

152. Ibid, November 4, 1987, p. D30.

153. Ibid., November 12, 1987, p. A1.

154. Ibid., December 17, 1987, p. A25, and December 15, 1987, p. B16.

155. Ibid., November 10, 1987, p. D34.

156. Ibid., November 12, 1987, p. B10.

157. Ibid., February 4, 1988, p. A18.

158. Ibid.

159. Ibid., November 12, 1987, p. A31.

160. Ibid., p. B10.

161. Ibid., November 11, 1987, p. B7.

162. Ibid.

163. See Stephen Gillers, "We've Wished For Too Long," *The National Law Journal*, December 21, 1987, p. 13.

INDEX

C

D